Research Misconduct
Issues, Implications, and Strategies

CONTEMPORARY STUDIES IN INFORMATION MANAGEMENT, POLICY, AND SERVICES
(formerly Information Management, Policy, and Services Series)

Peter Hernon, series editor

Technology and Library Information Services
   Carol Anderson and Robert Hauptman, 1993
Information Policies
   Robert H. Burger, 1993
Organizational Decision Making and Information Use
   Mairéad Browne, 1993
Seeking Meaning: A Process Approach to Library and Information Services
   Carol Collier Kuhlthau, 1993
Meaning and Method in Information Studies
   Ian Cornelus, 1996
Library Performance Accountability and Responsiveness Essays in Honor of Ernest R. DeProspo
   Charles C. Curran and F. William Summers, 1990
Curriculum Initiative: An Agenda and Strategy for Library Media Programs
   Michael B. Eisenberg and Robert E. Berkowitz, 1988
Resource Companion to Curriculum Initiative: An Agenda and Strategy for Library Media programs
   Michael B. Eisenberg and Robert E. Berkowitz, 1988
Information Problem-Solving: The Big Six Skills Approach to Library & Information Skills Instruction
   Michael B. Eisenberg and Robert E. Berkowitz, 1990
Deep Information: The Role of Information Policy in Environmental Sustainability
   John Felleman, 1997
Database Ownership and Copyright Issues Among Automated Library Networks: An Anlysis and Case Study
   Janice R. Franklin, 1993
Research for School Library Media Specialists
   Kent R. Gustafson and Jane Bandy Smith, 1994

The Role and Importance of Managing Information for Competitive Positions in Economic Development
Keith Harman, 1989
A Practical Guide to Managing Information for Competitive Positioning to Economic Development
Keith Harman, 1990
Into the Future: The Foundations of Library and Information Services in the Post-Industrial Era
Michael H. Harris and Stan A. Hannah, 1993
Librarianship: The Erosion of a Woman's Profession
Roma Harris, 1992
Statistics: A Component of the Research Process
Peter Hernon, 1991
Statistics: A Component of the Research Process, Second Edition
Peter Hernon, 1994
Research Misconduct: Issues, Implications and Strategies
Ellen Altman and Peter Hernon, 1997
Service Quality in Academic Libraries
Peter Hernon and Ellen Altman, 1996
Microcomputer Software for Performing Statistical Analysis: A Handbook for Supporting Library Decision Making
Peter Hernon and John V. Richardson (editors), 1988
Evaluation and Library Decision Making
Peter Hernon and Charles R. McClure, 1990
Public Access to Government Information, Second Edition
Peter Hernon and Charles R. McClure, 1988
Federal Information Policies in the 1990s: Views and Perspectives
Peter Hernon, Charles McClure, and Harold C. Relyea, 1996
Statistics for Library Decision Making: A Handbook
Peter Hernon, et al., 1989
Understanding Information Retrieval Interactions: Theoretical and Practical Implications
Carol A. Hert, 1997
Reclaiming the American Library past: Writing the Women In
Suzanne Hildenbrand (editor), 1996
Libraries: Partners in Adult Literacy
Deborah Johnson, Jane Robbins, and Douglas L. Zweizig, 1991
The National Research and Education Network (NREN): Research and Policy Perspectives
Charles R. McClure, Ann P. Bishop, Philip Doty and Howard Rosenbaum (editors), 1991
Library and Information Science Research: Perspective and Strategies for Improvement
Charles R. McClure and Peter Hernon (editors), 1991

U.S. Government Information Policies: Views and Perspectives
Charles R. McClure, Peter Hernon, and Harold C. Relyea, 1989
U.S. Scientific and Technical Information Policies: Views and Perspectives
Charles R. McClure and Peter Hernon, 1989
Gatekeepers in Ethnolinguistic Communities
Cheryl Metoyer-Duran, 1993
Knowledge Diffusion in the U.S. Aerospace Industry: Managing Knowledge for Competitive Advantage
Thomas E. Pinelli, et al., 1997
Basic Research Methods for Librarians, Third Edition
Ronald R. Powell, 1997
Silencing Science: National Security Controls and Scientific Communication
Harold C. Relyea, 1994
Records Management and the Library: Issues and Practices
Candy Schwartz and Peter Hernon, 1993
Assessing the Public Library Planning Process
Annabel K. Stephens, 1996
Depository Library Use of Technology: A Practitioner's Perspective
Jan Swanbeck and Peter Hernon, 1993
For Information Specialists
Howard White, Marcia Bates, and Patrick Wilson, 1992
Public Library Youth Services: A Public Policy Approach
Holly G. Willitt, 1995

In Preparation:

Into the Future: The Foundations of Library and Information Services in the Post-Industrial Era, Second Edition
Michael H. Harris, Stan A. Hannah and Pamela C. Harris
The Dissemination of Spatial Data: A North American-European Comparative Study on the Impact of Government Information Policy
Xavier Lopez
Silencing Scientists and Scholars in Other Fields: Power Paradigm Controls, Peer Review, and Scholarly Communication
Gordon Moran
Information of the Image, Second Edition
Allan Pratt
Computer-Supported Decision Making: Meeting the Decision Demands of Modern Organizations
Charles L. Smith, Sr.
The Information Systems of International Inter-Governmental Organizations: A Reference Guide
Robert Williams

Research Misconduct
Issues, Implications, and Strategies

Ellen Altman
Peter Hernon
editors

 Ablex Publishing Corporation
Greenwich, Connecticut
London, England

Printed in the United States of America

Library of Congress Cataloging-in-Publication Data

Research misconduct: issues, implications and strategies / edited by
    Ellen Altman and Peter Hernon.
        p.   cm.—(Contemporary studies in information management, policy,
    and services)
    Includes bibliographical references and indexes.
    ISBN 1-56750-340-3.—ISBN 1-56750-341-1 (pbk.)
    1. Research—Moral and ethical aspects.   2. Fraud in science.
    3.   Scholarly publishing.   I. Altman, Ellen.   II. Hernon, Peter.
    III. Series.
    Q180.55.M67R49   1998
    001.2—dc21   97-18061
                                                                          CIP

Ablex Publishing Corporation
55 Old Post Road #2
P.O. Box 5297
Greenwich, CT 06830

Published in the U.K. and Europe by:
JAI Press Ltd.
38 Tavistock Street
Covent Garden
London WC2E 7PB
England

We dedicate this book in the memory of Walter J. Johnson,
our long-time friend and publisher

CONTENTS

ACKNOWLEDGMENTS

We wish to thank Helene Woodhams, who untangled some of the ideas and prose with helpful suggestions; Dora Suarez, who spent many hours in the library searching for and copying articles; Allan Pratt, who patiently read all, well nearly all, the drafts and whose helpful comments made this a better work; and Timothy Jones, our eagle-eyed copy-editor, who pointed out many gaffes and inconsistencies in the nicest possible manner. We also appreciate funding from the Human Ethics Committee Standing Committee, Victoria University of Wellington; and the comments of all the students, faculty members, and university administrators who contributed to the data collection.

PREFACE

In the past decade a number of books and articles have dealt with the subject of misconduct in research. Some of these works recounted details of one particular case, whereas others covered a number of cases. Some authors chose to structure misconduct in terms of the denigration of truth or objective reality; others described cases of shoddy science and engineering that defrauded the U.S. federal government and taxpayers. Edited books, composed of chapters written by different scholars, usually academics, have focused on the reasons that misconduct occurs, speculated on the magnitude of misconduct, and offered suggestions on how to combat or reduce its occurrence. Articles and book chapters have also discussed the roles and responsibilities of academic institutions in dealing with allegations of misconduct among their faculty and staff, the protection of the rights and reputations of those accused or suspected of engaging in false research, and the treatment of whistleblowers: those who alleged having evidence of wrongdoing.

Interest in research misconduct has spread across many disciplines as more and more instances are uncovered. Although medicine has had the most cases exposed, misconduct has surfaced in disciplines such as history, psychology, chemistry, and literature. Journals in sociology, business, medicine, and higher education have devoted whole issues to the topics of research misconduct and professional ethics (see Table 8.1).

With the exception of Marcel LaFollette (1992), author of *Stealing into Print*, who discusses misconduct and its linkage to journal editing and publishing, few writers on research misconduct have been concerned with the impact of false research and tainted publications on the scholarly literature. None has addressed the impacts on libraries or on the bibliographic apparatus that underpins the identification and retrieval of scholarly writings. None has discussed how the literature present on library shelves might contaminate the scholarly record and whether librarians have any obligation to notify users about materials found to be bogus. The present volume deals with such issues.

The issues discussed in this volume focus on publications tainted by deception that has been committed by one or more of the authors, and the implications of that deception for library collections and information services. Information presented here about cases and the journals named as having published fabricated and false articles has been taken from public sources, including news reports, books, and other articles, and from the publications of the U.S. government agencies that deal with scientific misconduct in connection with federal research grants. Our criteria for selecting cases is that a published work resulted from plagiarism, fabrication, or falsification. Cases selected for inclusion had to have been decided by an institutional investigation, a federal investigation, a court case, or an admission of guilt on the part of the accused. We do not claim that the decisions resulting from these investigations and court decisions are correct, but, clearly, they do give pause to those who might use the writings of those deemed guilty of research misconduct.

In preparing this work, we identified a number of other cases of misconduct, including falsifying patient records in clinical trials, claiming non-existent academic and professional credentials, listing spurious articles and citations on curriculum vitae for grant applications, and plagiarizing grant proposals to government agencies. Although none of these cases were incorporated into the text of this volume, the number of instances uncovered does indicate that ethical lapses are not uncommon, even among the most educated and most advantaged in society.

The volume also presents the results of surveys and focus group interviews conducted in the United States and in New Zealand, where both of us have held a one-year position as Visiting Professor at Victoria University of Wellington. The purpose of the research was to gain insights into the perceptions of faculty members, students, and university administrators about the existence and use of tainted research. We also probed how universities might deal with a faculty member suspected of (or shown to engage in) wrongdoing.

The research reported here is not definitive; rather, it is exploratory, and provides a foundation from which others, within and outside library and information science, might build. There is clearly little known about research misconduct, despite the increasing amount of literature on the topic. Those of us within library and information science, in our opinion, must be aware of misconduct and its implications for library collections and information services, including the teaching of critical thinking and information literacy to students, as well as for the education of students intending to become information professionals.

Ellen Altman & Peter Hernon
October, 1996

1

SCIENTIFIC AND RESEARCH MISCONDUCT

Ellen Altman

Science is regarded in Western societies as the ultimate arbiter of truth.

—Broad & Wade, 1982, p. 7

"Deviant Science and Scientific Deviance," "Stanford Inquiry Casts Doubt on Eleven Papers," and "Researcher Convicted of Falsifying Data" are titles of articles chronicling cases of scientific misconduct that have come to light in the past few years. Hundreds of such articles have been published over the past decade. Reports of scientific misconduct have appeared not only in journals aimed at the scientific and medical community, but also in general circulation magazines and newspapers. The bibliography accompanying a National Academy of Sciences (NAS) report of scientific misconduct included over 1,100 items (National Academy of Sciences, 1992). The National Science Foundation (NSF) awarded a grant for the preparation of a bibliography on the same topic in the late 1980s. This bibliography provided the foundation of the widely acclaimed book, *Stealing into Print* (LaFollette, 1992), which examined specific cases of proven misconduct and the ramifications of these cases for scholarship, support from the U.S. government and universities, and the journals in which articles based on the tainted research had appeared. While some of Marcel C. LaFollette's instances were in the humanities and social sciences, most were in scientific fields. This is especially troublesome since scientific misconduct has the potential to influence people's lives in significant and harmful ways, as Congressman John Dingell (1993) pointed out:

Scientific findings largely determine the agendas of government agencies with thousands of employees....the publication of a paper claiming that a food additive causes cancer or that a building material retards the mental development of infants can trigger a massive public outcry and demands for government action. (p. 1610)

Although misconduct is a serious charge under any circumstances, an allegation of misconduct becomes a matter of particular gravity when levelled against an individual understood to be dedicated to the discovery of knowledge. To protect professional reputations and to safeguard the privacy and legal rights of those who might be unfairly accused, the concept of what constitutes scientific misconduct is quite narrowly defined. Misconduct, however, need not be limited to the sciences. As discussed in this book, there is evidence of research misconduct in other disciplines.

A DEFINITION OF SCIENTIFIC MISCONDUCT

Professional organizations, such as the Federation of American Societies for Experimental Biology, U. S. governmental agencies, such as the National Institutes of Health (NIH), the NSF, and the NAS, along with the scientists who have written about scientific misconduct, agree that fabrication, falsification, or plagiarism in proposing, performing, or reporting research constitute scientific misconduct. "Fabrication is making up data or results, falsification is changing data or results, and plagiarism is using the ideas or words of another person without giving appropriate credit" (National Academy of Sciences, 1992, p. 5). Both the NSF and the Public Health Service (PHS) definitions of misconduct include the phrase, "other serious deviations from accepted research practices," presumably to allow action for egregious behavior not yet envisioned (Buzzelli, 1993, p. 584). Gerald Dworkin's (1983) description captures the essence of these practices in a more vivid way:

A key element in determining scientific misconduct on the part of investigative bodies is false representation...of passing off as genuine what is only a simulation of the real. Plagiarism is the passing of another's work as one's own. Reporting data that have not been observed is passing off for the observation of nature what is a product of one's imagination. Faking an experiment involves passing off as nature what is really man's design. (p. 69)

A certain level of obfuscation, however, persists in newspapers and journals, even scientific/scholarly journals, in which cases of misconduct are referred to as fraud, and the terms are used interchangeably. The two differ "in a legal sense," according to Frederick Grinnell (1992, p. 105). Although both misconduct and fraud are based on deception, claiming something to be true which is false, fraud, in law, requires that the victims suffer damages. As more and more stories of doctors submitting inflated bills and charges for treatments never made surface, the term fraud is most appropriately applied to false billing of insurance companies and government health programs. Scientific misconduct, as currently defined, makes no mention of damages, but one could argue that misconduct arising from government-funded research could be categorized as defrauding the taxpayers. Despite these legal distinctions, most writers on the subject use the terms "scientific misconduct" and "fraud" interchangeably. Throughout this book, however, plagiarism, falsification, and fabrication of research will be called scientific misconduct or, more broadly, research misconduct.

Error, even error caused by sloppiness, is not misconduct. Error is a by-product of all research because the process itself is complicated. The definitions presented here, however, make it clear that simple or even careless error does not constitute misconduct, nor does what might be called questionable interpretation of data. It is not uncommon in any field to have sincere, but opposing, views about the meaning of a set of data. Misconduct, even criminal behavior, unrelated to the research itself (for example, harassment of a co-worker) would not be deemed research misconduct.[1]

A number of other dubious practices are omitted from the widely accepted definition of scientific misconduct. Although the NAS excluded them from its definition of scientific misconduct, it did label the following practices as "questionable" and itemized them in its report (National Academy of Sciences, 1992):

- Failing to retain significant research data for a reasonable period;
- Maintaining inadequate research records, especially for results that are published or are relied on by others;
- Conferring or requesting authorship on the basis of a specialized service or contribution that is not significantly related to the research reported in a paper (for example, listing the lab director as a co-author even though that person did no work related to the paper);
- Refusing to give peers reasonable access to unique research materials or data that support published papers;
- Using inappropriate statistical or other methods of measurement to enhance the significance of research findings;
- Inadequately supervising research subordinates or exploiting them; and
- Misrepresenting speculations as fact or releasing preliminary research results, especially in the public media, without providing sufficient data to allow peers to judge the validity of the results or to reproduce the experiments. (p. 6)

CONFLICTS OF INTEREST

Another practice with ethical implications, although not specifically part of the definition of scientific misconduct, is conflict of interest. Such cases typically arise when research on a product is funded by a company hoping to capitalize on positive conclusions about the product's efficacy. Drug companies frequently fund research on how their particular drugs cure certain diseases or alleviate symptoms. Food companies fund studies to bolster claims about the healthful effects of products like oat bran and to counter claims about the likely effects of products containing caffeine, fat, or other consumables that current medical dogma recommends be used sparingly. Accepting corporate funds for research is not considered a conflict of interest *per se*. However, the potential for such conflict exists, in that the findings of the research could be biased to satisfy the funder. Cynthia Crossen (1994, p. 172) points out that "today, researchers and even university endowments may also have an equity stake in a drug company and much to win or lose if the treatment is proven effective or not."

A former University of South Florida laboratory technician and student is serving a three-year prison sentence for theft of trade secrets for removing notebooks describing research related to a patent application for a product to clean sewage. The student-technician had actually developed the product. The university charged that he had "jeopardized the university's contractual obligation to the company paying for the research" (Navarro, 1996, p. A22). University-business partnerships vastly increased after 1980 when federal government policy changed to allow universities the right to patent discoveries made as a result of federal research grants.

Conflict of interest is also likely in cases in which a particular social advocacy group hires an academic to conduct a survey which is intended to highlight the great social need which the group represents. Obviously, surveys that found neither a great need nor a large number of sufferers would not likely meet with the approval of the group funding the study. The tendency, therefore, is to hire surveyers who have already demonstrated sympathy for the group's objectives.

HOW WIDESPREAD IS MISCONDUCT?

> Of all the questions that remain unanswered about scientific misconduct the simple one, "how much is there?" has inspired the most discussion.
>
> —Knoll, 1992, p. 174

It is understandably difficult to get precise data on the extent to which misconduct occurs. There are, however, three general sources of information on the topic. In increasing order of concreteness, they are: opinions of knowledgeable observers, surveys of scientists and graduate students in various disciplines, and actual cases brought to light, usually by whistleblowing co-workers. "Disparate opinion" places "the extent and the significance" of scientific misconduct "between minuscule and monstrous," said Judith P. Swazey, Melissa S. Anderson, and Karen S.

Lewis (1993, p. 542). Some scientists dismiss concern about misconduct as isolated to a few "bad apples," whereas others believe it is more widespread. For instance, Robert Petersdorf (1989), who was vice-chancellor for health sciences at the University of California, San Diego, during the investigation of a young professor found guilty of serious misconduct, claimed that fraud is "a major affliction of science and medicine" (p. 121). How much scientific misconduct actually exists is not known, for the obvious reason that the perpetrators try to conceal it. Although a number of those accused have admitted guilt when confronted with the evidence, most people who engage in deceptive research are unlikely to turn themselves in, and surveillance close enough to catch the perpetrators is inimical to the independence that society accords professionals.

Opinions about the Magnitude of Misconduct

> There exists a bitter argument whether deviance in science is better represented by the "iceberg theory" or by the "bad apples theory."
>
> —Ben-Yehuda, 1986, p. 17

Denial is the first reaction most scientists exhibit when questioned about misconduct. After discovery of misconduct in the Chemistry department at Columbia University in New York City, Pamela Zurer (1987), a reporter for *Chemical and Engineering News (C&EN)*, contacted several chemists in academia for their reactions to this news development and its likely impact on the field. Most downplayed it, as did Sir Derek H. R. Barton, professor of chemistry at Texas A&M University, who insisted: "We're different because our experiments are reproducible. Fraud is rare in chemistry as opposed to biomedicine" (Zurer, 1987, p. 12).

Zurer concluded that "Barton's opinion is echoed by almost every chemist *C&EN* spoke with in preparing this article. Yet, every one had at least heard of cases where chemists had fudged their results, and several had direct experience of such behavior themselves" (p. 12). Another example seems to indicate that personal experience with misconduct is not that rare:

> The evidence suggests…that the fraud cases that come to light are but a small fraction of the whole. A study at a major university showed that of the 32% of researchers who suspected that a colleague had falsified data, 54% did not report it or try to verify their suspicions. (Bell, 1992, p. xii)

By 1990, after several cases had been publicized, the matter was taken more seriously. "We're staggered under the cases we're looking into now," said Peter Stockton, former chief investigator for the House Commerce Subcommittee on Oversight and Investigations looking into scientific misconduct (Bell, 1992, p. 257). Stockton lamented that limited resources hampered the subcommittee's ability to do more investigations.

Elizabeth Knoll (1992), while an editor for science materials at the University of California Press, was quite familiar with the scientific literature and some of the unethical, or at least questionable, practices, of which most people are unaware. She summed up her observations of the situation by saying:

> Those who regard scientific misconduct as a relatively trivial problem are increasingly in the minority among their scientific colleagues and the general public. Younger scientists, of the generation that feels the most competition and that is closest to its vulnerable graduate student past; editors of scientific journals, who know that they and their peer reviewers are virtually defenseless against skillful dishonesty, but who will be the most visibly embarrassed and inconvenienced should they print dishonest papers; members of congressional investigating committees and their staffs, deeply exasperated when scientists' arguments that science should police itself become an excuse for clubby self-protection; and the readers of dramatic newspaper accounts—significant numbers of these groups see fakery, plagiarism, and abuse of power as issues that must be taken very seriously, investigated, and punished. (p. 175)

Surveys about Misconduct

> Although I would not characterize these findings as scientific, it is difficult to call them inconsequential.
>
> —John Dingell, 1993, p. 1611

While allegations proven about scientific misconduct cases are few in number, the responses to surveys asking about research misconduct indicate that such cases are not unusual. In 1988, the Acadia Institute surveyed 118 deans of graduate schools, which, of course, included units in the social sciences and humanities. Forty percent of the respondents admitted that they had received reports of possible faculty misconduct in research during the previous five years (Swazey et al., 1989). This survey also found a relationship between the amount of external research funding a university received and the number of allegations of research misconduct: 68% of the university deans whose departments usually received more than $50 million annually in external research funding admitted that they had been told of possible misconduct. Only 19% of the deans at institutions receiving less than $5 million had been so informed. Of the allegations investigated, 59 (20%) had been verified as true. Again, those receiving the most money had the most verified cases, possibly because the more research undertaken, the greater the opportunity to deceive.

Also in 1988, Stephen Lock, then editor of the *British Medical Journal*, polled editors of 15 other medical journals in the United Kingdom, along with professors of medicine and surgery, about their knowledge of research misconduct. Among the 79 persons responding, 46 knew of cases involving medical misconduct—

many had first-hand knowledge. Yet, "only three out of the 29 institutions reported mechanisms for investigating misconduct" (p. 1532). Clearly, misconduct is not confined to research in the United States; subsequent chapters support this fact.

A doctoral dissertation completed at Ohio State University (Davis, 1989) reported on the responses of 609 faculty members in six disciplines (i.e., astronomy, chemistry, biology, economics, psychology, and sociology) to a survey about misconduct in academia. Respondents were asked if they knew someone who had intentionally falsified data; 23% said that they did. They were also asked whether or not they perceived that their own work had been misappropriated by others; 40% believed that they had been so victimized. No information was given about their personal reactions to this misappropriation of their work.

In 1992, the Acadia Institute conducted another survey, headed by Swazey, of misconduct in research, the "Project on Professional Values and Ethical Issues in Graduate Education of Scientists and Engineers." The survey contacted 2,000 doctoral candidates and 2,000 of the faculty from 99 of the largest graduate departments in chemistry, civil engineering, microbiology, and sociology. All those contacted had received federal grants for research. Both groups were asked about their "rates of exposure to perceived misconduct" and given 15 different examples of ethically questionable behavior (Swazey et al., 1993, p. 542).

The Acadia Institute researchers maintain that, because of close agreement between the responses of faculty and students, the data were "highly reliable" (p. 544). In a backhand fashion, the surveyors claim that "examples of behavior that fall into the NAS's definition of science-related misconduct are not rare" (pp. 544-545). Specifically, 6% of the students and 9% of the faculty reported direct knowledge of faculty members plagiarizing or falsifying data. Faculty reports of student plagiarism and falsification are considerably more common; nearly one third of the faculty claimed to have observed student plagiarism. The highest percentage of plagiarism on the part of colleagues (18%) was reported by faculty in civil engineering departments. Twelve percent of microbiology students believed that their instructors had falsified data. The researchers agreed that questionable research practices, such as sloppy use of data and suppression of findings contradicting one's own previous research, were far more common than plagiarism, fabrication, or falsification (p. 545).

The American Association for the Advancement of Science (1992) (AAAS), the world's largest scientific society, sent a questionnaire to 1,500 of its members. Of the 469 respondents, 27% claimed to have personally encountered fabrication, falsification, or theft of research in the past decade. Moreover, they said they had witnessed, on average, 2.5 cases of suspected fakery in that period. In 48% of these cases, the suspected individuals left the institution, admitted misconduct, or were found guilty. Yet, most respondents (54%) considered their universities lax in investigating allegations of scientific misconduct.

In all fairness, the rate of one in four is probably inflated, since those witnessing or suspecting misconduct were more likely to respond than those without such experiences. On the other hand, only 2% believed that incidences of scientific misconduct were declining. Most (44%) said the amount was pretty much the same, and 37% said misconduct had risen over the past decade.

Congressman Dingell (1993), who was at the time Chairman of the House Commerce Subcommittee on Oversight and Investigations, which conducted investigations on scientific fraud, made caustic comments on the laxity of the scientific community with regard to enforcing proper standards. Commenting on the AAAS survey, he characterized as "notable" that the "vast majority [of scientists] had done little or nothing" about reporting the misconduct that they suspected (p. 1611). Arthur Caplan (1996), a highly respected bioethicist, however, noted how would-be whistleblowers who sought his advice reacted:

> after talking to me, most people do not pursue their complaints out of fear. The system has not yet evolved techniques for protecting them and the culture of the university still equates complaining or airing suspicions with snitching, disloyalty or worse. (p.1)

Allegations Made to Federal Agencies

> Before 1980 very few cases were known. Except for a handful, research fraud was privately and discreetly handled within the institutions where it occurred.
>
> —Woolf, 1991, p. 595

The NIH, the Food and Drug Administration (FDA), and the NSF are the agencies primarily concerned with reports of scientific misconduct. Only the FDA actually audits research reports. These audits concern the efficacy and ill-effects of drugs and medical devices awaiting approval as safe. No other agencies audit or monitor any research they fund. Their primary charge is to award research grants. These awards are made on the basis of proposals submitted by the applicants that describe the work proposed and the methodologies to be employed. Panels of scientists in the specialty review and evaluate these research proposals. Obviously, these review panels can detect only plagiarism at this stage, and, indeed, they have done so. Because these agencies do no after-the-fact analysis of research findings or methods, allegations of misconduct involving the funded research must be specifically reported to them, usually by co-workers of the individuals suspected of misconduct. Perhaps this circumstance has influenced the low incidence of reports to NIH and NSF, although these agencies have become much more aware of the likelihood of misconduct in the past decade or so. M. L. Miers (1985), from the NIH, commenting on allegations of misconduct in NIH grants, writes:

Until recently, NIH tended to treat reports of misconduct as isolated events, employing ad hoc procedures for each case on the assumption that the probability of encountering a similar incident was minimal. In the past few years, it has become clear that more explicit and predictable procedures are needed to deal with the same level of recurring activity involving allegations or evidence of misconduct. (p. 832)

There has been "an average of two reports per month of possible misconduct that appears to go beyond the traditional kinds of issues encountered in the fiscal and administrative management of grants" (p. 831). With about 20-25 allegations of misconduct per year compared to 25,000 active grants and contracts, NIH's alleged misconduct rate was less than 1:1000, according to Congressman Don Ritter in comments to the House Science, Space, and Technology Subcommittee (Grinnell, 1992, p. 116). The NAS report made a similar observation about the NIH research awards and also stated that in the two-year period from March 1989 to March 1991, more than 200 allegations of misconduct in science were recorded by U.S. government agencies. From this number, about 30 cases have so far resulted in confirmed findings of misconduct. Although the possibility of under-reporting should be considered, these statistics indicate that the reported incidence of misconduct in science is low (p. 2).

Donald E. Buzzelli (1993), a senior scientist in the Office of the Inspector General at NSF, said that from early 1989 until June 1992, the Office "added" 124 cases to its misconduct files, but the number "seems to be settling down to about 50 a year" (p. 584). The Office for Research Integrity (ORI) of the PHS published the number of cases brought to its attention between June 1992 and October 1995. These are:

- 1992:   56 (beginning June);
- 1993:   118;
- 1994:   100; and
- 1995:   69 (through October).

In all, ORI received over 675 allegations of scientific misconduct from the time it was established in June 1992 through October 1995. Cases deemed worthy of investigation totaled 343 ("ORI Assessing Allegations Quicker...," 1995, p. 1). Although these numbers comprise small percentages of the total grants awarded, both the NIH and the NSF now require that institutions have policies in place for dealing with misconduct before any grants or contracts can be awarded to them. ORI has developed a handbook for institutions to use in dealing with charges of misconduct.

Compared with figures from NIH and NSF, a high incidence of what have been termed "serious deficiencies" were uncovered during routine data audits conducted by the FDA on drug trials from 1977 to 1988. Of 1,955 research studies audited, 211 (11%) had serious deficiencies; half of these were investigated for possible misconduct. Of those investigations completed, 16% led to disciplinary action. Another finding of the FDA data audits was that a number of the scientists who had tested the drugs failed to maintain acceptable records documenting their research (Shapiro & Charrow, 1989).

Since the responses to surveys about knowledge of scientific misconduct contrast rather dramatically with assertions made to federal agencies involved with scientific and medical research, knowledge about the pervasiveness of misconduct is still elusive. However, two social scientists who have studied instances of scientific misconduct liken the answer to crime statistics; "only those crimes reported are counted" (Bechtel & Pearson, 1985, p. 238). Dworkin (1983) provides an analytical and philosophical analysis of scientific misconduct that sums up the ethical view quite well:

> Unlike the rich literature of lying in which casuistry provides us with a wealth of interesting cases, putative justifications, and excuses, there seems little to be said in defense of scientific fraud. I know of no scientist who has tried to justify his dishonesty in terms of the promotion of the greater good, or in terms of certain persons' not having a right to the truth—the two commonest justifications for lying to others. There does not seem to exist the equivalent of the "white lie"—the trivial offense against the truth in the interest of not hurting others. Nor does there seem much room for paternalistic justifications in terms of protecting others against their mistakes in judgment and self-control. (p. 71)

WHY BE CONCERNED?

Fraud compromises science in every regard.

—Poling, 1992, p. 141

Fraud in science may...do damage by opening false leads that are pursued by other scientists.

—Poling, 1992, p. 145

Trust is the glue that holds society together. Since few of us are self-sufficient, we have to trust that the products we buy and the services we obtain from others are reliable—that food and medicine are safe to ingest, that banks and financial service companies will keep reliable accounts of our money, that the airline keeps the planes in good mechanical condition and employs pilots who are competent, and that products will perform as advertised. For the most part, that trust is justified. Science and medicine, especially in the 20th century, have a special place in society because scientists have created the impression that their work is rational and objective and that the pursuit of truth is a basic tenet of science. The public at large seems to accept that impression and is willing to spend money for scientific research. The sciences, including medicine, have grown enormously in discoveries, importance, and respect in the last half of this century. Newspaper and television reporters monitor science journals for stories of broad interest (e.g., the claim of discovering a gene associated with breast cancer) and warnings (e.g., the claim that lead-based paint can cause mental retardation in children), and they report their findings in articles and in broadcasts to the general public. As a result, "misconduct comes at a high price both for scientists and for the public," according to the report of the National Academy of Sciences (1992, p. 2). The high price paid by the public can be represented in actual dollars: in 1995, for example, U.S. taxpayers funded scientific research at a cost of $25 billion or $100 per person (Alberts & Shine, 1994).[2]

False results represent a waste of money, especially at a time when federal spending is under scrutiny. "Health and Human Services Secretary Donna Shalala, who oversees much of the federal funding of science, has said that scientific misconduct and mismanagement are becoming such a serious problem that the taxpayer's willingness to pay for research is threatened" (Flint, 1994, p. E5).[3] Furthermore, some people may suffer injuries or illness as a result of scientific misconduct. Treatments touted as beneficial for patient use may cause harm, or at least delay treatment by more effective means. One of the most extreme examples was the claim that giving amphetamines to hyperactive mentally-retarded children calmed their behavior, a treatment described by Stephen Breuning, who later admitted that his research was fabricated. The state of Connecticut changed its policy regarding the treatment of hyperactive mentally-retarded children because of Breuning's published claims (Schmaus, 1988).

Alan Poling (1992), a colleague who was tarred by Breuning because his name was listed as a co-author on some articles, describes the consequences of the Breuning case on the field of mental retardation thusly:

> The recognition that Breuning's work cannot be trusted has seriously eroded the data base concerning psychotropic drug effects in mentally retarded people. We now know less about how psychotropic medications affect this population than we appeared to know when Breuning's data was accepted. This has implications for patients, as well as scientists. (p. 146)

Scientific progress is often likened to building a brick wall: each contribution is a brick. The implication is that science is built on previous work. Therefore, fabrication, falsification, and plagiarism breach trust and confidence among scientists and erode "the trust that allows policy makers and [non-scientists] to make decisions based on scientific evidence and judgments, especially in instances when definitive studies are not available" (National Academy of Sciences, 1992, p. 2). Federal regulatory agencies rely on scientific studies as a basis for many decisions affecting the public at large, such as standards for air and water quality, requirements for safety equipment for certain kinds of work, and the permissibility of food additives. Some policy decisions made on the basis of social science research have far-reaching effects as well, including those about busing school children to achieve racial balance in the classroom, and hence improve scores on educational assessment tests, and the assignment of children to certain types of classes based on IQ test scores.[4]

MECHANISMS TO COUNTER MISCONDUCT

> The system of incentives in science does not encourage workers to devote their
> efforts to repeating past accomplishments when the record of such accomplishments
> is available in libraries.
>
> —Hagstrom, 1965, p. 69

A common response to expressions of concern about scientific misconduct is that science is essentially self-correcting. Three mechanisms supposedly ensure that only quality research gets funded and/or published in the scientific literature: peer review, refereeing, and replication of the research. The terms peer review and refereeing are commonly used interchangeably to mean the screening of research by colleagues in the discipline. Peer review, as used here, refers to reviewing applications for research grants by committees of specialists in the field (peers) to determine the significance of the work proposed and the methodology to be employed. Refereeing evaluates manuscripts submitted to scientific journals. The manuscripts are sent to knowledgeable people (referees) who scrutinize the work again for correct methodology, the quality of the research, and the novelty of the topic. They recommend whether the manuscript should be published, reworked, or rejected. The value of both peer review and manuscript refereeing have been debated over the past few years: are they "linchpins of science or merely the informed prejudices of old men?" (Lock, 1994, p. 60). Critics claim that peers and referees (frequently the same persons) demonstrate bias and unwillingness to accept new ideas.

Self-correction is the tenet that work presented in the literature can be replicated, and misconduct will be detected and corrected. This mechanism is considered reliable because scientific knowledge cumulates—one study builds on another. The assumption is that these three mechanisms protect the validity of claims of scientific discovery, and for the most part they do. Scientists themselves, however, concede that these mechanisms are far from being perfect safeguards. The National Academy of Sciences report (1992, p. 32) admits "although mechanisms of self-correction may expose false claims, they are not designed to detect or deter misconduct in science."

Both peer review and refereeing rely on supposedly knowledgeable people reading about experiments that will be or have been done. The level of scrutiny depends on the readers' familiarity with the type of work described, the care taken in reading the document, and the diligence in preparing the comments for the funder or editor. Reader reactions can be influenced by knowing or guessing who wrote the document and how important or insignificant the readers consider the topic of the research. In addition, as Herbert S. White (1993, p. 293) points out, "scholars often play the simultaneous and conflicting roles of author, reviewer, editor, reader, academic credit dispenser, and credit recipient." While peer review and refereeing are both valuable, neither is foolproof. It is not difficult for a knowledgeable scientist to write a plausible paper using fabricated or falsified data because he or she can anticipate the points that the referees are likely to raise about the work. Marcia Angell, executive director of the *New England Journal of Medicine*, said:

> Peer review looks at methods, analysis, interpretation, the importance of a question and the logic of it, whether the question is an interesting one. But peer reviewers are utterly reliant on authors to tell the truth about what they did, what they found, what they observed. (Robinson, 1994, p. 834)

Replication of results, theoretically the best safeguard against error and false data, is seldom useful in practice because it is rarely done. Unless the research is on a current topic or one of great interest and the findings inconsistent with the consensus of experts (e.g., the claim of creating cold fusion), it is unlikely that anyone will try replication.[5] There are a number of reasons why replication is rare, as many scientists will agree:

- Peer review panels are unlikely to recommend funding proposals intended to replicate previous work.
- Employers are not interested in supporting replication; they want to use previous work to make new findings, not simply reproduce already published results.
- Scientists want to be known for original research, not as tweakers of someone else's research. Even proving that the original research was wrong is not considered significant.
- The information given in published reports is usually not sufficiently detailed to reproduce the work. This lack of information is sometimes deliberate on the part of the authors, to secure their discovery, and sometimes because of journal policy and its space limitations for articles.
- Some projects take years and the participation of many scientists. These projects cannot be replicated because of costs in time and money.
- Some studies use large animals, such as monkeys and dogs, who are killed at the end of the experiment. These studies cannot be easily reproduced.

Replication is simply not a realistic safeguard against scientific misconduct for the reasons outlined above. According to Poling (1992), another reason is, that if a replication is not exact, it is difficult to determine what is responsible for the failure. He concluded that:

> unless there is reason to believe otherwise, scientists must assume that their peers are honest; cheating characteristically is the last variable suspected to be responsible for unreplicable findings. (p. 145)

Clearly, the traditional mechanisms of peer review, refereeing, and replication are inadequate to detect false and fabricated research. How then is it detected? Usually misconduct is uncovered by co-workers or others familiar with the perpetrator. Those close to the action are the most likely to suspect it. As will be noted later, most instances of discovered fraud are due to such whistleblowers, though, in some instances, journal editors uncover it.

THE ENVIRONMENT OF SCIENCE AND SCHOLARSHIP

> Where "Science the Noble Calling" and "Science the Nobel Profession" intersect is where many of the problems begin.
>
> —Leibel, 1991, p. 601

Most scientists realize that they are unlikely to win the Nobel Prize, but the atmosphere in which science is currently conducted creates strong pressure to produce, while the likelihood of misconduct being uncovered is low. The atmosphere is largely due to the development that Derek J. DeSolla Price (1963) termed "Big Science," and the employment pressures it has generated. A *Newsweek* article, "How Many Scientists Does It Take to Screw in a Quark?" (Begley & Holmes, 1994), illustrates how complex Big Science has become. It took 440 physicists from 34 countries working at the Tevatron accelerator at Fermi National Laboratory, outside Chicago, 17 years to find "the first experimental evidence…for the existence of a long-sought elementary particle called the top quark." The top quark "was formed when the Tevatron smashed protons into antiprotons." No matter that the top quark was invisible; these days "in virtually every cutting-edge field, from astrophysics to molecular genetics, the object of discovery is often completely inaccessible to the senses, and the process of discovery has become inferential rather than direct" (p. 54).

This complexity has led to collaborative research involving several laboratories. With the information superhighway allowing for almost instantaneous transfer of data, it is fairly common for scientists in different laboratories, even in different countries, to cooperate on projects and to co-write scientific papers.[6] Sometimes collaboration causes disputes which then lead to one or several of the parties alleging fraud. Charges of misconduct were made by French physicians at the Pasteur Institute, in Paris, against Dr. Robert Gallo, who was then head of the Laboratory of Tumor Cell Biology at the National Institutes of Health, during a dispute over whether or not the French had provided the culture that subsequently led to the discovery of the AIDS virus. Scientists recognized that both honor and money were involved for those who could claim priority. Gallo, credited for the discovery and the resulting patent, was initially found guilty of misconduct. ORI at the NIH decided not to continue, however, when it became apparent that Gallo's appeal would be heard by the Research Integrity Adjudications Panel, which had overturned several previous ORI findings of guilt. Gallo subsequently left the NIH and started a new laboratory at the University of Maryland, Baltimore Campus, in 1996.

Gallo's virologist, Mikulas Popvic, was deemed guilty of misconduct because of statements he made in a paper about the AIDS virus discovery published in the journal *Science*. Popvic appealed to the Research Integrity Adjudications Panel, composed primarily of attorneys. After 12 days of hearings, the panel concluded that the ORI did not "prove that the *Science* paper contains untrue statements or data, much less that it contains intentional falsifications" (Marwick, 1993, p. 2666). ORI claimed that the term "intentional falsifications" created a new definition of misconduct and a difficult one to prove, so it decided to drop the Gallo case because his appeal would have been heard by the same group.

Big Science is a consequence of federal funding for research over the past 50 years. The recipients, mostly large and prestigious universities, have grown to depend on these millions of dollars arriving every year to keep certain departments at full strength. Federal funds support large laboratories employing many graduate students and post-doctoral fellows (with limited terms of employment, typically lasting a year or two) as well as laboratory and office support staff. Equipping these laboratories is expensive. Technology constantly develops new equipment which researchers claim they need to keep current with colleagues who are also competing for the same federal grants. The supervisors of these laboratories—the professors who have received grants—are known as principal investigators. It is not unusual for one professor to be principal investigator on three or four grants for different federal programs. Frequently, professors have insufficient time to monitor closely all the junior scientists working on all the grants. In turn, these junior scientists feel pressured to make a name for themselves. The fastest and simplest way to do so is to publish articles (as many as possible) in respected journals in their discipline.

That these pressures lead to cheating is confirmed by Jules B. Lapidus and Barbara Mishkin (1990), who write:

The vast majority of cases [of fraud uncovered between 1978-1988] concerned biomedical research, usually being carried out in a medical school environment....The culprits were junior colleagues with M. D. degrees who were doing research under the supervision of well-regarded, heavily funded senior scientists. There was no formal adviser-advisee relationship, no graduate program, no advanced degree being sought. (p. 290)

Untenured professors are under similar pressure to gain a professional reputation which, in turn, enhances their chances of obtaining tenure. Robert Slutsky of the University of California Medical School, San Diego, was found guilty of fraudulent and falsified research by a committee of his peers. He produced, on average, one paper every 10 days over a period of several years and attempted to stave off questions about his high productivity by listing other professors as co-authors, sometimes without their knowledge.

Although the Slutsky case is an extreme one, honorific authorship—listing as co-authors people who did not actually perform any of the research—has been relatively common in the sciences for a number of years. The practice has been questioned because, in a number of cases, those listed as co-authors claimed no knowledge of research later deemed falsified or fabricated. In several instances, the individuals did not even know that they were listed as co-authors. Robert Bell (1992) characterized honorific authorship as a form of "academic payola" (p. xii).

Honorific or not, the number of persons listed as authors for some papers has become enormous. The most egregious examples are the two papers published in *Physical Review Letters* announcing the top quark. A total of 831 people were listed as authors for one or both of these papers. Physicist Roy F. Schwitters (1996), commenting that it is not uncommon for 100 or more persons to be credited as authors on a single article, wryly noted: "The number of sentences in the text may be lower than the number of authors on the title page or pages!" (p. B1).

Today, tenured and untenured professors at major universities in every branch of science and most of the social sciences and education are expected to bring in grant funds. It is common in medicine and other scientific disciplines, even in prestigious universities, to expect professors to win grants large enough to pay for the operation of their laboratories, to support graduate student assistants, and sometimes to subsidize or underwrite their own salaries. Grinnell (1992) claims that, as of the early 1990s, "principal investigators' salaries account for about 30% of the funds awarded by NIH" (p. 126). Grant funds are commonly referred to as "soft" money to distinguish them from "hard" money supplied by the university from state appropriations, tuition, or other institutional funds.

All this grant money being competed for comes from two primary sources—the federal government and private industry. Foundations and non-profit organizations, such as the American Heart Association, make some grants, but the total amount of their awards is small in comparison with the other two sources. Congressmen Rick Boucher (1993), who, as chairman of the Subcommittee on Science of the House Committee on Science, Space, and Technology, wrote a statement on science policy. He noted that, between 1977 and 1989, the number of academic scientists with doctorates increased by 41%, while the federal appropriations for research rose by 72% after accounting for inflation. Now, however, even though appropriations are still increasing, but at a lower rate, the competition for federal grants has grown more intense. "Individual investigators were spending ever-greater portions of their time trying to raise money" (p. B2). The situation is unlikely to improve as "there is little sense on Capitol Hill that voters view academic research as a special national priority" (p. B2).

Grinnell (1992) worried that the keen competition for outside funding (federal or industrial) constitutes a potential problem for integrity in science:

> For these researchers, getting ahead in science may be secondary to keeping one's position and modest salary. The stakes are not only who will have the most intellectual impact, but also, who will have a job. (p. 126)

Grinnell's assessment, made in the early 1990s, was reinforced by statistics released in 1995. The American Chemical Society announced that finding employment was a problem for 17% of recent Ph.D. graduates in chemistry. Another study conducted by researchers at Stanford University and the Rand Corporation estimated that there are about 22% more doctoral graduates in science than there are jobs for them (Goode, 1995). Pressures like those described here offer temptations toward misconduct, but until fairly recently it was taken for granted that scientists and scholars would resist them. Thus, neither institutions nor funding agencies were concerned with the detection of misconduct.

GOVERNMENT OVERSIGHT OF FUNDED RESEARCH

> The subcommittee would not have needed to pursue any of the cases…had the institutions and people involved pursued them properly from the start….There is absolutely no good reason why a congressional subcommittee should be doing a job that scientists can and should be doing themselves.
>
> —Dingell, 1993, p. 1614

The federal government showed no interest in investigating misconduct in the research funded by agencies until the spring of 1981, when the House Committee on Science and Technology, chaired by then-Representative Albert Gore Jr., held hearings. Since that time several other House committees have followed suit. Representative Ted Weiss chaired two hearings of the House Committee on Government Operations, Subcommittee on Human Resources and Intergovernmental Relations, in 1988, to learn (Congress. House. Committee on Governmental Operations, 1989):

- How prevalent are scientific fraud, misconduct, and inaccuracies?
- Are universities, medical schools, and research institutes effective in preventing and investigating fraud?
- How does the Department of Health and Human Services (HHS) respond to allegations of fraud, misconduct, and inaccuracies, and should they do more to prevent, investigate, and resolve these cases? (p. 2)

Basically, the first question remains unanswered; the committee concluded that the answers to the other two questions are that neither the universities nor HHS were effectively preventing or investigating fraud.

The granting agencies, reacting to congressional outrage at their lack of policies to bar funding for scientists accused, or found guilty, of fraud, instituted procedures for responding to charges of misconduct on the part of grant recipients. In 1987, the NSF began requiring that institutions—primarily universities—establish policies and procedures for investigating allegations of misconduct, and that NSF be notified if the investigation determined that the allegations were valid.

NSF also established an Office for Ethics and Values Studies to fund projects about research ethics, such as the LaFollette and Swazey studies mentioned previously. Additionally, the Office supported publication of a book, *Ethics and Policy in Scientific Publication* (Bailar et al., 1990) under the auspices of the Council of Biology Editors, and a study of "questionable incidents" in the social and behavioral sciences (Hollander, 1992, p. 194). The NSF Office of Inspector General (OIG), established in 1989, however, undertakes the actual investigations. The OIG prefers that the employer of the researchers in question do its own investigation in-house, although in special cases the OIG may "supplement the institution's investigation" or conduct a full investigation of its own (Buzzelli, 1993, p. 584). A majority of the allegations made to NSF concern misappropriation of intellectual property (plagiarism, theft of research ideas, and failure to credit). A surprisingly large percentage of cases investigated involve plagiarism in proposals submitted for funding.

HHS, which awards more research dollars than any other agency, created the Office of Scientific Integrity (OSI) in 1989. The following year, HHS required that institutions receiving its funds establish policies and procedures for handling allegations about scientific misconduct. OSI established general policies and procedures for the handling of PHS grant misconduct charges, and it then reviewed the final investigative reports. If an institution was unwilling to investigate the charges, the OSI conducted the investigation. One regulation requires that "principal investigators keep their research notebooks and other records for three years following submission of the final expenditure report or until the conclusion of any ongoing investigations involving the notebooks" (Grinnell, 1992, p. 119). The availability of laboratory notebooks was central to the investigation of a well-publicized case in the 1980s.[7]

In a 1992 reorganization, the OSI was absorbed into the Office of Research Integrity (ORI) under the Office of the Assistant Secretary for Health. The ORI consolidated responsibility for oversight of scientific misconduct reported to the HHS within a single office. Less than two years later, Secretary of HHS Shalala appointed a Commission on Research Integrity to evaluate the workings of the ORI in light of criticisms from scientists accused of misconduct and their university employers, by attorneys for these defendants, and by whistleblowers frustrated by the glacial pace of investigations.

By 1993, the ORI was under fire for its failure to win a single case when scientists deemed guilty appealed to the next level, HHS's Research Integrity Adjudications (RIA) Panel. The Panel has stated that the ORI "should reach a finding of misconduct only...[when the deceit is intentional] and where the fabrications or falsifications are central to the conclusions of the research paper" (Burd, 1993a, p. A22); the previous standard of proof had been a preponderance of the evidence, as used for administrative law. As a result of the RIA Panel ruling, a commission of scientists and attorneys was established to consider the definition of scientific misconduct. The commission's report, released at the end of 1995, recommended that the term "scientific misconduct" be replaced by the term "research misconduct" defined as (Commission on Research Integrity, 1996):

> significant misbehavior that improperly appropriates the intellectual property or contributions of others, that intentionally impedes the progress of research, or that risks corrupting the scientific record or compromising the integrity of scientific practices....Examples of research misconduct include but are not limited to...misappropriation...interference...or misrepresentation. (pp. 13-14)

The statement developed by the Commission is now under review by the Secretary of Health and Human Services and other governmental agencies, but the recommendation has already been publicly opposed by the Federation of American Societies for Experimental Biology for its breadth of coverage.

As a result of testimony presented at congressional hearings about misconduct involving recipients of federal grants, in 1986 Congress amended the False Claims Act of 1863 to allow whistleblowers reporting fraudulent use of funds from federal contracts or grants to receive an award of up to 30% of any money that the government recovers. The intent was to encourage people with knowledge of misconduct to come forward. Curiously, the first known case of criminal prosecution for scientific misconduct was for violation of the False Claims Act, but without use of the whistleblower amendment. Stephen Breuning was charged for submitting false information in order to obtain money. He pled guilty, was fined, and was sentenced to community service. The University of Pittsburgh, his employer, was required to return a portion of money received from the grant.

The first case involving the whistleblower amendment occurred in 1990, when J. Thomas Condie, a former laboratory technician, accused Professor John L. Ninnemann of falsifying data. Both Ninnemann's current and former employers, the universities of Utah and California at San Diego, were required to return $1,575,000 from his grants to the federal government. Condie collected $311,000, plus $265,000 for legal fees. Ninnemann was barred from the receipt of federal grants for three years.

In a more recent case, the plaintiff, dissatisfied with two inquiries by the university, bypassed the usual federal mechanisms for dealing with scientific misconduct and went directly to the courts. Epidemiologist Pamela Berge claimed that four researchers at the University of Alabama Medical School in Birmingham plagiarized parts of her doctoral dissertation. She sued, not for plagiarism, but under the False Claims Act, charging that the four had used the material that she claimed was hers as part of a grant application to the NIH. A jury found for Berge. The University of Alabama, Birmingham is appealing the $1.65 million judgment (Taubes, 1995).

Formal punishment of those deemed guilty of misconduct is rare. Federal agencies typically "punish" the guilty by barring them for a specific period of time—usually three years—from receiving federal grants and from serving on committees that award those grants. Even such relatively mild punishment is frequently blocked by legal action or an appeal on the part of the accused, and those who appeal to the next level within the HHS usually win. In 1995, a panel of outside experts recommended that ORI uncouple its investigatory activities from its judgmental activities, a recommendation likely to be adopted. Whether ORI should notify state medical boards about physicians found guilty of misconduct in research is an issue in dispute. The ORI stance is that such notification would reduce the likelihood of cooperation on the part of the accused (Dalton, 1996). Indeed, there was much negative reaction when the PHS began publishing the names of those found guilty of scientific misconduct in 1993. Prior to that time, names of the wrongdoers were made public only by request under the Freedom of Information Act (Burd, 1993b).

Hearings before the House Committee on Governmental Operations, in 1993, highlighted concern about conflict of interest involving federally-funded research. Such conflicts center around: (1) accepting simultaneous funding for essentially the same research from both the federal government and a drug company, and (2) research by principal investigators owning stock in fledgling companies hoping to profit from the results of that research. Both situations have occurred.[8] While neither of these acts, per se, are considered misconduct under the present system, there are fears that misconduct may occur to protect financial interests.

The House Committee clearly is not satisfied with the misconduct-monitoring activities of the granting agencies. In a report titled, "Are Scientific Misconduct and Conflicts of Interest Hazardous to Our Health?" (Congress. House. Committee on Governmental Operations, 1990) the Committee said:

- At the present time, it is not possible to rely on institutional or PHS oversight for the handling of misconduct allegations or the prevention of misconduct. The examples in this report indicate that many cases of scientific misconduct would have gone undiscovered, and many of the scientists would have continued their fraudulent or misleading research, without the courageous and sometimes single-minded efforts of one or two individuals, many of whom were sharply criticized by the institutions involved as vindictive or jealous colleagues. (p. 67)

- The Department of HHS should immediately promulgate PHS regulations that clearly restrict financial ties for researchers who conduct evaluations of a product or treatment in which they have a vested interest. If PHS fails to meet this responsibility, then Congress should enact legislation to achieve that goal. (p. 68)

Research misconduct is an issue not confined to the United States and the federal level of government. It can (and does) occur at other levels of government and in other countries. Thus, other countries are considering how to handle their own cases of misconduct.

DEALING WITH MISCONDUCT IN OTHER COUNTRIES

Every country that conducts scientific research experiences research misconduct... countries that have gone looking for misconduct have found it.

—Smith, 1996, p. 789

Other countries also are becoming aware of the need to deal with cases of scientific misconduct. The European Medical Research Council, a subdivision of the European Science Foundation, cited dishonesty in science as a national problem, and recommended the establishment of good practice guidelines for use in member countries. The Danish Committee on Scientific Dishonesty, established in 1992, handled allegations involving 15 cases, ranging from authorship disputes to data fabrication and falsification, during its first year of operation. After the Swedish Medical Research Council held a conference on research misconduct, it concluded that a Swedish initiative was needed. A similar council in Norway is working on developing a statement and procedures for investigating allegations of dishonesty.

As a result of two widely-publicized cases, one involving scientific misconduct in a major study of breast cancer treatments and another in which four faculty were murdered, the Canadian government now requires its research universities to develop guidelines for handling alleged cases of misconduct or risk losing government research funds.[9] The three major research councils in Canada—for science and engineering, medicine, and social science and humanities—have all adopted a statement on integrity in research and scholarship.

Britain, for reasons which are unclear, has been slow to act even though cases there have come to light. In 1991, the Royal College of Physicians called on medical institutions to "recognize scientific fraud and act to stop it" (Brown, 1991, p. 21). After the false articles of J. M. Pearce were exposed, Lock (1995), who was secretary to the working party of the Royal College and also former editor of the *British Medical Journal*, urged that Britain adopt procedures similar to those of the ORI in the United States. The next year, the *British Medical Journal* and *The*

Lancet jointly urged that a central agency be established to deal with misconduct in research.

Because of several highly-publicized cases, universities and research hospitals in Australia have instituted procedures that instruct scientists on how to avoid misconduct. The National Health and Medical Research Council followed this step by publication of guidelines for good scientific practices that applicant institutions must follow. The Council has also developed guidelines for dealing with misconduct allegations.

THE SCIENTISTS RESPOND

...an institution which is endowed with $100 billion per year of government money is not going to risk self-criticism or self-analysis; those in charge are not going to look.

—Higgins, 1996, SCIFRAUD listserv

The scientific community has been generally indignant about both the publicity concerning uncovered misconduct and the regulations designed to deal with it. The typical response is simply denial. Some scientists characterize the reports of misconduct as exaggerated, and others continue to cite Daniel Koshland's claim that "99.9999% of scientific reports are accurate and truthful" (see Koshland, 1987, p. 141). On the other hand, cases such as that of David Baltimore, winner of the 1975 Nobel Prize for Medicine, give pause. When Baltimore became president of Rockefeller University in New York City, he left Thereza Imanishi-Kari in charge of the NIH-funded project that he had supervised at The Whitehead Institute associated with Massachusetts Institute of Technology. When she was accused of falsifying data in the study and in the article published jointly with Baltimore in the journal, *Cell*, his reaction was not what might have been expected of a respected Nobel laureate. He "cast the conflict as one of outsiders invading the sanctuary of science" (Hilts, 1992, p. 30). Instead of checking on the science in question, he urged eminent scientists, including other Nobel laureates, to write letters to Congress and to newspaper editors on his behalf. "Baltimore and his lobbyists arranged for a bevy of distinguished scientists to go to Washington..." to sit behind him while he testified at Michigan Representative "John Dingell's second congressional hearing in April 1989" (p. 30). Evidently these scientists accepted Baltimore's words in favor of proof, certainly failing to demonstrate adherence to the scientific method. (Imanishi-Kari was exonerated of misconduct by appeal to the Research Integrity Adjudications Panel in June, 1996).

Some noteworthy cases from the recent past demonstrate that scientists are sometimes less than virtuous. German scientists were acknowledged as the world's best before World War II, having won more Nobel prizes than any other country from the time the first awards were given in 1901 (Cole, 1983). Yet, there is no evidence that they challenged the infamous Nazi "medical experiments." The Tuskegee Study, conducted by the PHS, "observed" the effects of untreated syphilis over a period of 40 years: the "subjects," several hundred black men, thought that the placebos given them were actually medicine to treat the disease. The U.S. military downplayed the harmful effects of radiation when it exploded nuclear bombs in the Nevada desert in the 1950s, and the Central Intelligence Agency (CIA) and the Army gave the hallucinogenic drug LSD to people without informing them of its dangers. As a result of the information released about government-funded radiation studies by Energy Secretary Hazel O'Leary late in 1995, some former residents of the Fernald School for mentally retarded children filed a $14 million lawsuit against the Quaker Oats Co. and the Massachusetts Institute of Technology for a study done in the 1940s and the 1950s to promote oats instead of wheat as the preferred cereal. The suit charges that the residents were "given radio-tagged milk so scientists could learn whether eating oatmeal inhibits the intestinal absorption of iron and calcium" (Kaiser, 1995, p. 1763). Scientists employed by the tobacco industry continue to maintain that the relationship between smoking and lung cancer remains unproven.

While NSF and NIH can investigate possible fraud under government contracts, no official oversight bodies have the power to investigate allegations of misconduct in research conducted with private funds—either from foundations or from the employing institution. Although employers can investigate suspected wrongdoing and take appropriate action, few would publicize either the investigation or the outcome unless the case had wide media exposure. Although the federal government has made employers responsible for conducting investigations of alleged misconduct in government-sponsored projects, criticism of the general laxness of these investigations was sharp before the government threatened to stop funding all research at uncooperative institutions.

Reputation, the currency of universities and hospitals, confers prestige, attracts donations, and gives the edge in winning grants. Most universities, hospitals, and corporations do not want to confront, investigate, or admit that their employees, especially faculty and physicians, might have engaged in dishonest research.

PLAGIARISM, FORGERIES, AND FAKES

...all the uses of history depend upon the integrity of the record....No concern could be deeper than assaults upon the record, upon the very idea of a record.

—Handlin, 1979, p. 408

The social sciences and humanities are not immune from misconduct in research. However, the number of cases discovered is smaller, for several reasons. First, the amount of such research funded by the federal government is quite small in comparison with science and medicine. Another reason is the dissimilarity in the research methodologies between these disciplines and the physical and medical sciences. Social surveys and textual analysis are quite different from formulating and assessing drug reactions or gene splicing. Common methods for misconduct in the social sciences and humanities are plagiarism, forgery of documents, and fakery of artifacts. Sometimes these practices are done under the guise of research and sometimes for money or power or both.

Thomas Mallon's (1989) book on plagiarism contains a chapter titled "Quiet Goes the Don," which describes how Texas Tech University allowed an assistant professor (or "don") to resign quietly after the history department's promotion and tenure committee learned of remarkable similarities between that person's writings and those of previously-published historians. The department and its faculty, fearful of litigation and bad publicity, kept quiet. As a result of their silence, the publisher had to insert an errata sheet into the assistant professor's book and was publicly embarrassed when the author had to issue a statement in prestigious history journals acknowledging his copying.[10]

The case from Texas Tech to some extent influenced the American Historical Association (AHA) to develop and approve a Statement on Plagiarism in 1986. This statement became part of the AHA Statement on Standards of Professional Conduct. Robert Zangrando (1991/1992), who was involved with the development of these statements, noted that the Professional Division "found itself regularly hearing plagiarism cases" (p. 59). The association, however, publicized neither the names of the "proven plagiarists" nor the titles associated with their copying. Zangrando considers this a mistake. Furthermore, he suggested establishing a clearinghouse "through which journal editors and book publishers [could] obtain information on authors who exhibit a tendency to plagiarize" (p. 62). Mallon (1989) noted that one thing that seems common among plagiarists is recidivism.

The charges of plagiarism became so public and so contentious in one case that the AHA, it would seem, is unlikely to want to reveal the names involved in any future disputes, especially if the accused threatens a legal fight. Robert Bray, a literary critic, presented a paper at the 1990 Illinois State Historical Society symposium claiming that Stephen B. Oates, a professor of history at the University of Massachusetts, Amherst, had copied large parts of his 1977 biography of Abraham Lincoln from another Lincoln biography. Historian Cullom Davis, who moderated this meeting, filed a complaint against Professor Oates with the AHA. Others also filed similar complaints against him. Oates, who was later accused of using large sections of books without sufficient attribution in two other biographies, fought back.[11] He claimed that, since he was not a member, the AHA had no authority in his case. To be more exact, he claimed that the AHA lacked jurisdiction; only his employer had any real influence in this situation. Oates claimed that the charge of "intertextuality," essentially using small phrases and rephrasing Benjamin Thomas' writing, did not constitute plagiary (Oates, 1994). He enlisted other scholars to write statements in his defense and hired an attorney who threatened legal action for slander and libel against those who attacked Oates.

Zangrando (1994) wrote of his frustration with both sides in the investigation. He claimed that Oates "embraced any tactic that might stifle and end the controversy" and that the AHA "discourag[ed] any discourse that might involve or seem to involve the Association" (p. 65). Basically, the AHA

> investigation, found Oates's Lincoln biography partially "derivative to a degree requiring greater acknowledgment of Benjamin Thomas's earlier biography." Thanks however to Oates's adversarial tactics and to the Association's fears, no such disclosure was made to AHA members. Silence descended and seems likely to remain....(p. 67)

Although plagiarism, which involves copying substantial parts of a published work, is technically a copyright crime, it is one that district attorneys are unwilling to "expend governmental resources" in prosecuting (Kozak, 1994, p. 72). Authors who find that their work has been plagiarized have the option to sue for civil damages, but, unless the plagiarist has earned considerable money from the copying (highly unlikely in scholarly publishing), the injured party will probably not collect much beyond vindication while, at the same time, incurring substantial legal fees. The publishers of the purloined and the tainted work are more likely to file civil suits, first to win damages and second to recover from the plagiarist the costs of producing the book.

A plagiarism case recently decided in Brazil has an interesting twist, in that the plaintiff's article was not published, while the plagiarist's was. The plaintiff, Yeda Lopes Nogueira, claimed that Carlos Augusto Pereira had usurped her ideas about the cytopathic effects of the rabies virus. She had presented her work at scientific meetings, and an abstract of her presentation had been published in the proceedings of one of the meetings. She had no other publications describing the research. Her claim was upheld in two trials, and Pereira was ordered by the appeals court to pay $50,000 damages (Neto, 1996).

Those who plagiarize from the dead and those who plagiarize journal articles and dissertations usually get away free. The former associate editor of Martin Luther King, Jr.'s papers has conceded that King appropriated, for seminar papers and for his dissertation, large sections from both published sources and from another dissertation written at Boston University in 1952.[12] The passages of King's writing and texts from which he borrowed are compared in the June 1991 *Journal of American History*; the issue contains eight separate articles, under the heading "Becoming Martin Luther King, Jr.: Plagiarism and Originality," on the impact on King's reputation (Thaler, 1991). Even the editors of his papers had to concede that the plagiarisms were obvious:

> In November 1990, the Martin Luther King Papers Project's director and senior editor, Clayborne Carson, announced the Project's finding of plagiarism in King's dis-

sertation....Boston University correctly convened a committee of inquiry, acknowledged the plagiarism in King's dissertation, and declared the case closed. (Luker, 1993, p. 155)

Keith Miller's book (1992), *Voice of Deliverance: The Language of Martin Luther King, Jr. and Its Sources*, identifies many of the sources from which King borrowed in sermons, books, and articles attributed to him.

Reinventing History

> The use of history lies in its capacity for advancing the approach to the truth.
>
> —Handlin, 1979, p. 405

The recently published *Lies My Teacher Told Me: Everything Your American History Textbook Got Wrong* (Loewen, 1995) has been characterized as an "exposure of our historical constructions" (Higgins, 1996, n.p.). That the victors write history to suit their purposes has been a common practice through the ages. Historian Bernard Lewis (1975) classified the types of history as: remembered, recovered, and invented. He readily concedes that remembered and recovered history may be inaccurate but not deliberately false. Invented history has a purpose:

> of changing the past, not to seek some abstract truth, but to achieve a new vision of the past better suited to [the historians'] needs in the present and their aspirations for the future. (p. 55)

The creation of myths to engender national pride or patriotism is a rather common purpose promoted by most governments. Other purposes are less benign, as when governments undermine history to create a new identity or deny past transgressions. The "revisionist" history of the former Soviet Union and Japan's refusal to teach schoolchildren about that country's invasion and occupation of China and Indochina prior to World War II are examples. The film director, Oliver Stone, sought to impose his own versions of "history" in the films *JFK* and *Nixon*, which unfortunately will be believed by some of those unacquainted with the remembered facts. Stone would probably characterize his interpretations as literary license.

Some cases of inventing history and buttressing the claim by producing forged documents have become quite famous. The German magazine, *Der Stern*, paid two million Deutschmarks, in 1983, to publish what were purported to be Hitler's diaries. Eminent news organizations, such as *Newsweek, Paris Match*, and the *Times of London*, purchased the rights to publish the diaries from *Der Stern*, and, indeed, printed some of the material before the forgery was exposed. The diaries were forged by Konrad Kaujau, a Stuttgart dealer in military memorabilia and documents. He was sentenced to prison for four and a half years (Rendell, 1994).

Another more talented forger is serving a life sentence for murdering two people to keep his forgeries hidden. Mark Hofmann had quite a successful career forging, by his own estimate, "hundreds" of historical documents purportedly signed by such luminaries as Daniel Boone, Paul Revere, Myles Standish, and assorted U.S. presidents. He sold these creations to the Mormon Church, individual collectors, auction galleries, and autograph dealers (Lindsey, 1988). The libraries of Utah State University, Brigham Young, and the University of Utah were also customers for Hofmann's forged creations. Many respected historians in the state of Utah, and even Charles Hamilton, the famous New York autograph expert, vouched for the authenticity of the ersatz documents that Hofmann forged. At the time of his arrest, Hofmann's forged copy of *Oath of a Freeman*, a broadside printed in Colonial America in 1636, had been exhaustively analyzed for authenticity by the Library of Congress (LC), which was sufficiently convinced of its genuineness that James G. Broderick, Assistant Librarian for Research Services, sent a letter to Hofmann's agent, Justin Schiller, asking that an offer to sell be made to the Library.[13] The parties were dickering over the price, originally set at $1.5 million, when Hofmann was arrested for murder. Although the sale to LC was not consummated, Hofmann estimated that he had made "at least $2 million" from his forgeries (Lindsey, 1988, p. 378).

The most famous forgery, and one that contributed to the worst massacre of the 20th century, is the so-called *Protocols of the Elders of Zion*, which were purported to be the text of a secret meeting held in Switzerland at which Jews plotted to take over the world. According to document expert Kenneth Rendell (1994) "the *Protocols* were fabricated by agents of the Czar in France and first published in Russia at the end of the 19th century" (p. ii). Supposedly both Kaiser Wilhelm and Czar Nicholas II believed them to be genuine. An article in the *Times of London* made the same assertion. Hitler later used them to stir up anti-Semitic feelings, later "less scrupulous Arab governments" used them (Lewis, 1975, p. 64).

ADVOCACY RESEARCH

Advocacy research's function of promoting public awareness is being compromised by the growing tendency to greatly magnify needs while asserting the scientific validity of these large numbers.

—Gilbert, 1994, p. 19

The media constantly bombard the public with statistics about social problems. The validity of these statistics, compiled usually by those who are connected with advancing some cause or promoting the interests of a particular group, has become increasingly unreliable. Christina Hoff Sommers (1994) highlights the oft-repeated assertion that 150,000 women die each year of complications from two eating disorders, anorexia and bulimia. Gloria Steinem (1992) and many others reported this figure, which actually refers to the number believed to suffer from the condition as determined in a survey taken in 1985. The number of deaths is fewer than 100 annually (Sommers, 1994).

During the 1980s, stories in the media reporting 50,000 child abductions by strangers per year created near hysteria as nervous parents took their children to be fingerprinted and their DNA recorded and placed on file in case the child was kidnapped. In truth, the number of children abducted by strangers is about 1% of that number.

A report,"A National Disgrace," from the Aging Committee's Subcommittee on Health and Long-Term Care estimated that 4% of aged persons (about one million in the United States) were victims of abuse by family members and other caregivers. The data were based on information from 73 people who responded to a survey of 433 residents in Washington, D.C. Three of the 73 "reported experiencing some form of psychological, physical or material abuse" (Gilbert, 1994, p. 22).

Inflated statistics on rapes committed on college women are another example of dubious social research. Mary Koss of the University of Arizona directed the *Ms. Magazine Campus Project on Sexual Assault*, and has published a number of articles based on that study. From these data, Koss asserted that 27% of college women had been victims of rape or attempted rape an average of two times between the ages of 14 and 21. Those numbers were unquestioned by the media that reported them and the scholarly journals that published Koss' articles, despite her numerous revisions of the data categories in light of scholarly criticism of her methods and interpretations. It was an undergraduate at Princeton, Katie Roiphe (1993), who raised a realistic question which showed that the statistic was inflated: "If I were really standing in the middle of an epidemic, a crisis—if 25 percent of my women friends were really being raped—wouldn't I know it?" (p. 26).

Advocacy research is probably more like propaganda than like scientific misconduct. It may illuminate real problems, but it exaggerates the extent of those problems by draining funds for research and prevention programs and public and governmental attention away from other areas. For example, members of Congress sponsored bills with the intent of governmental intervention to improve situations highlighted by advocacy research.[14] Irresponsible advocacy research "creates an unreliable foundation for social policy and does little to advance the credibility of social science" (Gilbert, 1994, p. 26).

Although logic is useful in questioning inflated and dubious statistics, identifying false or fabricated data in the social sciences is exceedingly difficult. Most social and behavioral science research cannot be replicated, in the sense that the results will turn out the same from study to study: human behavior, the subject of the social sciences, is not nearly as consistent as that of atoms or molecules in physical objects. Nachman Ben-Yehuda (1986) notes that scientific truth can be influenced by the character and beliefs of the researcher:

Furthermore, in sciences where "interpretations" prevail (e.g. sociology), the "truth" of a statement can be negotiated, and clearly depends on the prestige and world view of the scientist who makes the statement. A Marxist sociologist and a Parsonian sociologist would not explain the Russian revolution similarly. (p. 3)

Just as in science, little research in the social sciences is replicated. Yet, later analysis of a researcher's data can sometimes lead to suspicions of fraud. The case of Cyril Burt, the noted British psychologist who won the American Psychological Association's Thorndike Prize in 1971, is an example. Burt specialized in measuring intelligence (IQ) and was the leading figure in promoting the concept of the inheritability of intelligence (i.e., that nature is more dominant than nurture). He supposedly studied twins separated at birth and reported that, in general, they were of equal intelligence, despite growing up in very different environments. His data about the twins' intelligence were widely cited and used by other psychologists. Because he served as a consultant to a committee charged with evaluating Britain's educational system after World War II, his ideas were highly influential. Then, after Burt's death, Leon Kamin, a psychologist at Princeton University, noticed that Burt's statistical results never changed, even though the participants did, in studies conducted over time. Nor could Miss Conway or Miss Howard, the two women who Burt claimed were research assistants, ever be found; they are now considered mythical. Biographies published since Burt's death first discredited, then rehabilitated, and still later, again discredited his research.

There is strong suspicion that Alfred Kinsey, whose work on sexual behavior in the 1950s influenced the loosening of social mores as the baby boomers came of age, based his findings about sexual activity in young boys on the diary of a child molester. At least that is the belief expressed by the director of the Kinsey Institute at Indiana University, where Kinsey was a professor for many years ("Weird Science," 1995, p. 62).

CONCLUSION

Bogus research may be forgotten, its perpetrators disgraced or dead, but tainted writings endure. As Mallon (1989) observes,

To put one's theft into print is to have it forever on the library shelves, guiltily stacked just an aisle away from the volume it victimized, a stain that doesn't wash but forever circulates. (p. 131)

Unfortunately, the mechanisms for notifying purchasers of bogus, falsified, and simply erroneous publications are even weaker than the mechanisms for detecting them. The next chapter will discuss this point in greater detail, as the book examines the implications of research misconduct for library collections and information services.

NOTES

[1] The NSF and the NIH include the term "other serious deviations from accepted research practices" in their definition of scientific misconduct. This clause is controversial because there is no consensus about how such deviations should be defined. NSF had a case of misconduct in which the principal investigator pressured undergraduate women on a field trip in Mexico for sexual favors by offering or withholding research data and equipment.

[2] "FY 1996 funding for R&D [research and development] totals $71.2 billion, just over 0.4 percent above FY 1995. Defense R&D is up 1.7 percent to $38.5 billion, while nondefense R&D is down 1.1 percent to $32.7 billion" (see "Congressional Action on Research and Development in the FY 1996 Budget," 1996, n.p.). See other documents, as well, at http://www.aaas.org/spp/dspp/ rd/fy96. htm; http://www.aaas.org/spp/dspp/rd/fy97.htm.

[3] Donna Shalala herself was embroiled in a controversy about scientific misconduct when she was Chancellor of the University of Wisconsin, Madison. Charges of misconduct were leveled against two scientists who had received federal grants. The government sought to obtain laboratory records to investigate the case, which also resulted in a lawsuit over who has patent rights to a form of vitamin D. Shalala refused to allow these records to be turned over to the government. The case was brought to a standstill because the government did not obtain the information sought (Burd, 1993c).

[4] The work of Cyril Burt, the English psychologist considered an authority on IQ and genetics, has been discredited as fabricated. Burt influenced both Arthur Jensen, professor of psychology at Stanford University, and the late Richard Herrenstein of Harvard University. Jensen and Herrenstein have been sharply criticized for their work tying intelligence to genetics. Herrenstein's last publication, *The Bell Curve*, with Charles Murray (1995), is based on the premise that intelligence cannot be significantly raised because it is determined by genetics which are, in turn, determined, to a large extent, by race.

[5] The two scientists, Martin Fleischmann and Stanley Pons, who claimed to have discovered cold fusion lost a 1996 lawsuit that they had filed against the Italian newspaper, *La Repubblica*. The newspaper had called them and their associated Italian researchers "scientific frauds" and compared them to "fornicating priests." Douglas Morrison, a physicist from the Swiss research center CERN, served as the paper's science advisor. (See SCIFRAUD@CNISIBM. ALBANY.EDU (April 8, 1996)).

[6] The forerunner of the Internet was developed for the exchange of information among scientists working on projects for the Department of Defense.

7 The importance of laboratory notebooks cannot be overstated. The Secret Service's analysis of the paper in the notes of Dr. Thereza Imanishi-Kari was considered proof that the data in the infamous Baltimore/*Cell* paper had been falsified (see Sarasohn, 1993). Imanishi-Kari was deemed not to have committed scientific misconduct after an appeal to the Research Integrity Adjudications Panel in June, 1996.

[8] Charles Bluestone, professor of medicine at the University of Pittsburgh, acknowledged receipt of money for the same research from a drug company and from the NIH. In another case, a Harvard University researcher worked on an eye ointment while he was a stockholder in a company intending to sell the same ointment.

[9] Following the murder of four faculty members by a member of the engineering department, Concordia University in Montreal launched an investigation. As a result, three professors agreed to leave after they were deemed guilty of fraudulent authorship and questionable financial practices.

[10] Evidently the professor's subsequent employer—the National Endowment for the Humanities, where he administered research grants—never contacted the department for a recommendation.

[11] Walter Stewart and Ned Feder developed a software program to scan and match passages for plagiary. Using this program, they claimed that Oates' biographies of Abraham Lincoln, William Faulkner, and Martin Luther King, Jr. "turned up what they interpreted to be...instances of plagiarism,...all of which were short phrases rather than conveniently unmistakable extended passages" (Swan, 1994, p. 44).

[12] King's dissertation, "A Comparison of the Conceptions of God in the Thinking of Paul Tillich and Henry Nelson Wieman," contained passages similar to those of Jack Boozer's "The Place of Reason in Paul Tillich's Concept of God," doctoral dissertation, Boston University (1952).

[13] *Oath of a Freeman* is supposedly the first document printed in Colonial America. It expressed the idea "that the people should control their own destiny" and "was incorporated into the Declaration of Independence. The fifty or so copies of the oath itself were lost" (Lindsey, 1988, p. 150) until Hofmann "discovered" one.

[14] The bills include: "Violence Against Women Act of 1993," introduced by Senator Joseph Biden in response to Koss' rape survey, and "The Gender Equity Education Act of 1993," introduced by Representative Patricia Schroeder in response to the Association of American University Women's report, "Shortchanging Girls, Shortchanging America" (Sommers, 1994, pp. 298, 138).

2

MISCONDUCT AND THE SCHOLARLY LITERATURE

Ellen Altman

Publication is the lifeblood of science, conveying the symbolic nutrients of new theories, research findings, credit, and critical scrutiny. Journals and the articles they contain are so characteristic of science and so firmly entrenched that today these regularly published collections of research results drive, and perhaps define, the scientific enterprise.

—Chubin & Hackett, 1990, p. 83

...the number of publications by U.S. scientists and the frequency with which these publications are cited by other scientists are the criteria that the National Science Foundation uses to measure U.S. contributions to world science.

—Grinnell, 1992, p. 72

Several scholars of academic life have advanced the idea that research is basically the process of making and proving claims. Scientific theories require consensus before they become incorporated as knowledge in their respective disciplines. Advocates of particular theories that have not yet been accepted by consensus and incorporated into the discipline are characterized as "thought collectives" (Grinnell, 1992), which may be thought of as "sub-paradigms" in the sense used by Thomas Kuhn (1962). A thought collective is the consensus of some group within a given specialty regarding acceptable research topics, acceptable methods of research, and respectable publication channels. That consensus may be at odds with the view of others in the same specialty:

...an investigator's work will be considered in the context of the prevailing thought style of the collective. Only research that can be assimilated by the thought style will be seen as acceptably scientific. At the same time, however, the thought style is changeable and will accommodate to newly assimilated observations and hypotheses. (Grinnell, 1992, p. 69)

Being the first to make a claim which later proves to have lasting impact on some aspect of the discipline is exceedingly important to ambitious academics. Professional journals are the primary arena for staking claims and the accepted means for communicating new discoveries to specialists in every discipline. Professional journals serve as arbiters for the knowledge base of the discipline, showcasing what the editors and referees consider the best among the claims submitted to them. Having one's claim published in a prestigious professional journal is the first step to having it incorporated into the knowledge base.[1]

Articles reporting research are essentially claims awaiting acceptance by other scholars in the specialty. Readers who disagree with a claim frequently attempt to refute it by writing articles espousing competing claims or by sending letters to the journal editor in which the disputed article appeared, denigrating the method, the conclusions, or anything else they deem lacking in the research. Corrections and disagreements are considered part of the normal progress of scholarship. Articles containing competing claims may even be published in the same issue of a journal. The intent is to allow the experts to evaluate the validity of each claim. These disagreements among the competing "thought collectives" are considered normal and necessary for the advancement of knowledge in the discipline.

All researchers recognize that the possibility for error (unintended mistakes) in any research is high because the process is quite complex. Researchers can deal with error in their published articles in several ways: by writing other articles acknowledging and correcting the previous error, by sending a letter to the journal editor admitting the error, or by asking that the article be retracted. These examples of simple error, acknowledged by the authors, reflect the uncomplicated situations. Other cases of correction and retraction are not so straightforward.

PUBLICATION, ITS INFLUENCE ON FUNDING AND PRESTIGE

Since publication is the return on the investments made in the research funding process, we often hear the formula, "money in, papers out."

—Chubin & Hackett, 1990, pp. 90-91

Regardless of discipline, scientists and academics earn tenure, respect, and reputation based on their publications. Publication confers expert status on authors and is highly desirable, if not essential, in securing grants to support future research. An anthropological study of a biomedical laboratory at the University of California, La Jolla, concluded that "the production of papers is acknowledged by participants as the main objective of their activity" (Latour & Woolgar, 1986, p. 71). Because academic research is seldom concerned with developing tangible products, publications are its primary products. Indeed, publication is the *raison d'être* for academic research; thus, it is extremely important to both the authors and their employing institutions.

The prestige of universities and other knowledge organizations, like hospitals and research institutes, derives from the perceived quality of their faculty and researchers. The *Chronicle of Higher Education*, the influential newspaper that covers colleges and universities, frequently contains stories summarizing articles from other publications that purport to identify the "best departments" in (whatever discipline). The criterion typically used to determine best is the combined total of publications written by the department's faculty.

Because researchers need outlets to publish and to distribute their writings, a complex system of organizations has emerged in the last half-century, not only to publish and to disseminate research, but also to index, to classify, and eventually to facilitate retrieval of these writings. This system involves editors, publishers, indexers, database producers, and librarians.

The number of professional journals and books issued each year has grown enormously during the past 50 years, as has the number of people writing them. As disciplines develop more and more specialties, likened to the twigs on the branches of a tree, the experts in each specialty require a forum in which to communicate with others having similar interests and expertise. Commercial publishers have willingly underwritten the development of specialized journals, confident that the libraries serving the universities where the potential readers work will purchase subscriptions—and they do. In fact, as subscription prices of scholarly journals have risen, the number of individual subscribers has steadily declined.

Indexing services record bibliographic information about recently published articles. Abstracting services provide summaries of the articles as well as bibliographic information (hereafter referred to, both singly and together, as Indexing and Abstracting Services, I&A). Early on, it was recognized that these services were needed for timely identification of published articles. By the 1970s, database vendors began purchasing records compiled by the printed I&A services. These vendors then offered electronic retrieval of bibliographic references formerly available only in printed format.

Citation indexes, popularized by Eugene Garfield and his Institute for Scientific Information, provide a different approach to indexing and document retrieval. "The basis of citation indexes is that, if a writer cites a previous work and it is referenced in the bibliography, then the article must be about the same or a related topic" (Fisher, 1995, p. 28). There are three major citation indexes: for science, for the social sciences, and for arts and humanities.[2] Each index contains two parts: the source index and the citation index. The source index lists all the articles, chapters, books, and book reviews indexed during the time period covered. The citation index lists, by author, all the sources used to prepare the writings listed in the source index. Authors can look under their names to see which other authors have referenced their writings during a particular time period.

Citation records have become a form of academic currency, in that having one's writings cited by others acknowledges expertise and confers prestige. Citation counts (quite literally, the number of times an individual's writings are cited) are often considered by committees deciding on a professor's worthiness for tenure, promotion, or a merit raise. Articles identifying and ranking the most heavily-cited authors in a particular discipline are often used to determine this worthiness.

Citation indexes would, of course, be virtually impossible to construct without the use of computer technology. Apart from law, in which precedent is vitally important, there were no citation indexes before there were computerized databases. These databases now far overshadow the printed indexes in both usage and importance. According to Martha Williams (1995), between 1975 and 1994 the number of databases covering scholarly literature increased from 301 to 8,776 and the number of vendors offering them from 105 to 1,691. The 301 databases available in 1975 contained "about 52 million records." In 1994, 367 databases contained over a million records each, and the number has continued to grow.[3] By 1995, the records totaled 6.3 billion. Database searches in libraries between 1975 and 1993 increased from 750,000 to 58.3 million. Richard T. Kaser (1995), executive director of the National Federation of Abstracting and Information Services (NFAIS), wrote that the Association's 46 members published 14 million abstracts in 1993. This interlocking network, involving thousands of knowledge workers, millions of articles, and billions of bibliographic records, although not comprehensive, represents the scholarly and scientific knowledge base of society. Considering the enormous number of authors and titles contained in these bibliographic files, ensuring the integrity of the literature and its bibliographic structures is a complex task, even without the complications described in this chapter.

THE EDITORIAL PROCESS

> In theory, editors set standards of authorship for their journals. In practice, scientists in the specialty do.
>
> —National Academy of Sciences, 1992, p. 55

These standards are set by authors' choices of the journals to which they send their manuscripts and by the opinions of those who decide which manuscripts to publish. One factor in establishing the pecking order among journals in a given specialty (and, thus, the reputations of the journals' authors) is the way in which the publishing decisions are made: at the top are journals that have high rejection rates and are refereed.[4] The implication is, of course, that articles published in such journals have successfully passed a demanding screening process, causing laypersons to assume that what is accepted is true and reliable, a totally erroneous assumption.

Although most editors of professional journals are themselves scholars in the journal's specialty and possess considerable knowledge with which to assess the quality of the submissions, they tend not to rely solely on their own judgment. The better-financed journals might employ full-time associate editors who select among the manuscripts. The "better" journals also send manuscripts to two or more evaluators (referees), who typically are more knowledgeable about the topic of the paper than the editor(s). These referees donate their time and expertise to evaluate manuscripts. Some journals provide referees with a rating form to be completed in the evaluation process; others do not. Whether or not a rating form is employed, the quality of the evaluations vary, from useless to insightful, as do the opinions about the merits of the research, even among experts reading the same manuscript. Thoughtful evaluations and those from widely known experts do, however, carry considerable weight in the decision to accept or reject a manuscript. More commonly, the referees want revisions in particular sections of the manuscripts. So, then begins a process of negotiation among editor, referees, and author.

In essence, the referees and the editors are gatekeepers responsible for selecting, presumably, the best among the manuscripts sent to them. Referees, however, can make only limited assessments, based on their expertise, about the importance or novelty of the topic and about the plausibility and significance of the research, which they are expected only to read, not to replicate. Indeed, except for articles in mathematics and theoretical physics that contain the equations used to "prove" the hypothesis being tested, most articles in the sciences are "reports of what went on in the laboratory, and the evidence for their conclusions ultimately lies outside of the papers themselves....Laboratory research reports are relatively easy to fake" (Schmaus, 1988, p. 110). Articles based on surveys in social science disciplines are easier to falsify and their veracity is even more difficult to ascertain.

Criticism of the refereeing process has been constant over the years for a number of reasons, one of which is that the term itself has no agreed-upon meaning, not even for journals which belong to associations such as the International Committee of Medical Journal Editors (ICMJE). Some journals allow referees to know the names of the authors whose manuscripts they read; others do not. A criticism of allowing referees to know a manuscript's author is the possibility of referee bias, either for or against the author or for or against the author's employing institution, that may influence the evaluation of the manuscript. Some journals ask referees to sign their evaluations, which are then sent to the author(s); other journals follow a policy called "double blind" in which neither the authors nor the referees are apprised of each others' names. There is no standard regarding the number of referees who read a manuscript; some journals use one or two, others use more. Some use referees only for particular types of articles or for those likely to be controversial. Very few journals publish their policies for selecting manuscripts, hence it is difficult to know the basis for manuscript evaluation. Charges that the system is erratic are given credence by the research of Douglas P. Peters and Stephen J. Ceci (1982).

Peters and Ceci, who tested the refereeing system in a widely-cited and controversial study, sent retyped copies of 12 articles to the same journals that had published the originals some 18 to 32 months before. The names and affiliations of the original authors were changed and some minor revisions were made in the text. Only three of the resubmitted articles were detected; eight of the remaining nine were rejected. Yet, in spite of the obvious flaws in the refereeing system, no better alternative has been found. To paraphrase Winston Churchill's remark on democracy as a form of government, "it is the worst possible system, except for all the others." Just as democracy does not guarantee good government, peer review does not guarantee reliable research.

THE INTEGRITY OF SCHOLARLY LITERATURE

> Since scientific papers are intended to be read, not "hidden under a bushel," their authors should anticipate that others will rely on them.
>
> —Schmaus, 1988, p. 100

With few exceptions, editing a scholarly journal is an assignment in addition to one's regular job—usually as a professor. Nevertheless, editors spend much time corresponding with authors and referees, reading and evaluating manuscripts, and proofreading pages prior to publication. They must also be alert for authors' attempts to inflate their resumes by submitting manuscripts that essentially duplicate their previous publications, or "salami" articles (also called Least Publishable Units) that describe only tiny slices of a research project. These "add considerably to the growing problem of sheer volume of the literature" (Weller, 1995, p. 59).

Then there are the manuscripts that are based on fabricated data or copied from the publications of other authors. Journal editors, however, are often ill-prepared to play cop.[5] Most journals lack policies on how to handle accusations involving fabrication, falsification, plagiarism, or disputes between or among co-researchers.

Although editors are not responsible for the accuracy of the articles they publish, they are concerned about the integrity of their journals and their reputations for quality. More importantly, both editors and scholars recognize that:

> The research community, regardless of discipline, cannot tolerate misrepresentation of experimental results or of authorship. Scientists rely on the literature in their fields as the basis for their own work, whether that work be pointed toward chal-

lenging, corroborating, or extending reported studies. [Therefore, it is important that] everyone…be able to assume correctly that experiments described in a research article were actually carried out, that the results reported were actually obtained, and that the individuals whose names appear as authors actually did the work and are responsible for it. (Lapidus & Mishkin, 1990, p. 289)

When trust is broken the price can be high. When Jack Schubert and Steven Krogh Derr published research that had implications for removing toxic chemicals (e.g., cadmium and plutonium) from the blood of persons who worked with these poisonous materials, other researchers tried to extend the conclusions presented in the article. As a result, "seven groups in various countries spent six months" and nearly a million dollars based on the fabricated information which Derr provided for the article (McGinty, 1979, p. 4).

A Cornell University tumor specialist and his graduate student spent several months trying to determine why they could not duplicate the reactions reported and published by another Cornell graduate student, Mark Spector, as did several scientists in other labs who had purchased a substance created by Spector (Wade, 1981a). The data, they came to learn, had been falsified. "Three competent biochemists (at University of Birmingham, England, and Max Planck Institute in Germany) spent four man years trying to repeat the exciting work of a Ph.D. student." Then that student admitted that the data were "figments of his imagination" (Muller, 1977, p. 522).

When law enforcement suspects that a crime has been committed, there is a clear procedure to follow. However, most people are confused about what to do about suspicions of scientific or research misconduct. To whom should it be reported, what exactly constitutes misconduct, and what standard of proof determines it? Editors and publishers are equally confused not only about the issues involved but also the lack of consensus in scholarly and scientific publishing about what Marcel LaFollette (1992, p. 87) calls "publishing tradition." Such consensus would provide editors with a course of action and a system of accountability when confronted with allegations of tainted research. She asks to whom editors should be responsible:

- The accused and his or her professional reputation?
- Federal sponsors and legislators?
- Subscribers who paid for what they trusted were "authenticated" results?
- The publisher who wishes to uphold the standards of good scholarship and to protect copyright?
- The journal's primary constituency? (pp. 87-88)

Obviously, all these parties have a stake in the integrity of the material published in journals. Charges of plagiarism, fabrication, or falsification in articles appearing in the pages of their journals are the stuff of editors' nightmares.

It is only in the past few years that journals, like the federal funding agencies, have begun to establish policies for dealing with allegations of research miscon- duct. Both the International Committee of Medical Journal Editors (1988) and the Council of Biology Editors (Bailar et al., 1990) have adopted statements on deal- ing with allegations. The decision to conform to these guidelines rests with each individual journal, however, and these decisions can be influenced by advertisers, by threats of legal action, and by the organization sponsoring the journal, which may even be the employer of the person accused.

Because editors do not know if allegations about articles already published are true, malicious, or baseless, their reactions are usually cautious, and certainly with good reason. Because professional reputations are at stake, care must be taken not to damage them with hasty actions. Increasingly, those accused of wrongdoing hire attorneys to threaten lawsuits. Not surprisingly, such threats have a chilling effect on most journals, as financial ruin might result from legal fees and perhaps damages awarded to the plaintiff.[6] Ralph D. Davis (1988, p. 67) has likened these threats of legal action to a new form of academic censorship. The journal, under such threat, is effectively silenced about the misconduct charge until a formal investigation is completed, if ever, and the results released.

Davis' comments were prompted by the difficulty that Walter W. Stewart and Ned Feder (1987) had in publishing their paper that analyzed the flaws in 109 of Dr. John Darsee's 116 published articles. (Darsee was found to have fabricated data for articles reporting on heart research while employed at the medical schools of Emory University and Harvard University.) The prestigious British journal, *Nature*, initially accepted the Feder and Stewart manuscript in 1984, but feared to publish it because of British libel laws, and because some of Darsee's co-authors threatened suit. Fifteen other journals also declined the paper, primarily out of fear of litigation. The manuscript, considerably revised, finally appeared in *Nature* in 1987, along with a statement written by the head of Darsee's lab (Braunwald, 1987).

Yet, some journals and aggrieved authors are taking action to expose problem articles. The journal *Human Biology* printed a letter charging that a large section of a recent article had previously been published by the same authors in a Japa- nese journal and that the last part of the article had been plagiarized from an arti- cle in *Science* by the British and American writers of the letter. They cited both the purloined and the copied publications, so that readers who wanted to follow up could judge the content of these three publications for themselves (Bittles & Mason, 1993). Similarly, the editor of the *Canadian Journal of Physics* dis- avowed an article published in that journal as one plagiarized from an Italian peri- odical (Betts, 1992).

Neal Bowers (1994), a professor of English and a published poet, wrote an arti- cle for *American Scholar* about the plagiaries of two of his poems by a person who changed the titles and the first lines, and submitted them as original work. The plagiarist's "variant titles help disguise the multiple publications while preventing detection through reference to indexes or tables of contents" (p. 546). Despite Bowers' diligent attempts to spread the word about the plagiaries among editors of literary journals, 18 of them published the tainted poems. Bowers charges that his "plagiarist has stolen from other poets as well" and names them (p. 546).

The editors of the *Journal of Laboratory and Clinical Medicine* recently conducted an investigation after questions were raised about two articles it had published. The author of both, a foreign national, had left the United States, and his former academic employer was not interested in the matter. The editorial staff felt that the journal had "a special obligation to its readers and to the scientific community" (Hammerschmidt & Gross, 1995, p. 3).

The author, Aws S. Salim, was suspected of fabricating data. He maintained his innocence but declined to produce the data on which his articles were supposedly based. The investigation broadened to include other articles by the author. Editor Dale E. Hammerschmidt noted that "each of the individual articles was credible when examined in isolation; it was only when they were placed in the context of the calendar and their fellow publications that…concerns arose" (Hammerschmidt & Gross, 1995, p. 5). For example, at his peak of productivity, the author in question had produced a paper every two weeks. The number of patients on whom he reported "exceeded 4,000 in an unusually short space of time" (p. 6). Some of the author's "studies" of patients preceded the animal studies on which they purportedly were based. In other cases, the work was done "before the disease in question had even been described" (p. 6). As a result of its investigation, the journal disavowed the two articles it published by "withdrawal of aegis" (p. 8).

The editors of the *Bulletin of Environmental Contamination and Toxicology* conducted an investigation after receiving four manuscripts between 1990 and 1994 that were found to be plagiarized. Herbert Nigg and Gabriela Radulescu (1994) expended considerable effort to determine the background of these instances of plagiarized manuscripts. They found that the four cases had common elements. When questioned by the editors, each of the principal authors admitted, in writing, to copying published material. However, the editors characterized three of the authors as "arrogant in their excuses" (p. 169). In two of the cases the first author had been involved in other instances of scientific misconduct. The plagiarized materials were not cited in the references. The editors placed these authors on a "List of Shame," essentially banning them from publishing in that journal. Nigg and Radulescu made some observations about these cases that have implications for the scholarly literature. People who are found to have plagiarized usually get away with little or no punishment from their employers, from funding agencies, or from any other source. Neither editors nor reviewers have organized to take "concerted action" against those guilty of scientific misconduct involving the misuse of literature.

Editors usually learn about problems with articles they have published from third parties, co-workers and/or other authors claiming that their research or their ideas have been stolen by the accused. If an allegation of misconduct seems plausible, some editors will write to the author outlining the charges and asking for an explanation. Should the author fail to provide a plausible explanation, supported by evidence such as research notebooks or completed survey forms, editors may write to the author's institutional administrators asking for a response to the charges. The guidelines adopted by the International Committee of Medical Journal Editors (1988) insist that "If substantial doubts arise about the honesty of a wor...it is the editor's responsibility to ensure that the question is appropriately pursued" (p. 304). The onus of investigation, however, should be on the institution where the work was done, because journals generally lack both the means and the authority to conduct investigations. As Philip Majerus (1982), in his presidential address on the topic of scientific misconduct at the 74th annual meeting of the American Society for Clinical Investigation, put it, "We are the JCI [*Journal of Clinical Investigation*], not the FBI [Federal Bureau of Investigation]" (p. 216). When institutional investigations are complete, however, journal editors expect to be notified, and they are annoyed when they are not. (The editor of a psychology journal was annoyed that the University of Calgary notified funding agencies of the findings of an investigation of false research, but not any of the journals in which the suspect articles appeared (Kaihla, 1994)).

Some authors and institutions stonewall these editorial inquiries by simply denying that any misconduct occurred. Acknowledgment of error is even less likely in situations in which "gift authorship" is conferred on individuals who contributed nothing to the actual research or writing. Laboratory directors frequently are accorded gift authorship solely because of their position. LaFollette (1992), commenting on what she called "irresponsible co-authorship" in the proven case of fraudulent publications by Dr. John Darsee, said many of his colleagues had willingly accepted credit as "co-authors" on "articles they had neither written nor read and then blithely disavowed responsibility when the articles were challenged" (p. 23).

The co-authors associated with Robert Slutsky, M. D., who was found guilty of publishing fraudulent research by two faculty committees at the University of California, San Diego, showed the same disinclination to come clean about their involvement. As Paul Friedman (1990) explains, "our experience with Slutsky's coauthors is that they were uninterested in taking any initiatives to reproduce research results or correct the literature" (p. 1419).

As a result of these cases and of continuing concern about honorific authorship, the International Committee of Medical Journal Editors (1991) recommends that journals require all authors to sign a statement affirming their contribution to the manuscript under consideration. This practice is now followed by some major medical journals, such as the *Journal of the American Medical Association* (JAMA) and the *New England Journal of Medicine* (NEJM). Journal editors have also found that conflict of interest, or at least the appearance of conflict of interest, should be made public. The dispute over treatment of children's ear infections with antibiotics illustrates how complex a case may become.

Charles Bluestone and Erdem Cantekin, both professors in the Department of Otolaryngology at the University of Pittsburgh, were co-investigators on a grant from the National Institutes of Health (NIH) to study the effectiveness of antibiotics for treating otitis media, more commonly known to parents of young children as ear infections. During the 1980s, the NIH had granted some $18 million to the Otitis Media Research Center (OMRC) at Children's Hospital, Pittsburgh, where the research was conducted. Unbeknownst to the NIH, Dr. Bluestone had accepted, on behalf of the OMRC, $3.5 million from pharmaceutical companies to assess their antibiotic treatments for the ear infection. Dr. Cantekin claimed that because he was "concerned over the ethics of mixing public and private funding in the OMRC's research into antibiotic effectiveness, he refused to participate further in privately funded clinical trials" (Cantekin, McGuire, & Potter, 1990, p. 1428). Bluestone and Cantekin submitted papers, with opposite conclusions about the effectiveness of antibiotics on otitis media, to the *NEJM* in the spring of 1986. The editor contacted the University of Pittsburgh and Children's Hospital; both institutions said that Cantekin had no right to submit an article and that he had acted improperly. The Bluestone version was published in 1987 without any editorial statement about Cantekin's manuscript and its contrary findings. Cantekin then submitted his paper to *JAMA*. One of the *JAMA* referees contacted Bluestone and suggested he obtain a copy of the manuscript, which he did. The Department of Otolaryngology then filed charges of "research misconduct" against Cantekin and banished him from the hospital. The editor of *JAMA* rejected the article because of the charge of misconduct, concern over Cantekin's inability to gain access to the data, and the fact that NIH was conducting an investigation.

Erdem Cantekin, Timothy W. McGuire, and Robert L. Potter (1990) raise some interesting questions about research and publishing that remain unresolved:

1. How should scholarly journals handle dissent among co-investigators? If co-investigators write competing articles should they published together or at least by the same journal?
2. "Should a scholarly journal deprive external reviewers of the knowledge that a dissenting analysis exists and has been received and fail to provide the reviewers with that dissenting analysis?"
3. "Should a scholarly journal refuse to publish the dissenting views of the co-researcher" because of factors other than scientific inadequacy?
4. "Is the peer review process adequately equipped to detect undisclosed conflicts of interest or undisclosed problems with the conduct of studies…?" (p. 1429)

Treatment for otitis media costs more than $2 billion every year, so the outcome of the debate had significant implications. A large epidemiological study published in 1991 concluded that antibiotics did not significantly speed recovery from otitis media, essentially verifying Cantekin's earlier position (Crossen, 1994, p. 165).

Whether influenced by the otitis media case or not, some journals "[have] required authors to disclose their economic ties as a condition of publication" (Relman, 1989, p. 934). The *New England Journal of Medicine* implemented this requirement in 1984. The *Journal of the American Medical Association* requires that authors "certify any affiliations with or involvement in any organization or entity with a direct financial interest in the subject matter or materials discussed in the manuscript" ("Instructions for Authors," 1994, p. 161).

Results of research conducted with corporation funds may be suppressed if the funder does not like the findings. Dr. Betty Dong, a clinical pharmacist at the University of California, San Francisco, agreed to test the efficacy of several drugs for hypothyroidism. The study was funded by Knoll Pharmaceutical, the maker of Synthroid, whose sales top $600 million a year in the United States. Dr. Dong's research, which concluded that Synthroid was no more effective than its competitors, was accepted by *JAMA* for its January 1995 issue.

Not only did Knoll Pharmaceutical threaten breach of contract if the study were published, but Gilbert Mayor, senior director of medical research at Knoll and also an editor of the *American Journal of Therapeutics*, "was the lead author on a lengthy critique of [Dr. Dong's] unpublished findings" related to the thyroid drug research (Wadman, 1996, p. 4). The article, published in June 1995, claimed that Dong's work was too flawed to reach any conclusions about the equivalence of the other thyroid medications to Synthroid. The few cases described here show that the scholarly literature is being affected. There are even more egregious examples.

EXAMPLES OF THE CONTAMINATION OF THE LITERATURE

> ...there is reason to be concerned with the literature of science and the research based on the findings of that literature.
>
> —Kochan & Budd, 1992, p. 492

Descriptions of the details surrounding some of the more famous cases of deviant research have been published in a number of sources. This section discusses only the effects of malfeasance on the literature. For a fuller listing of perpetrators and the journals in which their contaminated articles appeared, see Appendices A and B.

E. A. K. Alsabti, a Jordanian national and a graduate of an offshore medical school, worked at a number of U.S. hospitals and medical centers in the 1970s and early 1980s. He retyped an estimated 60 previously published papers, changed the titles, claimed authorship, and sent the papers to relatively obscure journals, mostly located outside the United States. His plagiary was difficult to detect because the words in the titles differed from the originals, thus preventing detection by keyword indexing. He was finally exposed because of the persistence of one of the authors he had copied. Even after his misconduct was exposed, the scholarly record has not been completely corrected. The report from the National Academy of Sciences (1992) notes:

> Many of the demonstrable plagiaries were eventually retracted, but his name still stands atop dozens of papers in the computer files of the huge scientific indexing services, the overlords and compilers of scientific track records. Spokesmen for *Index Medicus* and the *Science Citation Index* say there is no precedent for retractions from their files, and that they would probably hesitate to set one, as it might force them in the future to pass judgment on disputes that sometimes arise over authorship. His legacy lives on. (p. 51)

Fortunately, Alsabti's plagiaries have been ignored by the scientific community as his work has not been cited, except in reference to his plagiary.[7]

Stephen Breuning's work was not ignored. He wrote 24 of the 70 papers published between 1979 and 1983 that discussed drug therapy for institutionalized, severely mentally handicapped children. He simply made up the data. Eugene Garfield, founder of the Institute for Scientific Information which publishes the major citation indexes, and Alfred Welljams-Dorof (1990) studied 101 citations made by other researchers to 20 of Breuning's writings. They categorized 33 of the citations as disagreeing with Breuning's findings or methods, 10 as agreeing, and 58 as neutral. Garfield and Welljams-Dorof concluded that "the frequency of citations…seems to indicate that [Breuning's work] was influential in the field…. 11 Breuning publications were cited between 10 and 26 times. In the 1955 to 1987 *Science Citation Index* files of 30 million cited items, only 7% achieved this level of citation. However, closer examination of the type and context of Breuning citations diminishes the apparent influence of his work" (p. 1426) in that many of the authors citing Breuning rejected his purported findings.

Paul J. Friedman, associate dean of the Medical School at the University of California, San Diego (1990), describes the School's attempt to notify journals and their readers about the tainted publications of Dr. Robert Slutsky. In collaboration with the chairman of the faculty committee investigating the validity of Slutsky's publications, Dr. Friedman sent a letter to 30 journals requesting publication of a statement and a list of citations representing Slutsky's fabricated and questionable publications. In all, 135 articles by Slutsky appeared in prestigious medical journals, such as the *Journal of the American College of Cardiology*. Slutsky, through his attorneys, sent letters disavowing the conclusions in 15 of the articles. A faculty committee concluded that another 12 articles were fraudulent, and that 48 others were questionable because no co-author could produce the original data or vouch that each phase of the research had been performed.

John Darsee published 116 papers in five years as sole or co-author. After investigating, Emory University declared as "invalid" 43 of 45 abstracts (short statements commonly used to report research findings). Later, the university announced that eight of 10 articles were invalid. Harvard University retracted nine of Darsee's articles in whole or in part. The effect of his publications on the scientific literature has been staggering. According to Bruce Dan (1983),

> the list of papers that cite Darsee's work covers more than 29 feet of computer print-out from the SCISEARCH data base. The ultimate validity of these 241 papers which cited Darsee's work as a foundation for all or part of their investigations is now open to question, including 13 in which Darsee cites his own previous publications. (p. 2872)

Darsee's deceit, which was exposed in 1981, has been difficult to eradicate because computerization of the bibliographical system was not as widespread then as it has now become. Many printed indexes covering the years in which Darsee's false articles appeared are still in use. Carol Ann Kochan and John M. Budd (1992) examined the citations to Darsee's articles and abstracts listed in *Science Citation Index* from 1982 through 1990. In all, they identified 298 citations in English-language journals, which they then categorized according to context: whether the citations dealt with Darsee's research positively (meaning that they agreed with it), negatively, or discussed his misconduct. As late as 1990, Darsee's work was still receiving positive citation. In fact, between 1982 and 1990, 256 of the citations to Darsee's work (85.9%) were positive. Kochan and Budd concluded:

> Analysis shows that 136 of the positive citations are to works deemed fraudulent or questionable by the committee [in 1982]....Darsee was cited in the journal *Circulation* as late as 1986, despite the fact that two of his papers had appeared and were retracted in that journal....Through 1990...Darsee is still cited, and cited positively, in the literature of cardiology. (p. 491)

In 1990, *The Journal of the Geological Society of India* asked readers to ignore all the papers it had published over the preceding 21 years written by paleontologist Viswa Jit Gupta, who was exposed for deceiving co-authors and journals about fossils and their locations. The Geological Society of India and the University of Panjab conducted investigations, and both concluded that Gupta had indeed seeded fossil finds, plagiarized, and misled his co-authors. John Talent, the Australian paleontologist who first charged that Gupta's work was both false and plagiarized, cautioned: "A major exercise is necessary to delineate just where reality and truth might lie. Until the facts are established it would seem advisable to doubt the rigor and even the factual content of any work bearing the name of V. J. Gupta among its authors" (see Talent et al., 1990, p. 582). Considering that

Gupta's publications are estimated at over 400, his impact on the credibility of the database of Himalayan paleontology has been significant.

Concern about the credibility of the literature led the editorial staff of the *Journal of Laboratory* and *Clinical Medicine* to investigate Aws S. Salim, the author suspected of fabricating research. His articles "supported a change in therapeutic strategy for common and serious illnesses, and citations to the problem articles were beginning to appear in the other authors' articles" (Hammerschmidt & Gross, 1995, p. 7). This author had over 50 other publications of which he was sole author. There is no information regarding the actions other journals that published his articles are taking to investigate their validity.

THE BIBLIOGRAPHIC APPARATUS

> Once published, a scientist becomes a bibliographic entity that lives in the literature and bears certain intellectual interests and competencies....Similarly, publication gives enduring life to a research enterprise....
>
> —Chubin & Hackett, 1990, p. 111

Once an article appears in print, it becomes part of the bibliographic record and is incorporated into the interlocking apparatus that creates the world's knowledge structure. On the simplest level, the article appears in a particular issue of a journal, that issue is bound to preserve it physically along with other issues covering a particular time span, and the bound volume is placed on library shelves where it sits awaiting readers. However, shortly after the article appears, the bibliographic apparatus incorporates it into the scholarly record. Its existence is noted in at least one indexing and abstracting publication, making it readily findable by the author(s) name(s), by the subject covered, and perhaps by all the keywords in the title. Each service decides on how completely to index each journal title, based on how important that journal is to the discipline. Some journals are more completely indexed than others, even by the same I&A service. Each has its own policy on how, or if, it will handle corrections to the literature. Some services index only articles, not letters or errata statements, while others index everything except advertising. Most, however, do not describe their policies about what, or how much, is to be indexed.

Traditionally, the printed volumes of I&A publications were purchased by libraries for consultation by users. Now, however, all the major printed I&A services are also available in digital format as an online database, as CD-ROM discs, or as both. Some newer I&A services are issued only in digital form. New services such as *FirstSearch* and *Tulip* provide the full text of some articles in electronic format, allowing anyone wanting to read an article included in a database to do so on a computer screen, or to print it off using the printer attached to the computer, rather than having to consult the print version of the journal that originally published it.

Other researchers working in the same area may read the article, either in printed or electronic versions, and use it in preparing their own articles. Once these new articles are published, their footnotes acknowledging use of other writings—which buttress the claims made in the new article—will be entered into a citation index. It is not unusual for bibliographic information about an article to appear in several different indexing sources and to be cited in other journal articles and books. If that article, however, is later proven fraudulent or plagiarized, how does that fact become known? How to incorporate such information into the bibliographic record and how to notify potential readers have been, and continue to be, issues largely ignored.

CLEANSING THE LITERATURE

Unfortunately, fake scientific knowledge is not like fake art—we cannot simply tear an offending page from a journal like we remove forged paintings from museum walls.

—LaFollette, 1993, p. 23

Detecting fraud in science may be difficult, but purging the literature of bad papers is even harder.

— "Setting...," 1989, p. 911

At present there is no organized alerting mechanism to identify retracted articles nor is there a consensus as to what form such an alert should take or even who should assume responsibility.

—Ratzan, 1992, p. 31

In a sardonic look at scientific misconduct, Lee Ratzan (1992) created a story about how a dictator in an African country was killed by clever use of the medical literature. A physician, whom the dictator had persecuted, escaped to the United States and became a medical researcher. Some years later, the dictator was reported to be ill from an undisclosed problem. The physician, aware of the cause of the illness, submitted a paper to a journal announcing a wonderful treatment for a rare disease, which was, of course, the same as the dictator's illness. The physician's apology for the error in computing the proper dosage of the medicine accompanied his retraction which appeared some time later. By then, of course, the dosage had already been administered by the dictator's current physicians, based on an online search of the medical literature. "But so very few online databases identify retracted articles and [the physician] knew that..." (p. 120).

Retraction is the process by which corrections to the published literature are made. In essence, a retraction is like saying: "please disregard this article as though it had never been published." If only correcting the literature were so easy. In reality, correcting the literature is a complicated and highly fallible process because a number of thorny issues are involved, such as:

- Who has the right to retract an article if the author(s) refuse or are unavailable? What happens if co-authors disagree that an article should be retracted?
- Do editors have an obligation to publish retraction notices pertaining to articles in their own journals? Do they have responsibility to publish retraction notices about articles published in other journals?
- Can part, but not all, of an article be retracted?
- What form should retractions take in terms of placement, size, and prominence in the journal's pages? Should they be placed with letters to the editor, in an addendum, or in any empty space? Should the type be bold, or the size larger than standard? Arnold Relman (1990, p. 27), former editor of the *New England Journal of Medicine*, endorsed having a standard and separate place for notices of retractions, but his advice has not been widely followed.
- How should words such as *correction, comments, amendment*, and *withdrawal of aegis* be interpreted? Does the phrase "Notice of duplicate publication" mean self-plagiarism or plagiarism by another person or persons? All of these terms have appeared in journal pages describing problem articles. Should these terms be construed to mean something equal to or less than retraction? If less, how much less? There is no consensus about the level of severity these words convey.
- How can retractions, sent years after, be tied to the original article so that potential readers will realize that the article is invalid?
- Should corrections, amendments, and withdrawals of aegis be tied back to the original article to alert potential readers?
- How can those who use I&A services know whether or not a service includes retractions, corrections, or any material other than articles?
- Should news accounts about allegations, investigations, or lawsuits about misconduct involving publications be tied to those articles by the I&A services to alert the scholarly community to the possibility that the work is unreliable?

These are all extremely complicated issues, as shown by examples from publicized cases. Although the International Committee of Medical Journal Editors (1988) adopted a statement on retractions that addresses some of these issues, many journals have not followed their guidelines.

Authors of tainted articles react in different ways after their misconduct is exposed. Some send rather straightforward statements acknowledging their guilt, or have their attorneys send statements attempting to silence the journal editor or to obfuscate the situation. Others provide noncommittal statements, do not respond, or, in the case of some foreign nationals, flee the country. Some journals will print retractions sent by one or more authors. Other journals have a policy requiring all authors to agree to an article's retraction, which means that a number of articles considered tainted will never be retracted, since joint authorship is more the rule than the exception these days. Some journals will print retractions at the request of the author's employing institution. The ICMJE guidelines state that the editor may accept retractions by responsible persons but does not define who these may be.

Dr. Robert Slutsky is among the most infamous authors in terms of number of tainted articles. After the investigation by the University of California, San Diego, Slutsky's attorney sent a letter to some editors saying that Slutsky was convinced that his results were "subject to serious question," but did not acknowledge that he had falsified or fabricated the data (Friedman, 1990, p. 1416). The university wanted Slutsky's entire record cleaned up, so it sent a statement to the 30 journals that had published his 135 papers, both valid and nonvalid. Editorial reaction to this request was highly mixed. Half of the editors did not respond to the first letter and received a follow-up request. Many journals took as long as two years to answer. Eventually, statements concerning 46 of the 60 non-valid articles were printed, but they took a variety of forms. Of the 17 journals that published work known to be tainted, only nine printed a retraction that specifically stated that the University had found evidence of "research fraud," accompanied by an explanation of how the investigation was conducted. "The others failed to include all the articles that were evaluated (valid or nonvalid) or published nothing" (Friedman, 1990, p. 1417). One journal refused to publish any retraction not initiated by an author.

Perhaps retraction is not as effective a means of notifying readers as might be expected. One study found that "general news articles and the three reviews published by the University of California-San Diego" were more effective than journal retractions in alerting scientists to Slutsky's tainted publications (Whitley, Rennie, & Hafner, 1994, p. 170).

Dan (1983) reports similar reactions on the part of journal editors when the Emory University Medical School attempted to clean up the false articles written by Dr. John Darsee. The assistant dean at Emory said "that at least one journal is looking into mechanisms for listing the retraction in its index. How or whether the articles will be identified as retracted in scientific citations systems is uncertain" (p. 2872). One journal refused to print a retraction on the grounds that it did not have a page for letters. Some journals will print retractions, but not corrections, amendments, or any statement not specifically labeled a retraction.

Allan Poling (1992) recounts his frustrations in attempting to get retractions published for articles which listed him as co-author with Stephen Breuning. The editor of *Archives of General Psychiatry* preferred to publish the retraction only after the university and NIH investigations had been completed, some four years after publication. The editor of *Pharmacology Biochemistry* and *Behavior* initially suggested a correction. Because Poling wanted to retract and Breuning did not, the editor suggested that Poling seek advice from the ethics committees of professional societies. After protracted correspondence, the editor agreed to publish a retraction upon the investigation's completion. According to Poling, however, the retraction never appeared. Some journals do not publish corrections as a matter of policy, and, especially in fraud cases, decline to publish them out of fear of litigation by the accused.

Consensus about the proper format for retractions does not exist. Some journals place them on unnumbered pages at the end of the issue, with letters to the editor, or with advertisements, and others display them prominently. Gwendolyn L. Snodgrass and Mark P. Pfeifer (1992), who have made several studies of retractions, noted that most retractions that they examined did not contain the title of the original article within the heading. They criticized the biomedical publishing community for its failure to establish and maintain a uniform format for retraction notices; the result has been a critical lack of visibility for retractions appearing in these publications (p. 331).

The words used in headings identifying the retractions also tend to be problematic due to a lack of clarity. Snodgrass and Pfeifer (1992) analyzed the headings used for 97 retraction notices. Although the word "retraction" was used for 66 of them, the other 31 were given 14 different headings, such as letter to the editor, notification to membership, correction, announcement, or statement. Each journal evidently chose its own heading without explaining exactly what the heading implied.

The content of retraction statements is another variable. Some statements simply give the bibliographic citation and say the article is retracted, a practice that, although common, has been criticized as insufficient. Keith Miller (1992, p. 97) considers it "unethical and collegially inappropriate not to report in a retraction some considered comment on the status of the science problems originally addressed." For example, some statements admit an inability to replicate original results by the authors, others cite new data or claim contaminated samples or materials, and still others admit misconduct on the part of named or unnamed coauthors. Many, however, simply ask for retraction. Miller says that, instead of placing blame, "retraction represents a judgment about the status of the science, not about the conduct of retractors" (p. 197).

Despite retraction, the printed version of a tainted article is not removed or destroyed. As an artifact, the article survives its retraction. A library would not extract the article from its bound volume, nor would most libraries mark the physical copy to note the retraction. Furthermore, the retraction notices in printed indexes can be many volumes removed from the citation to the tainted article because of the passage of time. Several years are likely to pass in the interval between an article's publication and the discovery of misconduct. For example, as a result of an Office of Research Integrity (ORI) investigation completed in 1994, Dr. John L. Ninnemann was to submit letters of retraction to three journals for articles that he had published in 1978, 1980, 1982, 1983, and 1984—10 to 16 years after their appearance. The volumes containing the retraction letters sit on the library shelves far removed from the articles disavowed.

For the most part, the bibliographic apparatus of indexes, databases, and CD-ROMs records only information published in other sources—mostly journals— and does not embellish or explain the information taken from these sources. While indexes in CD-ROM format can sometimes tie retractions to the citations for the original article, most CD-ROM indexes cover a particular time period, typically one to three years. If the article and its subsequent retraction appear within the time period covered by the disk, they are easily connected. However, "an archival database on CD-ROM...can be corrected only through the release of a complete replacement disk" (Beutler, 1995, p. 67). The CD-ROM vendor is unlikely to issue replacements to accommodate a few retractions; thus, CD-ROM archives suffer from the same time-delay problem as the printed versions.

It is technically feasible to tie retractions to the original article in an online database, that is, if the original publisher sends the information and if the database producers have a policy of making such corrections. Not all do, and some do only partially. As a result, other researchers continue to cite fraudulent articles. Another study by Pfeifer and Snodgrass (1990) used *Index Medicus* and other sources to identify 82 completely retracted articles published between 1970 and 1989. They then used *Science Citation Index and Social Sciences Citation Index* to measure subsequent use of the retracted articles. Comparison with a control group of non-retracted articles revealed that retractions reduced citations by approximately 35% (p. 1420). The researchers had difficulty in locating retraction notices, because of the problems noted previously. Indeed, Pfeifer and Snodgrass found that the majority of the retractions were not even included in the annual index for the journals in which they appeared (p. 1422). Their findings are similar to those of N. D. Wright (1991), who analyzed the context in which retracted articles were used in later publications. Wright found that although citations declined after retraction, reactions to 90% of the retracted articles were positive, meaning acceptance of the false claims. Even worse, some of the retracted material appeared in review articles, and, in some instances, articles cited works that had been retracted in the same journal. Evidently, these journals kept no record of tainted works that they had published.

The National Library of Medicine (NLM), which prepares the largest medical index in the world, did not begin indexing retraction notices in its MEDLINE database or its printed *Index Medicus* until 1984. At that time, NLM initiated the subject heading "Retraction of Publication." This was augmented in 1989 by the subject heading "Retracted Publication." The first heading is linked to the notice retracting the original; the second is linked to the original article itself. MEDLINE began retroactively tagging retractions in 1988. The printed versions of *Index Medicus*, however, cannot be retroactively corrected.

Despite the policy, scientists tracking scientific misconduct continue to find it difficult to identify fraudulent articles, even when they know the articles that they are seeking. Friedman's (1990) study of the Slutsky case revealed that, of a sample of 60 non-valid articles, only seven notices concerning 15 articles appeared in MEDLINE under the "Retraction of Publication" subject heading (p. 1418). Likewise, Pfeifer and Snodgrass (1990) found that only 56% of 82 articles that they identified as retractions appeared in *Index Medicus* (p. 1422). Miller (1992) noted that "a search of MEDLINE, Chemline, and Cancerlit (the last two draw largely from MEDLINE) show problematic inconsistencies in how indexing services report a journal's printed retractions" (p. 94). One of Alsabti's retracted articles, he noted, had been included in MEDLINE, but another retracted article had not. Neither retraction appeared in Chemline, and Cancerlit did not include the original reference to the article dealing with cancer.

The reason for the inability to identify all the retracted articles is that the NLM has adopted policies regarding certain words that both facilitate and hinder notification of tainted research. "Retraction" means disavowal and implies scientific misconduct or the conviction that the results reported cannot be replicated. NLM indexers make no independent decisions to categorize "problem" articles. They use only the information given in the journals and assign errata (for corrections such as drug dosages) or retraction headings only when those terms specifically refer to the problem article. The notices given in the journals must be citable, meaning that there must be a way to identify them clearly by heading and page number. The bibliographic information about the work being retracted must be complete, and the page on which the notice appears should be numbered. NLM will accept retractions by the institutional sponsor, editor, or publisher as well as the author (Colaianni, 1992, p. 536). By 1992, however, only 141 articles had been retracted during the preceding 26 years. None of Breuning's articles have been labeled as "retracted" because no responsible party—author, employer, or journal editor—requested retraction. BIOSIS, the biological index, has a similar policy; it indexes only retractions specifically designated as such in the original journal.

To somewhat compensate for the strictness of its retraction policy, NLM created the category "Comments." Comments are defined as substantive articles, editorials, or letters that have as their major purpose to challenge, refute, support, or expand upon another article or letter. Comments, according to this definition, cover a wide spectrum, and do not indicate whether or not the reader should be wary of an article to which a comment is tied. Theoretically, it would be possible to write a negative but inconclusive statement disavowing one's own article, and have it listed as a comment rather than as a retraction. The cause of the muddle is that the indexers at NLM have to rely on statements as they appear in the journals being indexed. As a result, some statements slip through the policy boundaries. Patricia K. Woolf (1991), who has studied misconduct extensively, claims:

My preliminary assessment of 46 instances of research misconduct shows that at least 246 articles have been designated as problematic. Retractions have either been recommended or sent in the case of 24 instances, but only 12 of these were indexed in Medline as retractions of publication as of February 1990. (p. 599)

Ann C. Weller (1995), commenting on the finding that tainted and retracted papers continue to be cited, "raises questions as to the effectiveness of these procedures and illustrates the difficulty of undoing what has been published and indexed" (p. 58). NLM will be even more cautious in the future. NLM flagged an article from Dr. Bernard Fisher's study of the efficacy of lumpectomy or mastectomy for breast cancer treatment, published in the *New England Journal of Medicine* (*NEJM*), because one of the 15 authors, Roger Poisson, had been found guilty of scientific misconduct by ORI in connection with the research described in the article (Fisher et al., 1989). The flagging was based on a new Public Health Service regulation allowing citations in MEDLINE to identify publications containing falsifications or misrepresentations with the explicit label, "Scientific Misconduct—see comments." The intent is to alert the scientific community and to "facilitate scholarly research on misconduct in research" ("Scientific Misconduct Identified in MEDLINE Citations," 1994, p. 4). Fisher's threat of legal action prompted the MEDLINE database to carry an apology. A re-analysis of the untainted data confirmed the findings reported in the flagged article (Marshall, 1995). The editors of the *NEJM*, which had published Fisher's 1989 article, were annoyed that ORI had not notified them about the misconduct case against Poisson. ORI adopted a policy ("Foster Research Integrity," 1994) to alert editors about "publications that might require correction or retraction as a result of confirmed scientific misconduct" (p. 8). This notification would be made at the time the news is published in the *Federal Register*. The editors would also get a copy of the ORI case report.

ELECTRONIC PUBLISHING: CAUGHT BY THE NET

Everyday, it gets harder and harder to hide from the Net.

—Kantrowitz, 1994, p. 59

The first peer-reviewed electronic journal, *Online Journal of Current Clinical Trials*, began in 1992. The fifth edition of the *Directory of Electronic Journals, Newsletters and Academic Discussion Lists* (1995) lists 675 journals and newsletters, up 235 from the 440 included the previous year. The number of refereed journals jumped from 74 to 142. The Office of Scientific and Academic Publishing within the Association of Research Libraries, which issues the *Directory of Electronic Journals, Newsletters and Academic Discussion Lists*, asked approximately one dozen scientific, technical, and medical publishers about their plans for electronic publishing. Nine of the 12 already have online versions of journals. Most are planning more.

The conversion from print to electronic journals presents both opportunities and challenges; some are anticipated and others are unforeseen. The anticipated ones include much faster dissemination of information. It is as yet unclear how the refereeing process will change. Although a number of e-journals continue to use referees, others foresee the end of refereeing in its present form. Paul Ginsparg (1995), a high energy physicist who has been active in the development of electronic journals, welcomes the end of traditional refereeing. He favors using pre-prints distributed over the World Wide Web (WWW) to allow any reader to comment on the papers. Thus, the gatekeeping function to select what, in theory, are the best manuscripts prior to publication would disappear. Some journals would still have an editor, to approve loading the file, but usually such approval is based only on the appropriateness of the content in relation to the journal rather than on the quality of the research. Essentially, that means that anyone qualified in terms of the discipline could send ideas to the e-journal and allow the readers to decide their value.

The way in which articles can be modified, changed, or deleted online (and by whom) will depend on the strength of the firewalls put in place to control those changes. These safeguards will have to be spelled out for readers and monitored to ensure that they are working properly. One advantage of this form of electronic publishing is that notification of retraction, comments, misconduct, or whatever could be placed directly in front of the article in question, greatly increasing the chances that these notices will be read. Increasingly, individual scientists are coming forward with criticisms of this or that study. Instead of writing to the journal for correction, and perhaps risking an unsuitable forum, some scholars have created pages on the WWW to serve as forums from which to attack studies that they deem incorrect, false, or inadequate.[8]

Electronic mailing lists are also rapidly spreading news about scientific disagreements. Frederick Seitz (1996), president emeritus of Rockefeller University, a leading medical institution, wrote a blistering statement to the *Wall Street Journal* about how a report on climate change released by the United Nations had been altered in substantive ways. Seitz, who was a member of the panel that drafted and approved the report, charged that key changes, which essentially distort the scientific consensus, were made after the scientists had met and approved what they thought was the final version. Seitz's comments were transmitted far beyond the readers of the *Wall Street Journal* to a wide audience of scientists around the world via the SCIFRAUD electronic mailing list.

Plagiarists will have a difficult time hiding their copying in the electronic milieu. Referees selecting papers for a conference in 1995 noted similarities between a paper submitted and one published. They used a program, the Stanford Copy Analysis Mechanism (SCAM), to detect "at least 13 cases of possible plagiarisms, involving Mr. X, who submitted the suspected paper. The 13 included seven articles already published." Peter Deming (1995), chair of the ACM (Association for Computing Machinery) Publications Board, noted that "that a would-be plagiarist can no longer rely on the immense size of the computing literature to avoid detection. The literature is being stored in digital libraries, where it can be scanned automatically by copy detectors such as SCAM" (p. 29). Fear of having one's work critiqued in a WWW page or having it discussed on a listserv may intimidate some from engaging in misconduct. Nevertheless, issues such as responsibility, liability, and fear of being sued will not be clarified simply by changing the format in which research appears.

The integrity of the scholarly literature is of concern to editors. The idea of auditing the data from one article from each thousand published has been mentioned a number of times in writings about false research. No one, however, seems to have specific suggestions on how such audits could be practically implemented. The House of Representatives has expressed not only concern but also frustration. In the three bills to authorize the annual appropriations for the NIH, amendments were inserted ordering the NLM to implement guidelines against publication of articles based on scientific misconduct. The intent was to force journals to issue retractions for "published articles when they are shown to be associated with scientific misconduct" (Anderson, 1992, p. 7) and when investigations found guilt in the misuse of federal grants. Any journal refusing to comply was to be dropped from the MEDLINE database. The Senate failed to pass similar legislation. Journal editors' reaction to government intervention was and is strong and negative. They prefer to do their own policing. They, however, are unsure just how to proceed. The editor of *The Lancet*, citing the withdrawal of aegis imposed by the *Journal of Laboratory and Clinical Investigations*, asked readers to help formulate a policy on how retraction and withdrawal of aegis should be "applied to instances of fraud, questionable scientific conduct and admitted lethal errors in the practice of research" (Horton, 1995, p. 1611).

Many groups have a stake in the integrity of the scholarly literature. Scholars need to be able to trust the literature as a basis for their own work. Editors and publishers want their journals known for publishing credible work. Taxpayers and the federal government want to be assured that they are getting real scholarship in exchange for research funds. Readers want to know that articles purporting to be fact are not, instead, fiction, and the libraries that are the largest subscriber bloc for scholarly journals do not want to purchase or stock false information. If only the information about false research were so easy to communicate!

NOTES

[1] Bruce Latour & Steve Woolgar (1986), in their study of laboratory life, observed that scientists through their publications "make claims." Subsequent publications by others turn those claims into fact.

[2] The citation indexes are: *Science Citation Index, Social Sciences Citation Index,* and *Arts & Humanities Index.* All are published by the Institute for Scientific Information in Philadelphia.

[3] The largest bibliographic database is MEDLINE, produced by the National Library of Medicine. That database, at the end of 1994, contained about 8.5 million records culled from 3,600 journals.

[4] Lois Ann Colaianni (1994) found that about 50% of the titles in *Index Medicus* are peer reviewed.

[5] The phrase "play cop" is borrowed from the title of the article "Should Journal Editors Play Science Cops?" (1988).

[6] Some attorneys now specialize in cases involving charges of research misconduct, especially those related to cases brought before the Office of Research Integrity.

[7] Stephen M. Lawani, a student at the School of Library and Information Science, Florida State University, Tallahassee, wrote a letter to *Science,* in 1989, claiming that no other scientist had cited any of Alsabti's purloined articles.

[8] As an example of such a WWW site, see http://panthron.cis.yale.edu/~ jmarks/dnahyb.html.2

3

STUDENT AND FACULTY PERCEPTIONS ABOUT MISCONDUCT: A CASE STUDY

Peter Hernon and Laura R. Walters

As far as I am concerned, anything "published" is as close to the truth as I need.

—Student survey respondent

I would never think a published piece was falsified to such an extent that I could not use it in a paper.

—Student survey respondent

The previous chapters have discussed misconduct within various contexts—that of the published literature, information provided through the World Wide Web (WWW), and the policies and practices of indexing and abstracting services. The purpose of this chapter is to see how faculty members and students regard misconduct. Do they perceive its existence as a significant problem? How discriminating are students in selecting the library resources they use, and what role, if any, do faculty and students envision libraries playing to minimize the impact of collections containing fraudulent information resources, and to ensure that their services do not refer users to discredited information resources?

The research presented in this chapter is exploratory, provides an everyday context to the previous chapters, and frames the approach taken in subsequent chapters.

Furthermore, the chapter identifies areas for further research. Our goal is to provide a base of understanding from which others can build and develop specialized methods of data collection aimed at specific disciplines and less global objectives.

STUDY PROCEDURES

Because the investigators wanted to solicit the perceptions of undergraduate and graduate students in the behavioral sciences, humanities, physical sciences, and social sciences, as well as the faculty from diverse disciplines, they conducted case-study research at one university, Tufts University in Medford, Massachusetts. One of the authors is affiliated with this university, which is a doctoral-granting institution known for its high-quality programs in assorted disciplines.

In February, 1996, the full-time Arts and Sciences faculty members on that campus received a two-page questionnaire soliciting their perceptions about the extent of misconduct they encounter in library resources, how they would cope with a work that they suspected resulted from misconduct, whether students have queried them about a work as potentially resulting from misconduct, how they expect students to cope with misconduct, whether they trust information received through the WWW, and the role of libraries and librarians in coping with the consequences of misconduct (see Appendix C for a copy of the questionnaire).

Of the 300 questionnaires mailed, 124 completed ones were returned, for a response rate of 41.3%. Given that the study was exploratory in nature and the responses provided useful insights, the investigators decided against the use of follow-up mechanisms to increase the return rate. At no time did they require findings generalizable to the campus' faculty.

One of the investigators asked two faculty members from the behavioral sciences, social sciences, humanities, and sciences to distribute the student survey, which was similar to the one administered to the faculty (see Appendix D for the questionnaire) in one of their classes. Thus, 198 students, both undergraduate and graduate, from eight classes completed and returned the questionnaire. The questionnaire attempted to gauge the extent to which students perceived the existence of a problem, the extent to which they were sensitive to the potential of the works they used as resulting from misconduct, how they would react if they suspected misconduct, and the role that libraries and indexing services might play. To repeat, both surveys are suggestive of the issues and are intended to provide a foundation from which other researchers can adopt multi-method techniques to explore the issues raised in greater depth.

FACULTY RESPONSES

Of the 124 respondents, 113 identified their departmental affiliation. Forty-six were in the sciences, with 10 in the behavioral sciences. The remaining 57 respondents were either from the humanities (including history) (35 respondents) or the social sciences (22 respondents).

The first question asked them to rate on a 5-point scale (ranging from "never" to "always") whether they ever wonder if the information or sources they find in the library might be falsified or fabricated. The mean response was 1.7236 and the median was 2. Marginal comments from 10 respondents reinforced the conclusion they give little thought to the matter.

If they suspected misconduct, responding faculty members were most likely to ask a colleague (80 respondents) or check the reputation of the author. Some respondents would check the reputation of the book publisher or the journal (e.g., "see who the journal editor is") (39), check for notices of retraction and letters to the editor in journals (37), check the reputation of the funding source (17), or ask a librarian (16). Twenty-two respondents ticked the "other" category and indicated they would query the author(s), search for other work on the same topic to see if it validated the findings, rely on their own knowledge of the field, replicate the experiment, or consult book reviews.

When asked whether students ever questioned the content of a library source or information as false or fabricated, the mean response was 1.6341 and the median was 1. Five respondents did insert, as a marginal note, "I wish they did!" One biologist commented: "Nearly all the material my students would use is in the scientific area where data get checked fairly regularly. It's the *conclusions* we question most, rarely the data."

If students were to question a work as falsified or fabricated, respondents did not have a clear view of what the students should do. Only 53 respondents (42.7%) marked that students should ask them. Other suggestions included:

- Ask a librarian (29 responses, 23.4%);
- Check the author's reputation (26 responses, 21%);
- Check the reputation of the publisher or journal (21 responses, 16.9%);
- Check for notices of retraction and letters to the editor in journals (19 responses, 15.3%); and
- Check the reputation of the funding source (13 responses, 10.5%).

Six respondents (4.8%) checked the "other" category and indicated that students should look for contradictions in the paper or book. Some respondents indicated that what students should do depended on whether they were undergraduate or graduate students; the latter had more of a responsibility to make their own determination.

Of the 115 respondents answering the question about who should have the major responsibility for teaching students to evaluate published sources to avoid using falsified or fraudulent work, 60 (52.2%) commented that the faculty should have that responsibility because they best knew the literature of their field and they had much more contact with students. Forty-eight respondents (41.7%)

believed that the responsibility should be shared with librarians, and 7 (6.1%) maintained that neither should have that responsibility. Instead, they preferred students to make their own determination.

When asked if library indexes and catalogs should forewarn library users when library materials come from falsified or fraudulent work, 116 faculty members responded. Fifty-five (47.4%) agreed and 61 (52.6%) disagreed. Those favoring the inclusion thought it a good idea but found it impossible for such notification to be comprehensive. Some of them also likened the notification to a "consumer warning to be alert and read cautiously;" they did not necessarily view the warning as a sign to avoid that material entirely. Those in opposition were concerned about the basis upon which the index or catalog made the decision and by whom the decision was made. Was there any doubt about the accuracy of such a notification?[1] If yes, they were concerned that publishers might be open to lawsuits. They also thought that students should be taught critical thinking so that, as readers of the research literature, they could make their own determination. Some respondents mentioned that "such boilerplate notices are pretty much useless" and that "anyone who believes everything he or she reads deserves whatever that person gets." One biologist suggested that "we should regard every published paper as an advertisement" and, thus, be skeptical of the findings. Also, there was concern that labeling would create "the impression that fraud is common."

Regarding the use or nonuse of the Internet or WWW, there were 120 respondents, 81 of whom (67.5%) did and 39 of whom (32.5%) did not. The major use related to e-mail (45 respondents). Other uses were identified much less frequently: use of discussion groups (20 respondents), searching for information (18 respondents), searching for information about software (8 respondents), seeking preprints (8 respondents), searching for information from the news (7 respondents), and miscellaneous "other" (6 respondents), including searching library catalogs.

When the 81 users of networked electronic information were asked if they were concerned that information they find on the Internet or WWW might result from falsified or fraudulent work, the mean response was 2.3333 and the median was 2. Those marking other than 1 ("never") commented that sources on the Internet and WWW are often not the subject of peer review, there are no safeguards, and anyone can place information in the electronic environment. They emphasized that honest mistakes were more likely to occur. Because the question did not place use within a context of purpose of use and type of use (e.g., e-mail), the implications of the findings should be regarded cautiously.

In response to the question about whether libraries should guarantee the accuracy of information contained in their collections, only 7 respondents were supportive. The others saw this as an impossible task that placed "unreasonable demands on librarians," and they did not regard it as the "responsibility" of librarians to verify all the information content of a library. Besides, as 10 respondents noted, "libraries are principally repositories" and the removal of material becomes "censorship:"

> Serious first amendment problems here. Also the logistics would make libraries the world's largest growth industry. You'd need thousands of employees working day and night.

The respondents did not see the issue as clear cut; there are shades of grey. As several respondents noted, focusing on accuracy and "truth" rules out works involving interpretation. Some regarded publishers as better able to perform the role of gatekeeper, maintaining high quality in their publications.

The final question asked "Should libraries attempt to identify as such, articles or books known to be based on fraudulent information or data?" Eighty-seven respondents (70.2%) were in favor of this, and 37 (29.8%) were not. Those in support regarded this as "helping scholarship by removing or labeling what is known to be bogus." Those in opposition believed that identification would take staff away from other responsibilities and would be expensive to do.

Finally, it merits mention that one respondent claimed to be a victim of plagiarism, "not once but (at least) twice." This person believes that the "presentation and notification of discovered fraud seem to me to be problems that do not lend themselves to general solution."

STUDENT RESPONSES

Of the 198 respondents, 185 (93.4%) identified their class level as:

- Freshmen (18, 9.7%);
- Sophomore (54, 29.2%);
- Junior (40, 21.6%);
- Senior (57, 30.8%); and
- Graduate student (16, 8.7%).

There was one unclassified student. The respondents were predominantly undergraduate students (170 students, 91.4%). Viewed from another perspective, 184 respondents characterized themselves as majoring in the:

- Behavioral sciences (23, 12.5%);
- Humanities, including history (14, 7.6%);
- Physical sciences (58, 31.5%); and
- Social sciences (79, 42.9%).

Ten students (5.4%) had not decided on a major.

The first survey question asked students to rate on a 5-point scale (ranging from "never" to "always") whether, upon finding information or a source in the library which might be useful, they ever wondered if the content might be falsified or fabricated. The mean was 1.5202 and the median was 1. Clearly, they do not give much thought to the possibility that they might be relying on a discredited or questionable work—a fact readily admitted by 25 students. As one sophomore respondent candidly admitted, "I usually take all information as being fact and have used this information in papers without any thought," whereas other students, especially mathematics majors, doubted that misconduct could ever occur in their discipline.

If students were to have questions about whether a work might be falsified or fabricated, they would, most likely, consult their course instructor (85 responses, 42.9%). Other possibilities included:

- Checking the reputation of the author(s) (37 responses, 18.7%);
- Asking a friend (31 responses, 15.7%);
- Asking a librarian (25 responses, 12.6%);
- Checking the reputation of the book publisher or journal (21 responses, 25.8%);
- Checking the reputation of the source of funding (17 responses, 8.6%); and
- Checking for notices of retraction and letters to the editor in journals (17 responses, 8.6%).

Of the 22 responses (11.1%) to the "other" category, the most common choice of undergraduates (15, 68.2%) was to do nothing. In fact, they would probably still use that source.

When asked who should have the major responsibility to teach them to evaluate published sources in order to detect falsified or fraudulent work, more than two thirds suggested both instructors and librarians (68.4%, 117 of 171 respondents), in the belief that the more assistance provided the more likely they would feel capable to evaluate the literature as part of their research. Forty-seven respondents (27.5%) believed that instructors should have sole responsibility, because they assigned the research paper, students had more contact with them, and they knew best the literature of their field. Furthermore, several respondents echoed the sentiment that "not to be cynical, but very few people go to 'library orientations' and their like. Also, not many listen to librarians' lectures; we listen to teachers."

It merits mention that 10 of the 47 respondents mentioned that they had either no or minimal contact with librarians. The remaining 7 (of the 171) respondents (4.1%) assigned that responsibility to either librarians or neither group. The four in the latter instance strongly believe "it is the sole responsibility of the individual."

Regarding the inclusion of information in library indexes and catalogs forewarning users that material came from falsified or fraudulent work, more than three-fourths (75.9%, 148 of 195 responses) concurred, but only when "there is no doubt, otherwise libraries and publishers would be engaged in censorship, making determinations which should be those of readers, and increasing the likelihood of lawsuits." Forty-seven respondents (24.1%), however, were quite forthcoming in their opposition. They did not see the need to go to such an "extreme;" they preferred course instructors and librarians to remind them about the possibility of misconduct but did not want labeling within reference tools. They tended to believe that "most authors are honest" and identification could "lead to panic or to a 'why bother' attitude." They also advocated "self-accountability; it's the researcher's responsibility to investigate if he or she is suspicious of material." There was concern that any identification "would bias students from looking at the work; we should make our own determination about the value of a work." Furthermore, they wanted to know the source of the information; as one respondent asked, "are we being told the truth?" Several students raised another question, "Should we assume that everything not so marked is *not* the product of falsification or deception?" One junior majoring in chemical engineering commented that "a warning would make it seem like tons of information was falsified and to feel like that would be unfortunate. People can't be naive, but this seems overly negative." A graduate student in biology pointed out that "I think it would make me question everything if it was in my face all the time, and I don't want to do that."[2]

Returning to those favoring warnings in library indexes and catalogs, some remarked that they had "a right to know if information isn't correct" and "we are trying to learn a subject, and would appreciate knowing that not everything in circulation at a library is true." One senior majoring in both biology and environmental studies would appreciate such notification because "I have always held the precept that if something is printed on research the results are as sincere as possible given that research does not prove a hypothesis true, but rather alternative hypotheses false." Another senior majoring in biology mentioned that for "much of what we learn, we don't have the *time* to cross-reference information content and to look for *better* sources." Such a comment perhaps explains, in part, why more students do not check for notices of retraction and letters to the editor.

To move the discussion from print to electronic sources, the students were asked if they used the Internet and WWW. More than two thirds (137 or 69.2%) do. The purposes for their use relate largely to:

- Entertainment (e.g., checking movie reviews and the availability of forthcoming CDs) (70 responses, 51.1%);
- E-mail (61 responses, 44.5%);
- Research (49 responses, 35.8%);
- Information-gathering (34 responses, 24.8%); and
- Other (e.g., job information and monitoring the news) (32 responses, 23.4%).

Of the 137 Internet or WWW users, 133 (97.1%) answered the question about the extent to which they were concerned that the information they find might

TABLE 3.1.   Selected Comments about the Internet and WWW

Those seeing no problem:

- I assumed that Internet is edited.
- Finding relevant information among the chaos of the Web is more important than worrying about if the information is true. I am so thrilled to find something, I never question it.
- I never question computers or technology.
- I don't think there is very much fraudulent information on the Web.
- I'm not that paranoid.

Those showing some awareness:

- Since the Internet is in the public access domain, you have to weigh the information found.
- You have to expect fraud on a system as easy to get on as the Internet.
- I rely on news from the media and we all know that the media may deal in half-truths.
- Since there is no policing of the Internet, everything on there should be taken with a grain of salt.
- I am skeptical about stuff on the Web because anyone can put whatever he or she wants on there.
- I only rely on homepages of highly reputable sources.
- It's very easy to falsify one's identity, even when using e-mail.

result from falsified or fraudulent work. On a 5-point scale ranging from "never" to "always," the mean was 2.0088 and the median was 2. Clearly, there is not a lot of concern or awareness about this issue (see Table 3.1 for some of the student comments). This conclusion must, however, be tempered by the fact that the investigators did not provide a basis to examine the finding within the context of the various purposes for which the respondents use networked electronic information services.

To gain additional insights into student perceptions about libraries and what role librarians might play in coping with research misconduct, the investigators asked:

- Should libraries guarantee the accuracy of information contained in their collections?
- Should libraries attempt to identify as such, articles or books known to be based on fraudulent data or information?

Regarding the first question, 44.1% of the respondents (82 of 186 respondents) answered in the affirmative and 55.9% (104 respondents) disagreed because they tended to regard this as "impossible to do with a finite budget" and the myriad of duties that librarians already perform. They also noted that libraries cannot know of every instance of fraud, "could not possibly function efficiently and effectively while checking the veracity of every resource," "cannot play the role of ethical police. Such is the responsibility of course instructors, their peers, and professional journals,"[3] and should not engage in censorship. Furthermore, as some respondents noted, "individuals must exercise their own personal responsibility regarding what information they rely on."

For the second question, more than 90% (92.8%, 180 of 194 respondents) concurred that libraries should attempt to identify books based on misconduct. Some again repeated that students have "a right to know." Still, there was some concern that librarians "might be biased in what they consider fraudulent" and mistakes would wrongly taint a work or individual. The 14 in opposition wanted the determination to be left up to them, echoing the importance of "self-accountability."

COMPARISON OF FACULTY AND STUDENT RESPONSES

Neither faculty nor student respondents really question the works that they use. Both respondent groups place faith in published sources, especially those known as high-quality or prestigious. The obvious implication is that they view science or research as self-correcting and assume that editors and editorial boards are effective gatekeepers in identifying and blocking publication of research resulting from misconduct.[4] Furthermore, both believe that misconduct is rare, and that they are more likely to find research in which "honest mistakes" were made. Clearly, it is more common to disagree about what a dataset means than to question a work as falsified or fraudulent.

Faculty members were more sensitive to the fact that networked electronic information and publications vary greatly in quality and they were more likely to evaluate such source material. Still, with their use most typically related to the sending and receiving of e-mail messages—and other non-research activities—they are not drawing upon a wide range of networked material for either teaching or research purposes.

IMPLICATIONS FOR FURTHER RESEARCH

A number of students, both undergraduate and graduate, admitted that they had never thought about research misconduct and tended to be trusting of printed sources in library collections. It is surprising that some students would do nothing if they suspected a work of being falsified or fabricated, and that more did not turn to their course instructor for guidance. Clearly, in-person interviews and focus group interviews, linked to actual examples of fraud in their particular discipline, might provide useful insights to place general questionnaire responses in a more meaningful context. Such methodologies could probe student understanding of notices of retraction and the purpose of letters to the editor, as well as how to find such sources of information. Why do not more faculty members and students look for retractions and letters to the editor?

Another area for examination is the belief that researchers, be they students or academics, should be "responsible for their own actions;" in other words, they should evaluate material and make their own interpretation. Presumably, if they were in error and used fraudulent work, they had not done a sufficiently good job of evaluation. How do they evaluate works and determine which ones to use?

Researchers examining student reaction to misinformation and disinformation on the Internet and WWW might focus on the categories of research and information-gathering. Presumably, faculty members and students are less concerned about falsified and fraudulent information in non-research contexts, including the use of e-mail. Respondents created the impression that they were selective in the number of people with whom they corresponded via e-mail.

It might also be useful to develop sampling frames that permit comparisons between graduate and undergraduate students, and by discipline. Such research might investigate the null hypothesis of no difference. In addition, studies might probe differences within the physical sciences, where a sizeable body of misconduct has been discovered (see Chapter 1).

It would seem that additional research on student perceptions of librarians might be in order. For instance, several respondents mentioned that "many students don't value librarians' information" and many students using the library for research purposes do not seek contact with library staff. Furthermore, 10 students suggested that librarians conducting bibliographic instruction sessions cannot get students to listen in the same way that teaching faculty can.

CONCLUSION

Students hold numerous misperceptions about library collections and services. For example, some respondents viewed libraries as mere repositories of information and could not understand why fraudulent work would ever appear in the library. One junior majoring in psychology expects librarians to guarantee the accuracy of information held because "it is the Library. I expect the information to be true. Thus, a library should stand behind its works."[5] Such misperceptions should be identified and addressed.

Faculty tend to assume that students, particularly graduate students, have gained or are gaining the ability to think critically and question material, whereas many student respondents tend to be very trusting and do not discriminate among materials. They do not question the material used and perhaps lack the background to recognize falsehoods. Several respondents commented that, if misconduct is something students might encounter in doing research for a class assignment, they should be forewarned by their instructors. Without such notification, they will assume that no problem exists. Thus, there is a need, on this campus at least, for teaching faculty and librarians to review class assignments and the extent to which students have the ability to question and think critically. It might also be useful to determine if, where, and how graduate students gain such faculties. Given the limited exposure that many librarians have to students, there must be further consideration of how librarians can make an effective and efficient partnership with teaching staff regarding information literacy, and, to some extent, how they can gain more credibility as educators.

Student respondents were, quite naturally, skeptical that fraud presented much of a problem,[6] undoubtedly in part because their instructors had not discussed the topic with them.[7] If there was a problem, they suspected that the responsibility for correction rested more with authors, editors, and publishers. The faculty respondents tended to concur. Like the student respondents, they perceive science, in the broadest sense, as self-correcting; it may take time, but fraud will be discovered and corrected. Thus, the perception of the respondents is that the investigators overestimated the extent to which a problem might exist. In the respondents' minds, sloppy and incompetent work is far more common than misconduct. As one psychologist summarized, "I am rarely concerned about fraud because I consider the weight of the evidence. If some result has only been found once, I remain skeptical, not because I suspect fraud but chance or limited applicability."

The next chapter provides additional respondent perceptions about fraud and misconduct. In this instance, librarians, students, and faculty members assess a falsified study. The remaining chapters build upon the findings of Chapters 3 and 4. Clearly, it is important to educate students, faculty, and librarians to the seriousness of misconduct for library collections and services, and for the resources which library users consult and cite.

NOTES

[1] They tended to view this question in the context more of an allegation being made than of a determination of guilt after an investigation had been conducted or of an admission of guilt.

[2] One junior majoring in clinical psychology summarized a concern raised by several respondents: "it seems that it would cause unnecessary doubt in the researcher/student." A senior majoring in biology summarized a perspective of several other students: "Widespread paranoia would be the result. While questioning information is a healthy thing, people do have a tendency to overreact. Tell them privately in a class and it's ok. Post it publicly and it'll suddenly become a big deal and nothing will be safe." Another biology major was concerned that "students might lose faith in the library or else ignore the warnings and use whatever works supported their own research."

[3] An unclassified student used the term "thought police:" "librarians should not be the thought police."

[4] One scientist noted: "Hoaxes or completely false studies eventually are uncovered by other scientists in the same field. This, of course, can be annoying or a waste of time, but we all know it happens. Most fraud is uncovered in the lab or department where it originate—usually *before* publication. In biomedical fields there will always be snake oil salesmen and even some government funding for them."

[5] One sophomore majoring in both economics and political science assumes that "a source is valid based on its existence in a library. Maybe that is naive but there has to be some truth in this world." Another sophomore majoring in political science echoed the same sentiment: "As far as I am concerned, anything 'published' is as close to the truth as I need." Another sophomore, one from an unidentified discipline, stated "I would never think a published piece was falsified to such an extent that I could not use it in a paper."

[6] As a senior majoring in psychology stated, "I'm assuming the problem is fairly rare. Thus, it might not be necessary to 'scare' students to be concerned every time they look something up."

[7] One student, who mentioned neither his or her class level nor major, revealed that "as students, we are ruled by books. It is our nature to trust everything we read. The only higher power is the instructor. If the instructor forewarns us about the possibility of falsified information, we'll take it to heart."

4

RESEARCH MISCONDUCT AS VIEWED FROM MULTIPLE PERSPECTIVES

Peter Hernon and Philip J. Calvert

> Unless a maladroit cheat fabricates results that are manifestly impossible or inherently contradictory, even the most rigorous peer review is not likely to uncover fraud.
>
> —Relman, 1983, p. 1416

> Lack of access to primary data forces social scientists to examine cases of fraud and misconduct "under glass."
>
> —LaFollette, 1994, p. 7

Research misconduct is a multi-faceted concept that includes the fabrication and falsification of data, findings, and conclusions. It also encompasses misappropriation (plagiarism and breaching the confidentiality associated with the review of manuscripts or grant proposals) and misrepresentation, when the intention is to deceive or demonstrate a serious disregard for the truth. As such, misconduct involves the falsification of evidence and, in some instances, a serious erosion of the rights of scholars and others to have the intellectual debt that others owe them acknowledged.

Although the exact prevalence of research misconduct is unknown, Chapter 1 does demonstrate that misconduct is far from unlikely (see also Lock & Wells, 1996). There is obviously some disagreement about the extent to which: (1) science is self-correcting, (2) deception detracts from one's reputation and career advancement, and (3) the ethical issues of today can be applied to the past (see Geison, 1995).

Misconduct, as used in this chapter, focuses on falsification and fabrication, not on over-generalizations, half-truths, outright mistakes, questions over interpretation, honest mistakes, and human error (e.g., as discussed in "Court Computers Can Get Reporters in Trouble, If Not Careful," 1995). Furthermore, the chapter does not address plagiarism or misrepresentation—"reporting citations of nonexistent articles in actual journals, articles in nonexistent journals, or [nonexistent] articles noted [in curriculum vitae] as 'in press'" ("Widespread Misrepresentation Found in Fellowship Applications," 1995, p. 2). Instead, the discussion focuses on higher education and the work of those individuals expected to engage in research and publication as part of promotion, tenure, and salary decisions.

Although there is no published evidence that a problem exists within library and information science, the investigators used this discipline as the basis for their research; however, they pursued the implications for other academic disciplines as well. To increase the value and relevance of the research, they examined the perceptions of librarians, library school students, university administrators, faculty members serving on ethics and promotion committees, and editors of scholarly journals and selected members of editorial boards, within and outside library and information science. The research reported here, therefore, has broad implications for academe and editorial practices. As Richard Smith (1996, p. 789) notes, there is "need to study research misconduct, horrible as it might be, so that we can better understand its epidemiology."

BACKGROUND

The popular press has recounted instances of faked e-mail services in which individuals have received messages that seemed to come from noted individuals, real, imaginary, and literary, or even God or Satan (see "Guess Who?," 1995; Quittner, 1995). As well, a professor at Mankato State University created a deceptive World Wide Web (WWW) page for Mankato, Minnesota, "where hot springs keep the air at a balmy 70 degrees Fahrenheit throughout the winter and vacationers come from all over the world to sun themselves on the beaches of the crystal-clear Minnesota River" ("Mankato, Minnesota Home Page," 1996, p. 1). The professor built the homepage, together with pictures, to demonstrate to high school students that they should not believe everything that they find on the WWW.[1]

While the faked e-mail service could be regarded as harmless, practical jokes might have harmful consequences, especially if, for instance, someone believes that he or she has been fired from work. Such examples address deception and raise ethical and other issues. They do not, however, deal with research misconduct associated with falsification and fraud. This misconduct can be investigated from three perspectives: (1) the use of self-reporting methods of data collection; (2) documented examples uncovered by researchers, whistleblowers, or investigative bodies; and (3) the policies and procedures of funding organizations, universities, investigative bodies, and journals. The research reported here relies upon self-reports and examines whether or not there is a failure "to respond to evidence of misconduct" (Smith, 1996, p. 789). It also examines systems for detecting, investigating, and punishing misconduct within selected universities, and for promoting greater integrity in the conduct and reporting of research.

Chapter 1 indicates that research misconduct is an international problem. Smith (1996, p. 789), who concurs, admits that he lacks "irrefutable evidence" to support his assumption, but notes that "countries that have looked for misconduct have found it." Expanding on his assumption, this chapter presumes that misconduct is not confined to the sciences, but could occur within any discipline, regardless of country.

PROCEDURES

For the research reported in this chapter, the investigators hypothesized that four groups of academics might be tempted to engage in misconduct:

- The new faculty member, who perhaps did not receive good mentoring or who did not have good training in research methods and design;
- The individual who will soon undergo a review for the possible awarding of tenure and needs one more publication;
- The habitual "liar" who likes to see his or her name in print, on a regular basis, but, for whatever reason, is unwilling to do and report legitimate research; or
- A person in ill-health, whether mental or physical.

With many academic institutions expecting faculty members to place a large number of publications in peer-reviewed journals, we assume that an unscrupulous individual could attempt to subvert the system of promotion and tenure through publications resulting from outright misconduct.

For this research, the investigators assumed the role of the new faculty member and wrote a falsified study, one containing a number of mistakes. The assumption was that this new faculty member, named Maxwell A. Mega for the purpose of the research, would not know better; his research might be regarded as sloppy but not totally fabricated. By submitting the paper to a reputable peer-reviewed journal, however, Max would likely receive a rejection letter containing suggestions for improving the quality of the research. More than likely, the editor would not welcome resubmission to that journal, but Max could take the suggestions, improve the quality of the paper, and submit the revised paper elsewhere. He might still receive a couple of rejections, but each time he would improve the quality of the paper and the likelihood of acceptance and publication.

As discussed subsequently in the chapter, we also viewed Max from a different perspective—that of a faculty member who knows better. He needs one more publication to ensure the likelihood of a favorable outcome in his review for tenure or promotion. It is also possible that Max has disdain for the peer-review process and is a habitual liar.

We assumed that we could write a falsified study that could fool an editorial board and be accepted for publication. Such a paper would not, however, have raised the types of issues which we intended to examine. We wanted to probe how trusting students are of what they read, how librarians would respond to having such material potentially in their collections, how much help editors provide to assist authors in revising a weak paper for resubmission or submission elsewhere, how they and other academic staff would react to having Max as a colleague, how they might identify him as a dishonest individual, and how the university might treat him.

Appendix E reprints the paper presumably authored by Maxwell A. Mega; this paper is reprinted because it comprises a data collection instrument, but the appendix clearly labels the work as fraudulent. The problem is real and so are the references. The research was never conducted and the findings are figments of Max's imagination. An assumption is that the findings, discussion, and conclusion of a fraudulent paper must be conservative; outrageous findings and interpretation would call attention to the research, its conduct and findings. We presume that Max would want to write the paper in such a way as to decrease the likelihood of detection.

Upon receiving approval of the Human Ethics Committee Standing Committee, Victoria University of Wellington, we asked the 135 master's level students, both distance and internal, taking the research methods course in the University's Department of Library and Information Studies to read and critique the paper without knowing that it had been falsified. Then, in a series of tutorials with the internal students, we informed them that the paper had been falsified and discussed the implications. As well, we conducted a similar discussion with distance students through an audioconference.

In a series of focus group meetings at all seven universities in New Zealand, we discussed the implications of the paper with librarians, soliciting their comments about the possible publication of such a paper and its subsequent appearance in their collections, their perceptions about the extent to which a problem exists, and how they would react if Max were a colleague of theirs. As well, we conducted focus group interviews at these universities with Deans and professors who would have to cope with the presence of Max on the academic staff, including the type of punishment he might receive. We also examined the types of policies and procedures in place for dealing with unethical behavior of the type that Max represents. The presumption was that he was a member of their department or college and that they had to deal with him.

LIBRARY SCHOOL STUDENTS

Both the distance and internal students found the fraudulent paper upsetting, and one even remarked "I feel cheated." They expect science and research itself to be self-correcting, within a relatively short time period. Almost all of them admitted that they were accustomed to believing what they read in scholarly journals, as they assumed that the peer-review process caught all instances of misconduct. Clearly, there is a misunderstanding of that process and how reviewers typically go about assessing the quality and value of a manuscript. The students expected them to review the actual dataset.

As we explained to them, there was a real dataset. It just happened to be fabricated. Of course, there was not a companion set of completed questionnaires. If administrators at the institution became suspicious of Max's work and demanded that an independent investigator examine the completed returns, similarities in handwriting might be uncovered. However, as the students queried, "how likely is this to occur?" They also commented that there are strict penalties against student misconduct and wondered if the penalties were as strict for faculty misconduct along the lines represented by Max.

There was concern about how they would ever spot research as fraudulent and how much library material might be the result of misconduct. A recurring theme in the discussions with students was a sense of helplessness that they had not seen the fraud in Max's paper, and many asked if they could be taught how to detect misconduct. They also asked if misconduct was prevalent in New Zealand or if it was limited to a few countries and disciplines, especially ones in the sciences.

UNIVERSITY LIBRARIANS

Regardless of site, the librarians participating in the focus group interviews expressed feelings of helplessness when confronted with a case of fraud. Even though they had been told in advance that data in Max's paper were fabricated, they did not feel confident that they could detect the fraud; many even did not believe they could find the "sloppiness" intentionally inserted into the paper.

The librarians expressed a belief in the honesty and integrity of scholars or anyone writing for scholarly publication. The point was made that in some professions a type of misconduct has appeared to have become acceptable, or at the least expected, because phrases had entered the communal vocabulary about "creative accountancy" and "cooking the figures" (e.g., in chemistry), but concerns about a librarian's dishonesty or that of the average faculty member going up for a decision regarding promotion or tenure are minimal.

They wondered how librarians could possibly identify cases of fraud, and why they might try to do so when the journal's editor, editorial board, and peer reviewers have better knowledge and the opportunity to validate a work prior to publication. They take the veracity of the journal's contents on trust both because that is their natural predisposition when dealing with scholars and because, in practical terms, they feel powerless to do anything else.

The serials librarians said that they made much of the journal's reputation and prestige when placing the library's subscriptions. When a journal's reputation is high they "buy into the reputation" of the journal. It was clearly a surprise to many of them that prestigious journals, such as the *New England Journal of Medicine*, carried articles later shown to be fraudulent. This caused a feeling of doubt that trust in the journal's integrity could ever be relied upon again, but the librarians rationalized their response by saying that one instance of error was no reason to create misgivings about a journal, but that if more cases were discovered and announced then the serials librarians would have to reconsider their purchasing decisions. Some said that the higher the initial reputation the journal has, the longer that reputation will take to collapse.

Collection Development

The librarians interviewed felt that they needed to develop some type of a response to the publication of fraud, but agreed that, since they had no way of identifying false data in printed materials, their responses had to come in other ways. A key observation was that their best response was to emphasise their traditional role of collection building, which, by its nature, provides a wide range of literature on the same subject, from which scholars and students can compare and contrast all items they find and read, and subsequently draw conclusions about the respective value of each item. This approach does not, in itself, identify fraudulent material, but it will aid scholars to identify doubtful items if it can be seen that the findings of one study are out of line with the rest of the corpus. There are clearly limits to any library's capacity to support this approach, for all libraries have a finite budget that can only purchase a limited number of items.

At a time when budgets are neither rising in line with book and journal prices nor keeping pace with an increase in volume of publication, librarians obviously cannot purchase as many items as they would wish. The librarians commented that, since many universities are expanding the range of subjects they offer to students, it is almost axiomatic that acquisitions librarians must stretch their budgets over a wider area than ever before. This, therefore, acts to counter the wishes of librarians who would build strong collections in limited subject fields—the activity which was identified as necessary before scholars can compare and contrast numerous items in a specialized field and identify items which may be out of line with the corpus. Thus, until the time (if that time ever comes) when acquisitions budgets rise faster than demand, the librarians interviewed are skeptical of their ability to continue to counter fraud through collection building.

Bibliographic Instruction

The librarians interviewed were extremely reluctant to act as arbiters of material in their own libraries and some preferred to rely on the phrase "let the reader beware" as a guide to their philosophical response, so the question had to be asked whether they could see a positive role for themselves in contesting scholarly fraud. A comment in several focus groups was that their best response was as educators, not as arbiters.

Bibliographic instruction (BI) was identified as a key response. Not all the libraries we visited, however, currently offer extensive programs of BI, and only one included the subject of information literacy, which takes the student from awareness of a citation to analysis of the content and encourages critical reading of all literature, in a course of study taken by undergraduates. The timing of this within a degree was open to dispute, as some librarians thought it unrealistic to teach it in the first year of the degree but hoped that by the time students graduate they will have acquired a critical faculty.

Student Use of Reading Lists

Despite the presence of collections that can support student learning with a wide range of literature, the librarians noted that there is an increasing tendency for undergraduate students to rely upon reading lists as the exclusive source of bibliographic references for their studies. This can only occur if it is made possible by the teaching staff, of course, but the ready acceptance and use of reading lists by students is a trend the students themselves seem to be encouraging. Almost all the librarians disliked the trend, as it seemed to challenge one of their traditional roles, that of collection building, except when it supports faculty research, but they recognized they had to accept the trend as a *fait accompli* by students and teachers. They observed that this increased the importance of teaching staff checking the accuracy of information in the recommended items before placing them on a reading list, because librarians assumed that once the item had got that far it had almost a "stamp of approval" from faculty guaranteeing its accuracy.

Librarians at one university that offers several programs by distance teaching pointed out that students remote from a good collection are bound to rely on reading lists or photocopied course packets, as they have no opportunity to visit the library in person and browse the shelves before making a serendipitous selection. Distance students, even more than those studying internally, must await technological developments that will encourage and enable their use of a wide range of literature.

Electronic Publishing

A second point that needs further discussion here is the growth of electronic publishing. On one hand, librarians greeted the greater availability of scholarly material in electronic form as beneficial. For reasons given above, they doubt their ability to support critical learning with hardcopy materials (e.g., books and journals) in the long term. They believe that electronic publishing will provide them with the ability to expand the range of literature accessible by faculty and students, yet at no great expense to the library. They noted the paradox in this: that if the scholarly content of electronically-published material proves to be less reliable than that of hardcopy texts, then it will fail to provide the expected benefits, despite its lower cost. This introduces a point that was made several times by the librarians, which is that, on the evidence so far, electronic publishing offers fewer guarantees of accuracy than traditional print-on-paper publishing.

No clear recommendations or even ideas emanated from the discussions on the implications of electronic publishing. The librarians interviewed see the potential of electronic publishing to provide an enormous boost to the material accessible by their own customers. On the other hand, there is great concern about the poor quality of much material currently found on the Internet, all of which, it was assumed, can be found by undergraduates without any need for intervention by faculty or library staff. There was little doubt that quite a lot of material on the Internet is either misinformation or disinformation, but, as those interviewed stressed, undergraduate students, in particular, will not have a sufficiently well-developed critical faculty to detect inaccuracies when they find them. The role of BI in developing critical ability in students was emphasized by this realization.

Censorship or Selection

For the most part, the librarians viewed their role as basically passive. They were, however, prepared to discuss the degree to which they became interventionists. The situation discussed was how far librarians would be prepared to go when they are given a clear statement that a journal article (the example used was Max's paper) includes fraudulent information. They expect that when editors and publishers discover that a published work contains bogus data, they will announce the fact, usually in the form of a printed retraction. An initial problem identified by librarians is that, since they do not actually read the journals, they are unlikely to see such retractions unless one is brought to their attention. They said that they are much more likely to see a separate letter from the publisher containing the retraction. Only a few of the librarians interviewed knew that some indexes listed retractions.

The focus groups discussed their reaction to a publisher's retraction. Should they try to bring the retraction to the attention of potential users of the item in as many ways as they can, including devices such as stamping the item with a disclaimer of some sort? If it is a book, do they withdraw it? Opinions differed sharply. On one hand, some librarians said that withdrawing items was the mirror of selection, and both were an essential part of collection management. On the other hand, some librarians said they would not withdraw items even if they knew the items were inaccurate, as once they had entered the public domain library users had a right to gain access to them. Influencing debate, to some extent, was a nagging doubt that, even if the publisher of an item issued a public retraction, the library was still not on strong ground if it marked the item in some way (a stamp on the first page, or a note on the OPAC record) as containing fraudulent information. There was doubt whether the publisher's decision was legally binding, so the fear of litigation from an outraged author or a publisher loomed large.

There was general agreement that research misconduct appearing in print was a problem that had not been given much attention in the past, and this raised issues for which many of them felt ill-prepared. They were prepared to accept any assistance that improved their capability of dealing with misconduct, such as providing access to the Office of Research Integrity's home page. One librarian suggested that a clearinghouse for scholarly misconduct be established. There was general agreement that library education needs to address the subject of research misconduct in an active way, such as including more courses on BI in the curriculum, for if the librarians do not believe they understand the issues clearly, then they will never feel competent to advise students.

UNIVERSITY DEANS AND PROFESSORS

There are different forms of misconduct, of which fraud is only one. As one group member put it, "the penumbra of fraud is unethical behavior," which is not true misconduct and is out of the realm of a legal response. Several academics said that instead of fraud they were more concerned about other forms of misconduct, such as using the same material in several different journal articles or going to many conferences and giving the same paper. It was pointed out that this misconduct was common, damaging to academe, yet tacitly condoned in many university departments ("it is part of the game") because it apparently increases their measured outputs.

There was widespread belief among focus group participants that science is self-correcting. As one (himself a scientist) put it, "when findings are pivotal they are likely to be tested quickly. If the research is archival it will be tested quickly. If it cannot be replicated it is not likely to be corrected quickly." Much depends upon the nature of the data. In the "hard" sciences the data, he explained, are available for all to see and use—for instance, the passage of a comet or the reaction of an element—but in the social sciences, such as shown with the Max Mega paper, replication may be difficult and ultimately unrewarding. Another said that it may take a long time before fraud is detected and corrected; it may even take generations; but science would eventually correct itself. He gave the instance of Cyril Burt as an example of how an academic discipline had apparently been distorted for generations by suspected fraud but had at last been corrected.

Academics in one focus group said that the definition of fraud became questionable in some subject disciplines. Whereas in LIS it was clear that Max Mega is a fraud, in the discipline of economics the technique of "data stretching" was well established and perfectly acceptable. In other subjects, the difference between deductive and inductive methods was now very fuzzy. With the crossover between quantitative and qualitative methods now common, "it must be tempting to mix up the data until you get what you want," as one focus group member put it.

Catching Misconduct

"In order to eliminate misconduct completely the necessary societal controls will have to be massive," said one academic who sat on his university's research committee. "In the process scholarship will be restricted and there will be a lessening of academic freedom." The cost, in monetary and scholarly terms, would be huge, and if it was all done for a few cases of fraud, then "why bother?" The cost-benefit equation of large societal controls to catch a few dishonest scholars is so poor that it is unacceptable. At one focus group, however, it was pointed out that "If one says that cost benefit means that tough auditing is not worth it then you have to establish a prima facie case that there is not much fraud in the system."

There were some suggestions about how the university might inhibit misconduct. In order to curb "data stretching" it was suggested that a detailed research methodology must be submitted in advance of the data collection and analysis phase of a project. If the research is audited, it will then be noticed that the researcher has deviated from his/her stated methodology. Another idea suggested was that all joint authors of an article must declare what their own contribution was to the whole. Another suggestion was that universities should require researchers to keep all datasets for up to six years so that they can be subjected to scrutiny if doubts are expressed about the veracity of the published results. If research has included a public survey, then an audit can ask every 10th person in the survey population if they have, indeed, been asked to respond to the survey.

Several academics said they believed they could spot a colleague who was committing fraud. The colleague may not be working hard yet would seem confident that his/her output will be satisfactory. He or she would not talk much about his or her research. This was contradicted by others who said that academics do not always talk about their research, but someone who was obviously chasing promotion might be suspected more readily than others.

Helplessness should not lead to inaction, said one academic. "It is critical that research be monitored in order to catch it," and this has to be done before the university can devise procedures to discipline the guilty parties, for "without procedures to catch fraud, why bother with the system to punish?"

The Response to Misconduct

The first reaction of the university, said one group member, would be "to take the high moral ground." This was partly because the organization has to observe all the normal rules of law and to be above criticism in its response. The accused staff member can use a number of defenses: first, denial; second, use a technicality as a defense; and, third, come to terms with the university. In the latter instance, it was suggested that the person (e.g., Max Mega) would receive a penalty graded according to the seriousness of the misconduct, but rarely would it lead to dismissal. It takes a lot to make an academic leave if he or she does not want to, and the worst the university can do in many cases is to ensure that he or she does not get promoted.

Some academics said they would be worried if a colleague was found guilty of misconduct because it would affect the reputation of the whole department and affect its collective, and their own individual, ability to secure research funding. They would therefore expect very strong action by their own departmental chairperson to show that the department did not tolerate misconduct and could be trusted to manage research funds properly. Another focus group felt that the reaction of the funding agencies would be fair if it was based upon the responses to fraud of the institutions.

There was almost complete agreement that the impact of the fraud should dictate the level of response to it. Fraudulent research that threatened life should be treated far more severely than Max Mega's fraud, for example. One focus group member pointed out an apparent irony when he said, "in this university the penalties for students found guilty of misconduct appear to be harsher than those for staff."

Although all the academics expressed the opinion that fraud was a very rare occurrence in academe, several individuals said they had first-hand experience of a case of fraud. One group member described a case which had marked similarities to Max Mega, in which a scholar on contract to a university (not in New Zealand) had fallen behind the research project schedule and so decided to invent responses to a questionnaire as a way of making up for lost time. The fraud was discovered by student assistants who first noticed a curious similarity in the responses they were entering into a computer, then on further investigation realized all the questionnaires were written by the same hand. The university's response was quick and severe. The researcher was sacked within 24 hours. Our focus group member felt this may have been excessive, as the person in question was clearly ill and needed help. This, though, was a rare case in which the guilt was obvious. One group member said he knew of a case in which a research proposal was submitted by his university to a national body for funding assistance only to see it rejected; later it was realized that the same proposal had subsequently been successfully submitted for funding by a different organization. "This is very suspicious," he stated. Others told us of their frustration with cases of misconduct dragging on while the accused used all the devices at his or her disposal to deny and delay.

Competition and Collegiality

In reality, the whole academic system is based on trust. Several academics questioned whether it is possible to change the culture of the academy without stifling it. There are, apparently, differences of opinion about the root cause of misconduct and hence how it can be treated. One academic said his response to a colleague suspected of fraud would be to "hit them with the full force of the university's disciplinary powers." He said that academe was competitive and could be "brutal," so there was no need to apologize for a harsh response by the organization. Another said that we had to look for the cause of misconduct in society, and blamed the increasingly competitive university environment for misconduct. He likened it to the rise in white-collar crime in general, in which competition among former colleagues encourages dishonesty. While some element of competition was healthy, there was now too much competition and it encouraged dishonesty, so some return to greater collegiality was needed. The university system has to articulate its mission clearly. At the moment it does not seem to place any emphasis on quality. "There are many within the system who believe quality has an important place, but the system and its rewards do not show any expression of that," said one group member. The system has to be balanced between collegiality and competition; to quote the same individual, "a system which only rewards the most prolific is not balanced."

SEEKING PUBLICATION

The assumption is that Maxwell A. Mega would not invest the time and effort in falsification of a study placed on an e-mail discussion group. In seeking publication of his falsified study, Max might make submission to print or electronic journals, ones that departmental guidelines recognized for purposes of promotion and tenure. Another assumption is that Max would probably not seek publication in the most prestigious journals; by approaching these journals and perhaps gaining acceptance (most likely after an extensive revision of the manuscript), the paper might attract more notice than perhaps a falsifier would want. This second assumption, however, is questionable in that very prestigious journals in the physical and medical sciences unknowingly have published fraudulent research (see Hernon & Altman, 1995).

Despite this second assumption, we approached editors of six prestigious journals in library and information science and asked for their participation. We requested permission to submit Max's paper for peer review with the proviso that the editors would alert their reviewers that the paper had been falsified. We realized that by alerting reviewers to the falsification, they might use the occasion to demonstrate an ability to spot fraud and to suggest they could not be fooled. Nonetheless, we accepted this as a study limitation. We were not interested in what the reviewers actually said, or in what the editorial outcome was. We only wanted to see how the editor (admittedly knowing the study had been falsified) would write either a rejection letter or a letter inviting resubmission after Max had made extensive revision to the manuscript.

Again, assuming that Max was a "beginning academic," we wanted to see if the editors provided guidance that Max could use to improve the quality of the paper for submission elsewhere or, later, to be published in that journal. The final assumption was that Max would eventually get published, especially if he or she pursued less prestigious journals, perhaps ones known to be off schedule in publication and suspected of having a manuscript flow problem. This beginning academic would be in a position to subvert the reviewing process by taking advantage of the desire of journal editors to be helpful.

A final observation is in order. We are not suggesting that library and information science is experiencing a problem with misconduct. Rather, we are using our discipline as the basis for an analysis much broader in its implications.

Responses from Journal Editors

Max's paper was submitted to six journal editors for editorial review. Three editors responded, in spring 1996, in time for inclusion in this analysis. One editor admitted that the paper would likely be accepted for publication, after revision, if the author had better tied the paper into that journal's scope. That editor did provide written comments for Max to consider in a revision and made suggestions for more appropriate journals for submission, in case Max did not want to make those revisions.

The second editor would not have accepted the paper for publication because it was not a good match for the journal's scope. Again, there were extensive suggestions for revision and an indication of choices for submission elsewhere.

The third editor rejected the manuscript and noted that Max was obviously a beginner. Nonetheless, this editor offered extensive suggestions for revision. The editor questioned the research design and the sampling procedure, the need for definitions (e.g., use and nonuse), and noted that reviewers challenged the numbers presented: "they do not add up properly." "For greater clarity, you might have used tables and graphics to reduce confusion relating to the presentation of so many numbers in the text." One editor, in an aside, noted that the narrative presentation of data is "a way of masking fraudulent data and encouraged the use of tables and graphics as a more effective way of presenting the basic data." Table 4.1 summarizes major problems that the various editors noted and that might guide Max in his revision.

Interviews with Academics

As discussed in the previous section, we conducted a series of focus group interviews with Deans and professors at New Zealand universities. In these interviews, we encountered members of editorial boards in psychology and the sciences. Before conducting the focus group interviews, each of them had read Max's paper. In the interviews, we asked "if the content of the paper had been changed to match their discipline and the journal(s) for which they review, how likely would it be that Max would be published in one of the journals in their discipline?"

Those serving as reviewers were quite consistent in their response to the question. If Max carefully targeted fringe and less prestigious journals—be they electronic or print ones—it is likely that he would get published. Furthermore, the chances for detection would decrease; "we tend to monitor such journals far less than the most prestigious journals."

Max, as they explained, would probably do as we had done: he would make conservative findings and not want to call too much attention to his or her work. This academic, either as a beginner or someone needing more publications before a tenure decision, would not want to risk letters to the editor or any questioning of the quality of the research.

They suspected that Max would not place his paper on an electronic discussion group because this would call attention to his work, thereby inviting comment. In effect, Max would want to say that he had been published, presumably in a peer-reviewed journal, but would not want to invite scrutiny of that publication.

If, by chance, there was harsh criticism of that work, it would be in Max's interests to admit sloppiness (but not outright fraud) as he rushed to publication, or to remain silent. As already discussed, if Max does not admit guilt, it is less likely that the university would take action against him. In effect, if Max already has tenure, he should deny, deny, and threaten the university with legal action. If, at some point, he had to leave the institution, more than likely there would be some legal settlement enabling Max to leave with his reputation untarnished.

If Max did not have tenure, however, there is still the chance that the university would show leniency in that he did not receive proper mentoring and the paper did not have life-threatening or major theoretical implications. In effect, there is a scale of misconduct and, as long as Max did not exceed it, he might be forgiven. Of course, a critical question is, "Is this an isolated episode or a pattern of misbehavior?" The university would be more concerned about that pattern. If Max refused to admit guilt, however, the university would have to proceed very carefully and not provide Max with an opportunity for successful legal recourse.

Those interviewed questioned whether or not it is the role of reviewers to detect fraud. Admittedly, they should differentiate between research worthy of publication within the journal for which they review and that which is of lesser quality. Reviewers lack the resources, time, desire, and ability to examine each dataset and

TABLE 4.1. Weaknesses in Max's Work as Noted by Editors and Peer Reviewers

- Lack of a theoretical framework placing the research in a larger context;
- Failure to address public policy issues;
- Poor focus on the research question;
- "Matter-of-factish" sample selection;
- Sweeping generalizations in the "analysis" for which quantitative data are near absent;
- A simplistic questionnaire;
- Poorly-phrased null hypothesis;
- Need for graphs and tables to summarize and interpret results;
- The section on topics for further research is general and remarkably devoid of relevance to the null hypothesis;
- The numbers do not always add up the way the paper claims;
- There is need for more discussion of the way in which those interviewed were selected, and the purpose of the interviews; and
- The quality of the writing could be improved.

replicate the study. "To do so would subvert the peer review process and the extent to which individuals would regard peer reviewing as a service commitment."

SUMMARY

According to an editorial in *The Lancet* ("Dealing with Deception," 1996),

> although exact data are lacking, the prevalence of fraud seems to be around 0.1-0.4% of research studies. Figures such as these have led several countries to develop a national mechanism to investigate alleged cases of scientific dishonesty. (p. 843)

Such estimates should more realistically be labeled as "guess-timates." Any estimate or "guess-timate" for the behavioral and social sciences, and the humanities, cannot be provided. Still, as the research for this chapter indicates, we cannot assume an attitude of casual indifference. Max would thrive in such a climate, especially if he refuses to admit guilt. At least, he might admit sloppiness or haste to produce a work and get a favorable editorial decision before the promotions and tenure committee met to deliberate on his future within the institution.

It would seem that universities, especially the ones at which we conducted the focus group interviews, are caring and forgiving institutions. They do not like long-drawn-out confrontations, especially if there are legal implications. The consensus of those university administrators and professors interviewed is that, if Max had tenure, he might remain on the staff. If he did not, he still might not be asked to leave.

If his future within the most prestigious institutions is limited, he may well remain within academe, but at an institution or institutions of lesser national and international reputation. By not being too ambitious and by carefully selecting where he published, Max could probably enjoy a somewhat distinguished career at some lesser-known academic institution.

As will be discussed in Chapter 7, academic institutions should review their policies and procedures so that they have recourse for coping with any Max who is a member of the faculty. Institutions have procedures for dealing with dishonest students but not always dishonest faculty members.

We did not probe reactions to Max as a student as opposed to a member of the faculty. Such research should be conducted; although the findings, like this study, would be based on self-reports, they are nonetheless illuminating and suggest areas for universities to pursue in addressing the implications of misconduct.

Students

Students are trusting of what they read, or at least what their instructors ask them to read. The library school students found the fraudulent paper to be disconcerting. Like a number of the librarians interviewed, they expect science or research to be self-correcting, and the peer-reviewing process to be infallible. They also expected an academic institution to deal with Max swiftly and decisively, and for the library and their instructors to caution against "blind acceptance of information," regardless of the medium in which it appears.

Librarians

The librarians interviewed assumed that misconduct is a rare occurrence and were unfamiliar with the literature on the topic. They were unaware of how to identify fraudulent research and maintained that they were too busy to consult the types of sources listed in Appendix F. The majority belief is that library collections should contain a diversity of material, without librarians' engaging in censorship, including the removal of fraudulent material. Their function is one of collection building, and faculty members enter a partnership with them in teaching information literacy.

University Administrators and Professors

Although most of the administrators and professors interviewed could cite particular instances of misconduct from the literature or in some instances from experience, they tended to regard misconduct as far from pervasive. Of course, Max or anyone else who might be accused of misconduct should have legal protection and due process should be carefully followed. Still, as long as Max does not admit guilt and hires legal counsel, universities, as conservative institutions, would probably try to avoid a prolonged battle. They might let Max remain on the faculty, isolated but still being paid a salary, or they might reach a financial settlement by which Max agrees to leave, but perhaps without his reputation tarnished.

Those interviewed held a strong belief that science is self-correcting; it may take generations, but self-correction does occur. They were not bothered by the fact that Max may have retired, died, or gone to another institution by the time it does.

Most of those interviewed would be more concerned about the type of falsification that Max did if his research harmed others. They also did not see his research as damaging the reputation of a university or discipline beyond repair.

Editors and Editorial Board Members

If Max, as a beginner, submitted to one journal at a time and rewrote the paper based on the criticism, he would improve the quality of the paper each time, presumably, at some point, resulting in acceptance for publication. We can also assume that Max might benefit from the criticism, in case he decided to falsify a future paper. If Max were not a beginner, he would not have made the glaring mistakes that we intentionally did.

LESSONS TO BE LEARNED

It is time to ("Ethical Tremors in World of Science," 1994):

> determine whether misdeeds are isolated events or signs of a wider problem driven by underlying institutional pressures to publish, succeed and win research grants from the government in a highly competitive environment. (p. B8)

As R. Glynn Owens and E. M. Hardley (1985, p. 331), however, note, "...as with so many things, it is easier to highlight a problem than to come up with a solution." Nonetheless, the research reported in this chapter reinforces certain lessons and suggestions. These are not original, but reflect the fact that previous recommendations have not always been heard or followed.

As noted in the editorial appearing in *The Lancet* ("Dealing with Deception," 1996, p. 843), "professional self-regulation has failed." As a result, there is a need to develop and widely circulate a whistleblower's "bill of rights," which covers "protection from retaliation, fair procedures, and timely processes." Furthermore,

> good scientific practice should become a routine part of research training in all institutions. A culture of accountability must be encouraged. Editors can help this process; we now ask authors to preserve their original data for five years in case we request a routine audit of their work. (p. 843)

Many journal editors would not be able to do such an audit, and authors might have legitimate reasons for resisting, especially if, as in library and information science, the majority of the research is unfunded and thereby not accountable beyond the investigator's own institution.

Thus, it is important that institutions review their own standards, policies, and procedures so that they will be able to cope with a Max, should they encounter someone like him. It is essential that students be taught critical thinking skills and how to evaluate information. They may be fooled at times, but they will become more adept at identifying the characteristics of good research and assessing where an individual study stands in relation to other scholarship on the same topic.

Another recommendation from the research presented in this chapter is that journal editors might demand that all authors of a work sign the contributor's or copyright agreement, thereby ensuring that each played some role in the publication.

To guard against plagiarism, to some extent, journal editors might send "reprints of any publication to all authors cited therein" (Owens & Hardley, 1985);

> Of course a plagiarist can carefully omit the name of the paper's original author, but if the policy were universally adopted it would be necessary to change the whole of the original publication's reference list. Where the paper was plagiarized from an unpublished document…the plagiarist would still have to gamble on none of the receiving authors being familiar with the original work. (p. 332)

The recommendations based on the lessons learned from the investigation of the work by the fictitious Maxwell A. Mega are admittedly small, but they are important. The cost of doing more than these suggestions may exceed the benefits derived;[2] many of the university administrators and professors were concerned that doing more might seriously retard the advancement of research and the publication process. They believed that research and publication depend on trust—trusting that the evidence has been honestly gathered and reported. Nonetheless, they recognized that some action was necessary. They were, however, more concerned about the scale of that action.

Turning to library and information science, is there a serious problem relating to misconduct by those in our discipline doing research? Our assumption, and those of others, is that the answer is "probably not." Still, as universities and journals in other disciplines review their standards, policies, and procedures, is it not responsible action to conduct a similar review in our discipline? In our case, that review might relate more to plagiarism than to falsification. But it should also recognize that Max might not have falsified the entire study. What if he had falsified just a few responses? As journal editors demand higher rates of return for surveys, might this not lead to instances of abuse?

As discussed, various actions can be taken. The first is to conduct a thorough review of an institution's or journal's policies and practices to cope with the eventuality of a Maxwell A. Mega. Colleges and universities have policies and procedures for coping with student misconduct, but not always ones for dealing with the possibility of faculty fraud and falsification. That review should address the types of issues raised in this chapter.

NOTES

[1] In another hoax, "a white 16-year-old high school student from Michigan" and some of his friends created the "Glock 3" Web site. Glock 3 is a gun that appears in some rap songs. The site "sparked outrage from church leaders" and at least one police officer. See http://www.infotech.co.nz/current/nxedu.html (November 1996).

[2] The assumption of those interviewed is that the amount of fraud in the academic system is small. If it were otherwise, they acknowledged that they would have to reassess the cost-benefit comparison.

5

MISCONDUCT: COPING
WITH THE PROBLEM

Peter Hernon

> Life is more complex than any institution is capable of dealing with adequately....
> [There is] a climate in which fraud could grow and the quality of scholarship
> decline.
>
> —Chapter 4 focus group participant

> Editors, editorial boards, and referees represent the front line of accountability
> against misconduct appearing in the scholarly literature.
>
> —Chapter 4 focus group participant

> How many times can a journal publish falsified research before we hold it account-
> able and cancel our subscription?
>
> —Chapter 4 librarian respondent

The evidence, as presented in Chapter 1 and Appendices A and B, continues to mount that misconduct—the fabrication, falsification, or plagiarism in proposing, performing, or reporting research—presents a problem of some magnitude to the medical and physical sciences. It would seem that the problem is less severe in the behavioral sciences and even less so in the humanities and the social sciences. In the humanities and social sciences, the problem may relate more to plagiarism and perhaps falsification of an occasional survey response in order to bolster the return rate or to make findings more dramatic, but not in such a way as to raise doubts about the conduct of the research. This is not to say that those in disciplines other than the sciences should be unconcerned about fraud and assume it could never occur within their disciplines. Rather, they should be alert to the possibility of a problem and implement corrective action as deemed appropriate. In effect, the problem may not require a cure with costly and numerous side effects. As this chapter suggests, the remedies must be balanced and reasonable.

The purpose of this chapter is to review the significant findings of the previous chapters and the types of sensitive practices that provide a degree of protection for systems based largely on trust—between faculty members and their academic institution, authors and the peer-reviewing process, those submitting proposals and funding organizations, the public and its tax dollars, and the public and the scholarly literature. As already noted, however, the sciences present particular difficulties and the literature addresses the need for greater accountability in record-keeping provided to project funders (to ensure replication of experiments and prudent expenditure of funds), protection of whistleblowers, and restructuring of peer-review processes for journals. The intent of this chapter is to add additional suggestions and not to repeat the existing literature.

MISPERCEPTIONS

The discussion in the previous chapters has disclosed some misperceptions that have gained wide acceptance. First, misconduct does not represent a significant problem in some disciplines. It occurs so infrequently that adopting corrective measures may be more bothersome than they are worth. Second, misconduct is far less of a problem than omission of data that do not support the alternative or directional hypothesis studied. Third, science is self-correcting. (In fact, it is not always so; when self-correction occurs, it may take generations. Not all social science research can be replicated in such a way as to verify the work of others.) Fourth, students, as part of their formal learning, gain knowledge about how to evaluate information. Furthermore, they will apply that knowledge as they sift through information to select the pieces needed to do term papers and other assignments. In other words, they are discriminate users of the literature, regardless of the medium in which it appears.

Fifth, academic librarians and academics are knowledgeable about scientific fraud and research misconduct, and have considered the implications from their respective positions. Sixth, they are willing to take action to determine the extent of the problem in their collections and the institution itself. Seventh, librarians feel a sense of responsibility for assuring the accuracy of material within the collection—that it is free from misconduct. Eighth, once aware of the problem relating to misconduct, all librarians will monitor the types of sources mentioned in Appendix F regularly to discover the magnitude of the problem and the immediate consequences for collection management, and to alert library users to evaluate material before using it. Ninth, the problem is confined to the United States and to funding within the sciences. Tenth, team research reduces the opportunities for misconduct. (In fact, medical research may involve teams focusing on narrow aspects of the problem, but the work of one team feeds into that of another team. Thus, misconduct might occur but be harder to detect.)

MAXWELL A. MEGA

In discussions with librarians, university deans, and professors (see Chapter 4), it became clear that, if Max were really devious, he might fool editorial boards of renowned journals, especially if he were not a neophyte in the conduct of research. Even if he were a neophyte, in all likelihood, he would be published at some point in his quest. He would benefit from a system in which editors, suspecting a neophyte and/or a person who produces hasty or "sloppy" work, want to be supportive and offer guidance for future submissions to their journals or elsewhere. Max would profit from the advice and produce a better product with each rejection or request for revision.

The consensus of the groups interviewed is that the best chance for catching Max would be if his institutional peers became suspicious. Had Max previously discussed his research with them, or did the paper mysteriously materialize? Did his colleagues notice Max's receipt of numerous completed questionnaires? This is not a foolproof system, however, for members of departments might become so specialized that they do not discuss their research with each other. Also, if Max were balancing a number of different research projects simultaneously, this one might slip through unnoticed. Furthermore, colleagues, most likely, do not pay attention to each other's mail.

It is also possible that Max might have used his home address or another location for the return of surveys. What if he co-authored the paper with a second Max—another falsifier—perhaps at another institution? Each could claim that the returned surveys were sent to the other. How likely is it that a departmental chair or dean would demand to see the actual completed survey forms?

Despite these problems, it is possible that some whistleblower at Max's institution might be suspicious and issue a formal complaint. The literature highlighted in Chapter 1 suggests that the whistleblowers themselves might be persecuted— not the offending party! The deans and professors interviewed suggested that, in some instances, the whistleblower, not Max, might decide to leave the institution. This is possible if Max refused to admit guilt and remained on the faculty. The whistleblower might become disenchanted with the institution and leave.

As already suggested (see Chapter 4), Max might admit guilt but not receive a severe punishment. Instead of being forced to leave the institution and being "branded" publicly with the scarlet letter F (for falsifier), he might receive a warning and counselling (about proper research techniques), and perhaps be ineligible for competing for research monies for a certain period of time.

If Max refused to admit guilt, the picture becomes cloudy. At this point, the scenario depends on whether or not Max has tenure. If Max does, then he might refuse to admit guilt and hire legal counsel, thereby forcing the institution to press charges, to reach a deal quietly, or to leave him untouched. Pressing charges would mean that the institution has irrefutable evidence and is willing to wait out any delays and stalling. As the university officials reminded us, academic institutions are conservative organizations, and Max could use this to his advantage. If Max remained in the department, he would probably see neither career advancement nor salary increases. Max would still, however, enjoy employment and a certain salary.

If Max left the institution, the departure might be part of a deal in which the misconduct does not go on his record. Max's history, therefore, does not follow him to the new place of employment.

The consensus from all the focus group interviews is that, from Max's point of view, it would probably be best to deny misconduct. To what extent could the university prove misconduct as opposed to sloppiness in Max's research? One dean commented "at one point or another, haven't all of us been sloppy in our research?"

Nobody refuted the summary characterization of the focus group interviews that Max would probably remain within academe. While he might not be at a first-rate institution, he might do fine at a less regarded academic institution. Furthermore, if science is self-correcting, the self-correction might occur after Max left the institution, retired, or died. To those deans and professors interviewed, the length of time is immaterial; what is important is that science is self-correcting. The social sciences are perhaps less self-correcting, especially when the research cannot be replicated in the same way. Clearly, such situations work to Max's advantage.

Motivation

Without having access to a real-life Maxwell A. Mega, we (and the focus group participants) were unable to probe Max's motivation. Some of those interviewed had heard of instances of misconduct but had not thought of Max being on the faculty at their insitution.

Chapter 4 summarized the situations suggested by the literature that might provoke Max to practice unacceptable behavior. The scientific literature offers another motivation—desire for research funding on a recurring basis. Some of the deans and professors interviewed suspected that Max might be seeking a short-cut to advancement, and possibly "he had not caught the eye of the head of the department, and, thus, produced a greater quantity of research hoping to gain notice and favoritism." Some of those interviewed thought Max would have high ambition but low capability to do research, whereas others agreed on the ambition but assumed Max might have medium to high capability. He might be lazy; on the other hand, he might not be.

There was disagreement over the amount of research Max might falsify. If he did it once and the misconduct went unnoticed, would this be license to repeat that behavior?

Max would be taking a risk. If caught, this would call into question all of his research, even the portions that are legitimate—assuming there are some. Why would someone potentially place his entire career at risk? The discussion in this chapter and Chapter 4 offers a partial explanation; still, so much remains unknown outside the sciences.

How Might the Questioning of Max's Work Have Occurred?

As already discussed, there might be suspicion on the part of a colleague at Max's own institution concerning the validity or even existence of his research. Perhaps someone at another institution working in the same field might question the research. The concern might be reported to the funding source, or, in the case of a publication, to the editor of the journal, perhaps through a letter to the editor. If the misconduct were discovered prior to publication, the paper might be withdrawn and an apology extended.

Recommendations

The consensus of the deans and professors interviewed was that, if they knew Max had engaged in misconduct and they had "the evidence," they would have to cope with the matter. Engaging in a coverup would only make matters worse. The work of others in the department could become discredited by association and the image of the department and university would be tarnished. As well, other scholars might leave the institution to avoid any damage to their own reputations. As discussed, however, dealing with the situation may not be so easy or clear-cut, especially if Max has tenure and refuses to admit guilt.

Academic institutions, including human ethics committees and promotion and tenure committees, should, at a minimum, review contracts for inclusion of a section on academic integrity and procedures for coping with a Max. It is clear from the focus group interviews that those university deans and professors interviewed had not considered the possibility that a Max could be a member of the faculty. As long as his research did not "harm others," they were likely to be forgiving. If this is so, there should be procedures for dealing with the situation presented by a Max. Good management involves preparation for the unknown, and the high number of incidents of scientific misconduct suggests that preparation is prudent disaster planning.

Human ethics committees might demand the submission of detailed proposals and conduct an audit on a random or systematic sample of studies in progress or recently completed. They might also comment on more than ethical issues; they might offer recommendations on study procedures. Of course, such procedures would not cover all the research performed, but would be an important step in formulating an institutional response to the possibility of misconduct and poorly-focused research.

When university promotion and tenure committees demand that candidates have a specified number of publications, of so many pages, of such and such a position within an issue (i.e., the lead article), and so forth, they might be creating a climate in which Max might be forced to conduct misconduct in order to remain at that institution or one of comparable prestige. This is another reason for review of procedures.

Another recommendation is for institutions to require auditing of outputs, and to implement an organizational culture resulting in greater accountability. More than likely, funding agencies will have to pressure institutions to develop more responsive organizational cultures. At the same time, departments might require, say, a six-year retention of datasets. If they did so, precautions about issues of privacy and access to the records would be necessary.

Faculty members teaching research methods courses should include a section on ethics, review the types of issues presented by Max's "research," and teach critical appraisal skills. As well, those supervising graduate student research should insist on the highest ethical behavior and warn against falsification of any data.

As a few focus group participants commented, there is a loss of collegiality in scholarship and research within a number of departments, when faculty members become highly specialized and less interested in the work of their colleagues. They wondered how that spirit could be regained. As a start, members of a department might hold brown-bag lunches and discuss research topics. One of them might even give a formal presentation for general comment. It is important to restart the dialogue.

CONTINUED RESEARCH INTO MISCONDUCT

It is important to have further investigations of research misconduct and to explore additional ways to understand its scope and nature, as well as to pursue cost-effective and cost-efficient remedies that do not alter the trust relationship upon which research and publication are based. Trust is important but should not become blind acceptance of whatever is reported.

Research might explore the different types of misconduct and the extent to which they occur in different disciplines. As survey respondents (see Chapter 3) and focus group participants (see Chapter 4) believe, misconduct cannot occur in disciplines such as mathematics, whereas in accounting and economics, for instance, practices that others might label as misconduct would be widely accepted.

The perception of the historians participating in the focus group interviews was that misconduct is rare but would involve, for instance, the failure to mention whether or not primary sources were consulted, failing to cite a secondary source, and citing sources that were not used. Clearly, for them, misconduct centers around acknowledging one's intellectual debt, plagiarism, and omission. How do other humanists' views of misconduct differ?

As discussed in Chapter 4, researchers into misconduct must be careful about the ethical implications of their own work. They should be careful about deceiving others as part of their data collection. Human ethics committees will weigh, as they should, the possible benefits of a project against the intrusion which results from deception.

While seeking approval from the Human Ethics Committee at Victoria University of Wellington to conduct the research based on the paper purportedly written by Maxwell A. Mega (see Appendix E), it was most distressing to learn that:

> One Committee member has suggested that all potential referees in participating journals could be advised in advance (for example, at the beginning of the 12 month period) that some manuscripts with fake data may be circulated for comment over the next 12 months, and their participation in the refereeing process is sought on that basis. This would ensure informed consent from the outset. It would, of course, alert referees to the possibility of fake data, which may reduce the usefulness of the results, although we are inclined to think that it would still be interesting to discover the extent to which referees are able to discriminate between fake and real data, even when they are alerted to the issue. (Personal communication)

In our opinion, this suggestion would serve to undercut the review process for one year. Every paper that consenting reviewers received would be considered as a possible test of their ability to detect fraud. In theory, they could accuse innocent authors of potential fraud; the accusation would be reported to the editor and presumably no further. In effect, for one year, every paper would be held to a higher level of accountability, as reviewers might insert new criteria into their recommendations. The peer-review process would be contaminated; no responsible editor would permit reviewers to be part of such a test.

A number of the professors and deans interviewed suggested that the chances of detection should not be underestimated. It is important that this assumption be examined, especially with electronic publication becoming one more avenue for publication rather than displacing the others.

The consensus of the deans and professors was that a Max would publish on "dull and unimportant topics," seek publication in less-prestigious journals, and want less visibility for his work outside the department. As one dean explained, "going for high visibility journals is more risky." When we responded that renowned journals had unknowingly published fraudulent work, however, the person had no response. Clearly, the whole range of assumptions merits review.

Librarians and professors at two universities mentioned instances in which a department evaluated the curriculum vitae of potential faculty members and the chairperson asked library staff to verify the accuracy of the claims on the vitae. The vitae contained misinformation (e.g., wrongly cited volumes and page numbers) and articles not in the journals claimed. Those whom we interviewed asked "How do we verify sources listed in difficult-to-locate journals and conference proceedings?" and "How do we treat works listed as 'in press' or 'forthcoming'?" It would seem that job seekers should be prepared to lend copies of works listed on the curriculum vitae.

PEER-REVIEWED JOURNALS

Scholarly journals, regardless of discipline, ought to review existing policies and procedures covering their peer-review process. Necessitating this review, in part, is the recent experience of *Social Text*, which unknowingly published a hoax paper on postmodern physics, in its May 1996 issue, by New York University physicist Alan Sokal. He admitted, in a paper appearing in the magazine *Lingua Franca*, that his paper was a prank (see http://www.nyu.edu/ gsas/dept/physics/faculty/sokal/index.html; see also Fish, 1996; Kimball, 1996; McMillen, 1996).

Journal editors and publishers should be prepared in case other individuals decide to conduct similar "stings" in other disciplines and fields. The motivation of these individuals might be to discredit science or scholarship, challenge peer reviewing (see Gross & Levitt, 1994), question the legitimacy of a field or discipline, or attack conventional thinking.[1] One supporter of Sokal's maintains that "if a field of thought is so lacking in rigor that its proponents can't even recognize gibberish and parody, what does that say about the validity of their views" (James Shea, communication on SCIFRAUD, May 17, 1996).

Editors might ask board members and other reviewers if they had ever questioned a paper as being based on misconduct or as a prank testing the peer-review process. The purpose of this query would be to make reviewers more sensitive to the possibility that misconduct might occur. Nonetheless, both reviewers and readers of a journal must recognize that the peer-reviewing process can only determine, for instance, that:

- Data are reported in a consistent manner.
- Findings are consistent with what is already known, or appear logical. The danger is that valid findings might be questioned because they do not conform to current beliefs.
- Conclusions are based on the data.
- Appropriate statistical tests are applied.

- Numbers and percentages are consistently and correctly reported.
- Study objectives, research questions, and hypotheses are clearly worded and addressed in a coherent and logical manner.
- Sufficient information is provided to replicate, in part, the *experiment*. Replication is important to ensure reliability in the sciences, but is more difficult to achieve in the social sciences, such as with a survey (similar to the one that Max used (see Appendix E)).

Publishers and editors might ask each author to sign a contributor's agreement, which contains a clause that the authors are responsible for the content and did not engage in misconduct, including plagiarism, or in defrauding the journal in jest. Journals in the humanities and many of the social sciences might not be able to go beyond such a step. In many disciplines and fields, it would be unreasonable for editors to require deposit of the dataset in some data archive or with the editor, or even to request occasional access to datasets. On the other hand, funding organizations might have such expectations.

Deposit does not guarantee that misconduct had not occurred or would be detected. After all, there was an actual machine-readable dataset created for Max's paper. There was, however, no print counterpart—no set of completed questionnaires. If university administrators became suspicious about Max's work, they might request both the machine-readable dataset and the completed questionnaires. If Max produced a set of completed questionnaires, they might be matched to the machine-readable records. Someone might also examine the handwriting on the questionnaires.

TEACHING INFORMATION LITERACY

The findings reported in Chapter 3 emphasize the importance of (and necessity for) instruction in information literacy. Somebody must do it, and it cannot remain a gap between what librarians and teaching faculty do. Each has a role to play, and neither should refuse the challenge.

One political scientist interviewed as part of the focus groups for Chapter 4 mentioned that he (and his colleagues) find it difficult to get undergraduate students to read! He did not want them to rely on the Internet and World Wide Web (WWW) because they become "so wrapped up in surfing that they become sidetracked and never develop their analytical skills." Clearly, the teaching of information literacy is complex and will not be easy to accomplish (see Chapter 6).

The amount and diversity of electronic information through the Internet and WWW will only make the problem worse. The problem here relates to both misinformation and disinformation. When information is not updated, misinformation may occur. At the same time, it may be difficult to separate the official record from other information produced by government. Clearly, the information that one uses might not be the most reliable and current; it might also be fraudulent.

MOVING TOWARD THE 21ST CENTURY

As the reading level of the public and many students in colleges and universities remains low, and as people blindly accept what they read as accurate and not the consequence of misconduct or sloppiness, the challenges will be enormous. Librarians and teachers from primary school through academe cannot ignore their role and obligation. They should not say that they lack the ability to change the situation. They have that ability and must emphasize critical thinking skills. More than ever, problem-solving is more important than rote memorization of facts and philosophies.

As we approach the 21st century, we have not yet seen the full magnitude of the information explosion. Not all information is of the same importance, value, or quality; selectivity is essential. The issue is: on what basis do people exercise that selectivity, and what are the consequences of their actions? While librarians are trying to cope with physical mutilation of journals and other print sources, they are now discovering the intellectual mutilation of knowledge. The scope of this problem is not well understood; future research might suggest its magnitude, and ways to minimize the problem across disciplines.

NOTE

[1] Jim Schnabel (1994) discusses examples of "hoax-like" deceptions to show that the purpose of such deception might be to discredit an idea, to demonstrate the arbitrariness of certain research findings, or to show bias in editorial decisions regarding which papers to select for publication.

6

IMPLICATIONS OF MISCONDUCT FOR BIBLIOGRAPHIC INSTRUCTION

Laura R. Walters

...to be information literate, a person must be able to recognize when information is needed and have the ability to locate, evaluate, and use effectively the needed information.

—American Library Association Presidential Committee
on Information Literacy, 1989, p. 22

In recent years, the problem of research misconduct has captured the attention of professional and lay people alike. The concern with misconduct beyond the professional community is only fitting, for it has ramifications for all segments of society. As Robert Bell (1992, p. xi) states, misconduct "affects...the medicines we take, the bridges we drive on, the buildings we live in, and the weapons that are supposed to defend us." Fraud in clinical research is of particular significance, for it can have dire consequences in the treatment of patients, leading to disability and even death. More broadly, misinformation and disinformation resulting from misconduct affect the understanding of issues and problems, and even knowledge itself. It may take generations to correct that understanding and knowledge. In addition, misconduct breaks down the trust relationship between scholarship and education, scholarship and policy-making, and scholarship and scientific advancement.

INFORMATION LITERACY

Concurrent with the increased interest in research misconduct is a growing focus on the subject of information literacy. Educators and librarians alike have explored the concept of information literacy and examined ways to turn students into independent lifelong learners (Rettig, 1991, p. 9). The detection of misconduct and the advancement of information literacy are closely-related concepts, for information-literate people are better able to assess the accuracy and validity of the research, scholarship, and general information that they encounter.

The role of academic libraries, particularly the bibliographic instruction (BI) staff, in contributing to an information-literate society is a topic of great debate. Inherent in the concept of information literacy is the ability to judge the quality of the information one has found. The American Library Association Presidential Committee on Information Literacy (1989, p. 22) states that "to be information literate, a person must be able to recognize when information is needed and have the ability to locate, evaluate, and use effectively the needed information." Similar reports from other professional associations, such as the American Association of School Librarians and the Association for Education Communications and Technology, identify the ability to evaluate the reliability of information as the foremost characteristic of an information-literate person. In addition, documents from these organizations "maintain that information literacy is an integral part of undergraduate education" (Rader & Coons, 1992, p. 111), and they urge librarians to take an active part in producing information-literate students.

A major component of information literacy is the ability to think critically. In the early 1980s, librarians and educators began to note the necessity of teaching students critical thinking skills. In 1983, Mona McCormick issued a rallying cry, stating that "it is now time to make critical thinking and the evaluation of information a focal point of library instruction" (p. 339). She bemoaned the encouragement of "sponge" readers who merely absorb information and urged librarians to at least hint "to students that the library can be used to evaluate information as well as to find it" (p. 339).

Many in the library community adopted McCormick's rallying cry, and a new component was added to the concept of information literacy. Teaching students simply to locate material was no longer deemed the primary goal of information literacy. Instead, higher-order critical thinking skills, such as understanding and evaluating information, became necessary attributes of an information literacy program (Behrens, 1994, p. 312).

Barry Beyer (1985, p. 271) has defined critical thinking as "the assessing of the authenticity, accuracy, and/or worth of knowledge claims and arguments." Essential to critical thinking is the willingness to question. Critical thinkers recognize underlying assumptions, evaluate evidence, question whether facts support conclusions, question the adequacy of data, and evaluate people and publications

(McCormick, 1983, p. 340). Above all, critical thinkers have a healthy skepticism about information and know how to recognize biases (Bodi, 1990, p. 254).

Scientists examining the question of misconduct also point to the necessity of developing a healthy skepticism concerning published works. Indeed, medical researchers Herbert Nigg and Gabriela Radulescu (1994) suggest that the lack of such skepticism contributes to the publication and perpetuation of scientific fraud. They note that "the task of gatekeeping to ensure the highest quality of science implies...a probing skeptical mind," and they urge editors and readers alike "to consider all authors 'suspect' until a thorough check of the literature establishes the honest authors" (p. 168).

Nigg's and Radulescu's words echo those of many in the library community who believe that the ability to suspend belief is an earmark of an information-literate person. Sonia Bodi (1995, p. 24) states this position succinctly when she notes that librarians "have a responsibility to educate students to know that resources are not uniformly valuable or relevant, and that students need to maintain skepticism and suspend judgment until they have assessed the text."

Despite the emphasis in the library literature on the role of librarians in producing information-literate students, Peter Hernon and Ellen Altman (1995) found librarians who still believe that "library users should draw their own conclusions about the reliability and validity of information" (p. 31). The majority of the librarians they interviewed concerning the role of academic libraries in coping with research misconduct in their collections and services felt that it was the faculty's responsibility to teach methods of inquiry and skepticism and not theirs. As Hernon and Altman note, "even when the library emphasized information literacy, the librarians interviewed did not consider [it to be] their role to inform students that fraudulent research might unknowingly appear in their class papers" (p. 31).

While the librarians interviewed by Hernon and Altman might not consider it their responsibility to teach students to evaluate information, some faculty members and scientists disagree. At Indiana University Southeast and North Park College in Chicago, freshmen composition instructors specifically asked BI librarians to address the use of weak, inappropriate, and unreliable sources by their students, and to teach students how to judge the academic soundness of the materials they cite in their papers (Bodi, 1990, 1995; Totten, 1990).

At Tufts University, 40% of the faculty members responding to a survey on fraudulent literature believed that librarians and faculty should share the responsibility for teaching students to evaluate published sources. Students at the same university felt even more strongly about this issue, with 68% of the respondents agreeing that faculty and librarians should share the responsibility (see Chapter 3). Comments provided by these students suggest that a joint partnership between faculty members and librarians would help them to feel more capable of evaluating published literature.

Scientist Mark Pfeifer and medical librarian Gwendolyn Snodgrass (1990) note the importance of librarians in addressing the problem of scientific fraud in the literature. They bemoan the fact that bioscience libraries have not historically addressed this issue, and they call for a multifaceted approach to deal with fraud, one that involves authors, editors, reviewers, and librarians. James Rettig (1991), who supports this multifaceted approach, states that librarians:

> must not take entirely upon themselves the burden for producing information-liter-
> ate adults. That is the responsibility of the entire educational system. However,
> because teachers at every level and librarians in every type of library have an equal
> stake in the development of information-literate people, all reference librarians have
> a common ground. (p. 20)

RESPONSES OF THE LIBRARY COMMUNITY

Librarians have responded to the call to produce information-literate students in a variety of ways. In teaching students to evaluate information, BI librarians have noted the importance of looking at both internal and external sources of validation (Bodi, 1988, 1990, 1995; Engeldinger, 1988; McCormick, 1983; Totten, 1990; Wesley & Werrell, 1985).

Internal sources are those present in the published material itself. By examining certain internal elements of a work, readers can assess the validity of the argument being presented, the bias of the author, and the adequacy of the evidence. Librarians teaching methods of internal validation stress the necessity of examining the following elements of a work:

- The author's stated purpose;
- The author's bias;
- Methods of data gathering;
- Methods of data analysis;
- The use of documentation; and
- Attribution of sources.

In studying these elements, students are taught to determine if data are reported in a consistent way, if the conclusion reached is justified by the data, and if the data are internally consistent.

External methods of validation take the reader beyond the internal elements of the work. By using the external sources noted below, readers are taught to assess the qualifications of an author and the status of the publication under review. BI librarians concentrating on external sources of validation teach students to examine biographical sources, determine the funding agency, note the publisher, distinguish between scholarly and non-scholarly publications, and identify refereed journals. In addition to these criteria, a primary component of external validation is a determination of the critical reception of the book or article under review.

Librarians teaching methods of external validation focus on the following tools and library aids:

- Distinguishing between refereed and non-refereed journals by using sources such as:
  - *Magazines for Libraries*; and
  - *Ulrich's International Periodical Directory.*
- Examining the qualifications of the author through biographical sources, including *Biography Index*, faculty guides, subject-specific biographical dictionaries, and encyclopedias.
- Determining critical reception by tracking the response to a work using:
  - Book review sources, including *Book Review Digest* and *Book Review Index*;
  - Citation indexes;
  - Newspaper and general journal indexes; and
  - Science indexes, including *MEDLINE* and *BIOSIS*.

Misconduct presents a potential problem for librarians, scholars, researchers, students, and others because it is difficult to identify even when the reader uses both external and internal sources of validation. Indeed, medical researchers have concluded that "scientists do not and probably cannot identify articles that are fraudulent" based on a reading of the articles alone (Whitley, Rennie, & Hafner, 1994, p. 170). This may be because articles based on research fraud are internally consistent. The author has falsified the data precisely so that internal validation may be achieved. This poses special problems for the reader and for the librarian attempting to teach information literacy. Fortunately, some of the external validation tools discussed above may be put to good use in exposing some fraudulent articles (see also Appendix F of this book).

CONFRONTING MISCONDUCT

Given the reluctance of academe to confront misconduct in a comprehensive manner, the lack of a consistent approach to dealing with retracted articles, and the continued citation of fraudulent publications, is it hopeless for BI librarians to attempt to alert students and others to the existence of fraudulent literature? We think not, for despite the difficulties imposed by misconduct, it is still possible to identify some fraudulent material. Using the tools that BI librarians have employed in teaching critical thinking skills, and suggestions found in other chapters of this book, students and others can learn not to take literature at face value and to evaluate the information they encounter. The first step in confronting misconduct is for BI librarians to accept their responsibility to deal with the issue and to alert students to the fact that fraudulent data or information may appear in the literature they are reading and citing.

The importance of informing students about the existence of research misconduct is borne out by Chapter 3 and the survey conducted at Tufts University. The majority of the Tufts student respondents indicated that they never consider the possibility of research fraud appearing in published literature. Indeed, many students echoed the sentiments of one respondent who noted that "I usually take all information as being fact." This type of response underscores the necessity of teaching critical thinking skills to students, concentrating on the tools needed to evaluate published material.

Addressing the topic of research misconduct is a natural component of any library instruction program that has the teaching of critical thinking skills as its major goal. BI librarians can integrate the discussion of research misconduct into a general instruction program that starts with such basic tasks as teaching patrons to distinguish between popular and scholarly literature, refereed and non-refereed journals, and primary and secondary sources. By introducing these critical concepts, library instructors alert patrons to the fact that all articles are not "created equal" and that a critical eye is necessary when assessing published material. From this base, instructors can move on to a discussion of research misconduct and the implications of misconduct for knowledge and society in general. The instructor might address the issue of self-correction in science and the length of time that it might take for self-correction to occur. There are several important studies on the continued citation of fraudulent data that can be utilized in this part of the instruction program (Garfield & Welljams-Dorof, 1990; Kochan & Budd, 1992; Pfeifer & Snodgrass, 1990; Whitley, Rennie, & Hafner, 1994). Starting with this base, the program could continue with a review of more sophisticated internal and external methods of evaluating published material.[1]

As stated earlier, internal methods of validation are least effective when dealing with research fraud. Research misconduct is difficult to detect precisely because the data have been "fudged." Researchers involved with fraud, such as Maxwell A. Mega (see Chapters 4 and 5), can either change the data to suit their needs or fabricate them entirely. Internal methods of validation will not be successful in ferreting out this type of fraud. They can, however, be helpful in determining the appropriateness and reliability of the sources used by an author. Readers can evaluate the author's use of documentation by examining the sources cited in a work. Students who are taught to review citations can assess whether the author has used weak and unreliable sources to back up his or her argument. Such an assessment may at least be helpful in judging the academic soundness of the article or book under review.

While it is necessary for BI librarians to point out the importance of examining the internal consistency of an argument, the nature of misconduct makes it unlikely that many readers will uncover fraud through this method. Of more usefulness in identifying fraud are the external methods of validation that BI librarians have employed when teaching students to evaluate material they have found.

A particularly effective external validation tool is the determination of critical reception. In determining critical reception, students are taught to track the reaction to the material for which they have found citations. Students can do so by using citation indexes, specialized subject indexes, newspaper indexes, general periodical indexes, and, if the material is a book, book review indexes.

Citation indexes are particularly crucial in tracking the critical life of a work. By using indexes such as *Science Citation Index* and *Social Sciences Citation Index*, students can find retraction notices, letters to the editor, and other critical commentary on the articles they have retrieved. Indeed, Eugene Garfield, the founder of the Institute for Scientific Information (ISI), had scientific misconduct in mind when he first suggested the production of the indexes. In his original paper, he proposed "a bibliographic system for science literature that can eliminate the uncritical citation of fraudulent, incomplete, or obsolete data by making it possible for the conscientious scholar to be aware of the criticisms of earlier papers" (Garfield, 1955, p. 108). Citation indexes are, therefore, an important tool when evaluating the validity of scientific material, and their use should be stressed in any BI program dealing with scientific information.

The use of citation indexes is invaluable in teaching students to evaluate any literature, not just the scientific. Misrepresentation of data and plagiarism are, of course, not limited to the sciences; they also occur in the social sciences and the humanities. Learning to evaluate material is critical to all academic disciplines. The ease with which one can do so, however, depends on the discipline. Indeed, it is possible that fraud is more public in the sciences because it is more likely to be uncovered. Scientific research is more easily replicated than social science research. Thus, it is more open to scrutiny.

This fact is reflected in the indexing and abstracting resources available in the sciences. Scientific indexing services such as *MEDLINE* and *BIOSIS* have added "retracted publications" fields that can help in the identification of fraudulent articles. With the addition of these fields, *MEDLINE* and *BIOSIS* can serve a similar purpose to citation indexes by leading students to criticisms of an original publication. Thus, when students retrieve scientific citations in other sources, they should be encouraged to search for the articles in *MEDLINE* and *BIOSIS*. In doing so, they might identify articles discussing retracted publications or making negative comments.

There are problems with retraction notices that should be pointed out when teaching the use of *MEDLINE, BIOSIS*, and other indexes. The inconsistencies in retraction policies practiced by indexing services and journals make it difficult to identify fraudulent publications (see Chapter 2). In 1988, the International Committee of Medical Journal Editors promulgated guidelines concerning scientific fraud in publishing. These guidelines state that "The retraction, so labelled, should appear in a prominent section of the journal, be listed in the contents page, and include in its heading the titles of the original articles. It should not simply be a letter to the editor." Despite these clear guidelines, the fact remains that most "journal editors are reluctant to print retractions or even report findings of investigations because they fear legal action" (Garfield & Welljams-Dorof, 1990, p. 1424).

Even when retraction notices are published, it is not always easy to identify retracted articles. This is largely because retracted notices are not usually linked to the original article. Thus, a retraction notice concerning an article published in a specific journal in 1983 might not appear in that same journal until 1990. Hence, the person reading the original article has a very high probability of missing the retraction notice.

It was to deal with this particular problem that the National Library of Medicine (NLM) began to link retraction notices to their original articles in *Index Medicus* and *MEDLINE*. In 1984, the NLM initiated the subject heading "Retraction of Publishion." This was augmented in 1989 by the subject heading "Retracted Publication." The first heading is linked to the article retracting the original; the latter is linked to the original article itself. In addition, both the retracting and retracted articles are linked so the user can locate all the references to the retracted article. *MEDLINE* began retroactively tagging in 1988, and all pertinent articles in the database should be so tagged (Kotzin & Schuyler, 1989, pp. 337-338).

The NLM will retract articles by the author and occasionally by the author's institutional sponsor, the editor, or the publisher (see Colaianni, 1992, p. 536). *BIOSIS* only includes published retractions that are specifically designated as retractions by the original journal.

The NLM realized the problems inherent in this policy and added another database field in 1989. This field, entitled "Comments," alerts the reader to the existence of comments on a previously published article. The comment may "criticize the referent article, question its findings, supplement it with additional data, or use it as a starting point for a discussion of the commenting author's own research or opinion" (Kotzin & Schuyler, 1989, p. 339). The "Comment" field is appended to the original article and simply lists the journal citation in which the comment is published. It does not include the nature of the comment.

While the addition of the "Comment" field to *MEDLINE* was a step in helping readers identify scientific fraud, problems remain with the retraction policies of both *MEDLINE* and *BIOSIS*. The database fields dealing with retractions and comments can be easily overlooked when reading a record, so care should be taken to point out the existence of these fields and their significance when teaching the use of these databases. In addition, the policies themselves are not listed in either the printed or electronic version of the indexes. Thus, it is necessary to make students and other patrons aware that the retraction policies of the databases follow the strict guidelines noted above.[2]

Whereas *Science Citation Index, MEDLINE*, and *BIOSIS* are specialized indexes that require rather specialized training, general periodical indexes can also be used to identify scientific fraud. As William P. Whitley, Drummond Rennie, and Arthur W. Hafner (1994) discovered, citations to the works of Robert

Slutsky, a cardiologist accused of research fraud in 1985, declined significantly after the case was reported in the news media. Although not all cases of scientific misconduct receive media attention, a number do. These cases can be identified through a subject search of the authors using newspaper indexes and general periodical indexes, such as *Readers' Guide* and *Infotrac General Periodicals Index*. This method is not, of course, limited to cases of scientific misconduct, and can be used to determine instances of fraud and plagiarism in social science and humanities research.

This method proved particularly fruitful when tracking the most notorious cases of scientific misconduct to appear in the last ten years. The cases of Robert Slutsky, John Darsee, and Stephen Breuning were all widely discussed in both the popular and scientific literature of the 1980s. A search of *Readers Guide*, *Infotrac General Periodicals Index* (1980-1991), and newspaper indexes revealed numerous references to the cases of scientific misconduct concerning these three individuals. The references were to scientific journals such as *Science* and the *New England Journal of Medicine*, as well as to titles such as *Time* and *Newsweek*. Although the popular periodicals do not mention the specific articles that contain fraudulent data, they do alert readers to the fact that the person under discussion is guilty of scientific misconduct and that his or her work should be approached with caution.

Articles concerning the misconduct of Slutsky, Darsee, and Breuning were retrieved through both a search of their names and a search of the *Infotrac* subject heading "Fraud in science—cases." Many indexing and abstracting services use this Library of Congress (LC) subject heading, and, when searched in *Infotrac*, it yielded articles about other doctors and scientists involved in scientific misconduct. This subject heading, and ones related to scientific fraud, should be discussed in any BI session focusing on scientific information and the retrieval of research. Indeed, the LC heading "Fraud in science" refers also to the social sciences and identifies cases of research misconduct in these disciplines. In addition, the LC subject heading "Fraud" covers all disciplines. When combined with keyword terms such as art or history, it can yield material on cases of research misconduct in a variety of disciplines.

Thus far, the discussion concerning research misconduct has focussed on printed material. Students and scholars examining printed works such as books and journal articles are assisted in their endeavors by book review sources and other evaluative resources. Library patrons can look to *Ulrich's* and *Magazines for Libraries* to distinguish between refereed and non-refereed journals, and they can count on the editorial staff at respected presses to filter the material they publish, although this is no guarantee that fraudulent research might not slip by undetected.

Some journals on the Internet and World Wide Web (WWW) are peer-reviewed, but such scrutiny may not detect fraud. A number of electronic journals are not peer-reviewed and are the product of unpaid individual effort. The credentials of the publisher or writer may be unknown and difficult to authenticate. As Walt Crawford and Michael Gorman (1995) note in their discussion of the Internet,

How can the user of an electronic resource be sure that the electronic text received is identical to the text requested? How can the user be sure that the text is in fact the text created by the person named as its author? In short, how can the authenticity of the text be guaranteed in an electronic environment? (p. 78)

These questions pose an enormous challenge to BI librarians teaching the use of the Internet. The teaching faculty may be wary of the material they find on the WWW. Indeed, they may inform librarians that they do not want students citing material retrieved on the WWW unless it is attributed and verifiable. Most students, on the other hand, have no such concerns about WWW resources. Many believe that if it is available electronically, it must be reliable. This belief is reflected in the survey comments reported in Chapter 3. One student stated that "I never question computers or technology," while another noted that "I assumed the Internet was edited." As with print material, students must be taught that healthy skepticism is the best tactic to take when approaching networked electronic information resources.

Library patrons must apply the same evaluative standards to information available through the Internet and WWW as they do to print sources. If the publication is a journal, they must ask who publishes it and whether it is peer-reviewed. If it is a text, they must also look for the name of the publisher, in addition to the edition of the text itself. This is particularly important when dealing with historical and literary texts, which often have several authoritative editions. The edition of a text is also important when dealing with statistical information. Patrons looking for the most recent employment data, for instance, must be taught to look for the date of the material they find on the Internet.

BI librarians can teach patrons to search for information about authorship on the Internet site itself and to be wary if it is not available. Often, a site will include the name and e-mail address of the person responsible for maintaining the site. If the patron is lucky, the site will also include the person's academic credentials. Unfortunately, this is frequently not the case. In these instances, students and others can be encouraged to contact the person by e-mail and ask for a listing of credentials and other important publication information.

Fortunately, librarians and library associations are starting to provide evaluative tools similar to those available for print resources. Patrons trying to determine if an electronic journal is refereed can look in the *Directory of Electronic Journals, Newsletters*, and *Academic Discussion Lists* (1991-). This annual directory notes whether a journal is refereed, in addition to listing its publisher, frequency, distribution, contents, format, cost, and contact agency. BI librarians can refer patrons to this source for electronic journals, just as they do to *Ulrich's* for print.

As its title denotes, the directory also lists academic discussion groups and electronic newsletters. Discussion groups provide an excellent way to see how experts in the academic community are responding to current publications, both print and electronic. Through electronic newsletters, patrons can find information about various Internet sites. For instance, *Current Cites*, a monthly current awareness electronic newsletter published by the University of California Library (ftp://ftp.lib.berkeley.edu/pub/Current.Cites), consists of annotated, evaluative citations of current literature in various fields of information technology.

In addition to discussion groups and electronic newsletters, the Internet itself is becoming home to more evaluative review sites. The Argus Clearinghouse (http://www.clearinghouse.net/) provides a central access point for value-added topical guides that identify, describe, and evaluate Internet-based information resources.[3] The ratings system used by the Clearinghouse includes such criteria as the quality of the content, its usability, and the authority of the resource authors. The Clearinghouse is but one of several Internet sites that evaluate and rate electronic resources. Others include *Magellan-McKinley's Internet Directory* (http://www.mckinley.com), *Point* (http://www.pointcom.com), *GNN* (http://gnn-e2a.gnn. com/gnn/wr/ index.html), and *GNN Archive* (http://gnn-e2a.gnn.com/gnn/wr/rev-index/ alpha.html).

Just as BI librarians teaching students to evaluate print material use resources such as citation indexes, book reviews, and periodical guides, so librarians teaching the retrieval of material on the Internet must also direct patrons to the relevant evaluative tools. Fortunately, these tools, be they electronic newsletters, academic discussion groups, WWW clearinghouses, or print material, are growing daily. Their use should be integrated into BI programs. As the philosophy statement of the Argus Clearinghouse noted,

> The Clearinghouse was founded on the belief that in order to make the Internet a more useful information environment, human effort must be combined with searching and browsing technologies....It appears that artificial intelligence technologies will not meet this challenge in the near future, so intellectual labor is necessary to provide qualitative assessment of the Internet's information. (http://www. clearinghouse.net)

CONCLUSION

Students, to become information-literate and critical thinkers, need a healthy skepticism about the information they encounter and plan to use. They should not assume that everything in print or available on the Internet and other telecommunications networks is accurate and of high quality. By teaching students to be critical thinkers and to question the validity of the information they retrieve, BI librarians will be playing a part in controlling the extent to which work resulting from fraud is mistakenly treated as accurate and authoritative.

It is important that BI, and other, librarians do not let students, faculty, and even colleagues forget that significant instances of misconduct have found their way into library collections and services, vitae of academics and others, fellowship applications, research proposals, and contracted work. The first step in attempting to minimize the impact of the problem is awareness that the problem exists and has serious implications for knowledge, understanding, future research, and the applications of research findings to improving society.

NOTES

[1] While a presentation of this kind may best be suited for a classroom BI session, some of the suggestions discussed below can also be utilized in a one-on-one BI encounter. In a one-on-one situation, librarians can point out the difference between primary and secondary source material, and popular magazines and scholarly journals. They can also teach a patron using certain indexes how to search for retraction notices.

[2] It would be helpful to have a copy of the retraction policies of both the NLM and *BIOSIS* available at the reference desk or with the indexes themselves. The NLM policy can be found in Lois Ann Colaianni (1992). Copies of the policy are also available from the NLM and *BIOSIS*.

[3] For a discussion of the clearinghouse, see Hope N. Tillman (1996).

7

THE IMPLICATIONS OF RESEARCH MISCONDUCT FOR LIBRARIES AND LIBRARIANS

Ellen Altman

The conduct of everyday affairs requires us to hold so many opinions and make so many decisions that we cannot possibly base them all on the personally examined evidence and the inwardly compelling logic that "good reasons" imply.

—Haskell, 1984, p. x

"Of course it's true, I read it in a book" is a statement commonly made to convince someone of the correctness of one's argument. Belief in the correctness of what one reads, whether on paper or via an electronic medium, remains strong, and library users rely on the accuracy of information found in the library. Surveys of patrons show that statements such as "The information you get from library books and periodicals is accurate" and "That staff answer your questions about library materials accurately" were rated as important aspects of library service with those users (Davis, 1996; Hernon & Altman, 1996). Gregory Crawford (1994), in a survey of four institutions, found that "most college students agreed on their preferences for academic reference service"—definite, not probable answers ranked high on the list of preferences (p. 265).

The students surveyed might perhaps be surprised to learn that many librarians take no responsibility for the accuracy/correctness of any of the information in their collections. In fact, one book written for librarians on the topic of intellectual

113

freedom versus censorship is entitled *Freedom to Lie* (Swan & Peattie, 1989). The stance adopted by the library profession is that librarians should promote freedom of expression and hence not restrict access to ideas which may go against popular opinion.

This stems from the "Library Bill of Rights," a policy that the American Library Association (ALA) adopted in 1939; this policy has significantly influenced professional thinking and practice in North America, and much of the English-speaking world, ever since. The statement, modified slightly over the years, affirms that "materials should not be excluded because of the origin, background, or views of those contributing to their creation" and that "libraries should provide materials and information presenting all points of view on current and historical issues. Materials should not be proscribed or removed because of partisan or doctrinal disapproval" (*Intellectual Freedom Manual*, 1992, p. 3). These policies have served libraries well in dealing with pressures from political, religious, and hate groups as well as self-appointed censors who sought to remove or restrict access to publications containing ideas contrary to their own. In essence, libraries are to be impartial, simply serving as a marketplace for ideas.

When the "Library Bill of Rights" was first adopted, the term "factually correct" was included in the text. The ALA decided, after some discussion over many years, to delete any mention of the factual correctness of library materials in 1967 (*Intellectual Freedom Manual*, 1992). Thus, by default, library users are responsible for judging both the accuracy and the relevance of any and all information obtained from the library.

An extreme interpretation of the "Library Bill of Rights" is that any material can be purchased for the library's collection regardless of content. In practice, however, professional standards have excluded potentially popular but extreme materials. For example, radically-alternative medical newsletters, such as the *Last Chance Health Report* (1990-), which claims to offer "cures" for cancer, AIDS, or other life-threatening diseases, are unlikely purchases.[1]

In selecting materials for their non-fiction collections, librarians traditionally have relied on two elements: the reputation of the publishers issuing the materials and the authority of the authors who write them. Many publishers specialize in certain subjects and become known for issuing important works on those subjects. Author authority includes academic qualifications as measured by advanced degrees, affiliation with a prestigious organization, such as a large university, and a record of publications on the same or a related topic. These criteria became guidelines for librarians in selecting particular titles for their collections because they were indicators of both quality and reliability, but not infallibility. Appendix B lists many prestigious journals that have inadvertently published articles based on research misconduct.

The tenet of providing materials representing all points of view has prompted librarians deliberately to seek materials offering conflicting assessments and opinions on many topics, which, of course, means that they take no side in any matter. Librarians also cite other reasons for denying responsibility for accuracy of materials:

- They lack the expertise to make such decisions covering all the different areas of knowledge represented in the collection;
- Scholarship in almost every discipline and sub-discipline is fraught with controversy over many unresolved issues with various thought collectives competing to have their claims accepted;
- The accuracy or correctness of certain facts is subject to change because of the discovery of new evidence or new methods;
- New discoveries and new scholarly interpretations of existing knowledge are constantly being published, as are new ways to treat diseases and to understand the universe;
- Outdated and/or discredited writings are not removed from large research libraries because such information is grist for future scholars who are interested in studying trends or the historical development of a certain field; and
- Inclusion in the collection does not mean endorsement of the ideas contained in all or any of the documents. The library is simply a marketplace of ideas.

These seem valid reasons. Most libraries, however, do not make it clear to customers that, for these very reasons, the library and its staff take no responsibility for the accuracy of any information in the collection.

An impartial stance seems appropriate for matters of opinion and for issues about which the facts are in dispute or unknown. Social questions, such as how to reduce teen pregnancy or how to improve educational test scores, are issues about which facts are lacking and opinions strong. On the other hand, impartiality in admitting all points of view may be unrealistic when users' questions concern matters of fact, and especially if they relate to health, safety, and business decisions.

The ALA, however, has not seriously discussed or considered the matter of factual correctness, especially as it relates to scientific rather than social, religious, or political topics. With the notable exception of the Holocaust denial literature, most of the conflicts about library materials publicized in recent years have concerned fiction, religious, or sociological materials.

Yet, concern about accuracy and admissibility to the collection may be rising. A 1994 article in *Library Journal* recommended books on alternative medicine. The article prompted several letters, including one from a physician who chaired the National Council Against Health Fraud. He complained that "a neutral position on false information seems both naive and absurd" (Sampson, 1994, p. 7). The author of the article responded to the criticism by saying that librarians provided information but did not judge it. John N. Berry, III, Editor-in-Chief, conceded that "the doctor has a point" (1994, p. 6). Although he was in favor of presenting diversity of opinions, he cautioned that librarians could not abdicate responsibility for guidance in using the materials. "At the very least the patron must be forewarned that there are unpopular points of view, inaccurate sources, and downright lies in the library. As a truly professional follow-up, the librarian owes the patron full assistance in seeking 'valid' information" (p. 6).

Positions adopted by some units within ALA seem to be at odds with interpretations about the statements regarding the collection. For example, ALA's Reference and Adult Services Division (RASD) reissued its guidelines for service in 1990. A commitment to accuracy as a professional standard is clearly evident. These guidelines, "Information Services for Information Consumers" (Reference and Adult Services Division, 1990), state that the library "should provide users with complete, accurate answers to their information queries regardless of the complexity of those queries" (p. 263).[2] Regarding collections, the RASD guidelines state: "The library should provide access to the most current reference sources available in order to assure the accuracy of information" (p. 264). Once a library accepts a question or a request for help in finding information about a topic, it seems that the library also assumes the responsibility for providing the best possible answer or strategy for locating appropriate sources. Otherwise, why mislead customers by offering personal reference assistance?

CHANGING RESPONSIBILITIES FOR CHANGING TIMES

> Librarians will have to unlearn some of the present attitudes and to realize that they are in the "information understanding business", rather than in the business of supplying information[,] and [they will have to] be generally more flexible and adaptable.
>
> —Wainwright, 1996, p. 1

Marcel C. LaFollette (1992) raised the questions about to whom journals and their editors are responsible when they publish fraudulent and falsified articles. The same questions can be asked about libraries and the professionals who purchase, store, and refer users to published materials. Are libraries and librarians accountable:

- To the university, hospital, company, or agency of government funding library operations, and thus to the people who pay the taxes and the fees?; or
- To the people who use the materials and services?

Merely acting as an impartial conduit between sources and users will no longer suffice to demonstrate value. Such impartiality gives the impression of indifference to knowing about their collections and the requirements of their users. Special librarians have known this for years. When they are asked to find something for a professional employee or an executive they know that the information they provide must be complete, accurate, timely, and focused; otherwise, their usefulness to the organization will be questioned and their continued employment threatened.

Independent information providers, many of whom are graduates of library education programs, are quite aware that they must provide answers, not choices, if they want to attract and keep clients. Anne Woodsworth and James F. Williams II (1993) predict that products and services that have been ill-defined or have been fuzzily presented to funding agencies will be subjected increasingly to harsher analysis (p. 18). They concluded that information services will be outsourced unless librarians can demonstrate their value to the organizations that currently employ them.

T. R. Halvorson (1995), an attorney knowledgeable about information services, has identified several negligent omissions that can result in legal action charging malpractice against information professionals, such as delivering false or incomplete data and neglecting to consult the correct source. The common defense is that the library simply purchased the information from a vendor, but this excuse may not be enough. Halvorson invokes the principle of shared responsibility. "Information flows down stream. At the headwaters is the information provider, then the service provider, the software developer, the network provider, the searcher and finally, the confluence with the river of end users" (p. 175). He maintains that pleading ignorance "might be fine as an insulator for other kinds of defendants, but for information professionals I believe that it would not be so fine" (p. 176).

Despite Halvorson's admonition, pleading ignorance might be acceptable in some instances, but hardly with respect to known fraudulent reports. For librarians to ask "How can we possibly know what writings are based on misconduct?" is a feeble response for a profession supposedly expert in finding information. These are not scientific matters, but bibliographic ones. Librarians are not expected to judge the research, but they should know the citations. Well-informed staff are essential to the provision of quality service. Librarians have a responsibility to keep current about events that impact the published literature, especially the information that appears in publications purchased for one's own library. Information about articles and books based on misconduct appears in publications widely available in libraries. *The Chronicle of Higher Education* covers all disciplines in academia and alerts readers when charges of misconduct are first publicized. The *Federal Register* reports misconduct involving federal grants. In both its quarterly newsletter and its annual reports, the Office of Research Integrity (ORI) publishes summaries of cases in which guilt has been determined. Lists of retracted articles can be identified in the MEDLINE database by the search terms "retracted publication" and "retraction of publication." Searches of other online databases also retrieve some retracted publications, but the applicable search term for retracted articles and retraction notices may be somewhat different from those used by NLM.

Medical librarians do not agree on their responsibilities to provide accurate information to their primary clientele. A nationwide survey of 127 U.S. libraries serving medical schools revealed that only 16% had policies for managing articles that report invalid science, that is, articles that were retracted (Pfeifer & Snodgrass, 1992). Eighty-four of the libraries manually reviewed copies of retracted articles in their collection, but 75 did not tag them to caution readers. The authors concluded that "the lack of stated policy and the disparate assumptions about the role libraries play in this area may perpetuate the use of invalid articles" (p. 109).

Ellen Cooper (1992), formerly of the University of Tennessee Health Science Library, surveyed some medical libraries about their efforts to alert customers to errors or fraudulent information. She noted that even the libraries that "do nothing...realized that there was a problem and that they should be doing something..." (p. 18). Cooper described three ways that medical libraries notify users about errata and retractions identified by the National Library of Medicine. All are based on a monthly search of the MEDLINE database using the terms "retraction of publication" or "retracted publication," and "errata" or "erratum." In the first method, the citation referring to the correction is tipped in the bound volume at the beginning of the article. The second method involves stamping a statement near the title indicating that the article has been retracted or contains errata. The statement refers the patron to a list at the Information Desk. The third method also uses the stamped statement, but also contains bibliographic information on where the correction can be found. The bibliographic information is handwritten by library staff. Cooper concluded that "it is important for librarians to identify and mark errata and retractions in biomedical journals due to the critical nature of the information" (p. 20).

One might believe that tying retraction notices to the original article in the online databases is sufficient notice to library users, and, therefore, that librarians need not be involved in notifying their own users of retractions of articles found to be tainted. Such a belief assumes that all users will actually do an online literature search in gathering material. Yet, Stephen K. Stoan (1984), who analyzed findings from a number of studies on the information-seeking behavior of researchers, concluded that "footnotes, personal recommendations from other scholars, serendipitous discovery, browsing, personal bibliographic files, and other such techniques that involve no formal use of access tools account for the great majority of citations obtained by scholars" (p. 101).

Gwendolyn L. Snodgrass and Mark P. Pfeifer (1992) write that "clearly, medical retractions should pose a professional challenge to health science librarians" (p. 332). They cite the "Medical Library Association's Mission Statement," which states that the Association is "dedicated to improving health through the professional excellence and leadership of its members in the...provision of information services and educational programs..." (p. 332).

One argument raised by some librarians reluctant to identify publications as fraudulent is that doing so would be tantamount to labeling. The "Statement on Labeling" is another intellectual freedom principle adopted by the ALA (*Intellectual Freedom Manual*, 1992, pp. 34-35). Essentially, the intent of the statement is that the library is not to characterize anything in its collection as to its appropriateness. In the discussions with focus group participants (see Chapter 4), they frequently mentioned that they would not place any notification on discredited articles because such a notice would constitute "labeling." Regarding this matter, we sought the opinion of Judith Krug, ALA's Director of the Office for Intellectual Freedom.

According to her personal interpretation (Krug, 1996), and not that of the Committee on Intellectual Freedom, a label is a statement that says in effect, "This is not good for you to read." A retraction notice, whether done by the author, the journal, or the employer of the author, is not a label, nor is a statement issued by the ORI that data in a particular article have been falsified. The notice of retraction is simply additional information to assist readers in making judgments about the worth of the material. To the best of our knowledge there has never been any complaint that retraction notices in electronic databases or in their printed versions constitute labeling.

Notices of retraction and correction are important information which users of the tainted article might find useful, even vital. Updated information adds value to the collection. Notices of errors or retractions are not censorious labels; instead, they assist users in making more informed decisions about the value of the publications' content. How can users make informed judgments about library materials without information pertinent to the judgment? As such, these notices do not violate the ALA stance on labeling, though it appears that many librarians misunderstand the intent of the "Statement on Labeling."

Since most of the examples of misconduct in publications concern medicine, a common response among public and academic librarians is that they do not dispense medical advice; they simply provide information. Another response is that the journals identified as having inadvertently published false articles are highly specialized and, therefore, unlikely to be read or understood by nonspecialists. Such responses ignore the profound changes occurring in health care. The public is repeatedly advised through print, radio, and television to become more informed about health and medical treatments, so that when medical decisions must be made about their own health or that of a member of the family, they have sound information on which to base decisions. Pharmaceutical companies and medical providers have begun to market directly to the consumer. The University of Pittsburgh Cancer Center, among others, now seeks patients via radio advertisements. Television is a new medium for pharmaceutical companies which urge viewers to "ask their doctor" about the prescription drug being advertised. General circulation magazines contain advertisements for prescription drugs, obviously aimed at the consumer. Many public libraries subscribe to major medical publications such as the *Journal of the American Medical Association* and the *New England Journal of Medicine* because research articles from these journals are regularly featured in newspapers, radio, and television stories, prompting public interest in reading the original articles.

The arguments that some librarians have raised against identifying retracted articles for their customers are of three kinds: "it's too much trouble to find out about them," "we can't label anything," and "our patrons don't read those journals anyway." These are convenient excuses for not doing something, but not very indicative of an interest in providing information service.

LET THE DATABASES BE RESPONSIBLE

> To date, there has been little attention paid to the quality of scientific information in databases, the focus has been on quality control in online bibliographic databases. Undoubtedly, this will be an important area for investigation in the future.
>
> —Crawford & Stucki, 1990, p. 226

Many academic libraries have declared their intent to "empower users." Essentially, this means more user self-sufficiency in identifying and locating information and greater emphasis on electronic databases rather than printed indexes. If users are to navigate successfully the library/bibliographic system, it seems incumbent upon the libraries to make the system as transparent as possible. Most databases, whether the format is CD-ROM, diskette, or online, are searched using "vehicles other than those provided by the organization that produced the data" (Beutler, 1995, p. 66).

A number of databases from different producers can be accessed in a library via one system's interface, such as CARL UnCover or Ovid Technologies Inc. By the same token, a single database can be used to create several information products, as is the case with PsycINFO. Prepared by the American Psychological Association (APA), PsycINFO is used to maintain several databases available in different formats—print, CD-ROM, and online. The online version can be obtained from at least five vendors of electronic information including OCLC, DIALOG, and Ovid Technologies Inc. The online version can also be accessed by subscribers to CompuServe through its Knowledge Index System. The CD-ROM versions are sold to libraries by subscription, but they are also available from the vendor SilverPlatter. As of 1996, SilverPlatter offered 235 databases covering a variety of subjects from architecture to zoology. The number of journals indexed in these databases varied from a few hundred (345 in *Business Periodicals Index*) to as many as 10,000 in one which covers agriculture, forestry, and allied disciplines. The compilers, such as APA, supply the information to SilverPlatter, which reformats it into CD-ROM and sells it, sometimes packaging several databases on one disk.

From examination of the SilverPlatter catalog, it is not at all clear how inclusive the compilers are in covering the journals and other sources indexed. Some descriptions include the terms indexing, scanning, covering, and monitoring. What, however, is really meant by these words? Is "scanning" being done by a person, to decide which articles will be indexed, or is it being done by a machine that converts print into digital form? Several companies are involved in producing, distributing, and licensing these databases. Each has its own policies and practices about updating information and making corrections. The database compiler may send corrections to the various distributors or licensees, but the corrections may or may not be incorporated into the database, whatever the format.

Another assumption inherent in relying on the database for alerting users to false research is that users will understand what the databases are telling them. Many users of the electronic databases will not understand the difference between such statements as retraction, comment, or erratum. It is unrealistic that they should when even the database producers and journals are grappling with how to define and present information about research misconduct.

Reva Basch (1995) observed that the accuracy/error rate—the criterion of database quality—concerns technical rather than substantive problems about the records. These include typographical errors, inaccurate or incomplete citations, misspelled words, and information entered into the wrong record field. Database producers and database distributors both, however, incorporate terms and conditions of use in their contracts that disclaim responsibility for errors, because they are essentially buying the database from outside producers. Anne P. Mintz (1990) notes that there are many errors in databases and proposes a "FIXIT" command by which users could communicate errors to online databases by logging into a free database and describing the error or other problem. This is a good idea that has not yet been implemented. Carol Tenopir (1995) urges searchers to test the quality of databases and to report errors and other problems. She notes that an "international *Consumer Reports*" on databases has been proposed. To date, however, virtually no attention has been given to finding a systematic method of both identifying erroneous or fraudulent papers and distributing information about them to the library community and thence to the users. Norman Stevens (1996) extends this idea even further by recommending that publishers of indexing and abstracting services establish standards to delete or to identify explicitly articles based on false research. He further suggests that the indexing and abstracting (I&A) services link the tainted article to "other publications that have exposed and commented upon the unethical behavior" (p. 91).

The Internet might well be the vehicle by which Stevens' idea could be carried out. As noted in Chapter 2, some scientists now use their own World Wide Web (WWW) pages to attack work that they consider tainted. Listservs have become another forum for specialists to argue the merits of various claims and to denounce work that they deem false. The C-Turtle listserv has been the locus of a debate about research claiming that sea turtles use the earth's magnetic field as a directional guide. Members of the SCIFRAUD listserv have debated many ethical issues and alerted each other about published reports of scientific misconduct. It is even possible that the rapid spread of information to a large audience via the Internet may deter scientific misconduct.

A mechanism could be set up on the Internet for citations to retracted articles; subscribers could automatically receive updates at regular intervals. The establishment of the list and its maintenance should be the responsibility of some generally-recognized impartial authority. The National Institute of Standards and Technology (NIST), formerly the National Bureau of Standards, would be one reasonable option.

A NEW ROLE FOR LIBRARIANS

We are taught to present choices to users, NOT to make choices for them. In a post-scarcity environment, there is likely to be little patience with these values.

—Keys, 1995, p. 29

There has been much discussion of new roles and responsibilities for librarians in this age of information technology. The identification of falsified and fabricated papers, however, is not a new role; it is a task that librarians should have been doing all along. It is not one they can do single-handed, but it is certainly one they have ignored. They cannot detect tainted works, but surely, when such are detected and announced as such in publications, librarians who take their responsibilities seriously will make every effort to inform their patrons about these works.

Another role suggested by several writers is that librarians should become filters between their users and the huge and growing volume of information;

...it's time to move beyond this librarian who still explains and then leaves the user on his or her own to do the research. It is time to replace that model with one in which the librarian actually does the search. No more library instruction in the guise of reference help.... (Mood, 1994, p. 28)

In fact, some see this role as a filter as the way to preserve librarians' jobs as more and more individuals take on their own computerized searches for information and need help in sifting through the mass of material to find what is relevant to their interests.

Marion Paris (1994) argues that it is now time for librarians to "assume a greater sense of responsibility for the information they provide" (p. 772). She is especially referring to medical information. Others are also urging librarians to take more responsibility for providing information rather than showing customers where and how to find their own information.

The role of filter between user and information appears especially pertinent at a time when the future role of traditional librarianship seems uncertain as the explosion of electronic information accessible at any time from any modem threatens an end to the traditional ways of doing library business. Users now do many of their own searches, and most assume, rightly or wrongly, that they are competent searchers. Yet, "it is all too common to see end-users accept what they find at the terminal as 'the truth, the whole truth and nothing but the truth'; in fact, this is rarely the case, and end-users have to be persuaded of this" (Armstrong, 1995, p. 237). Surely, there is a role for librarians.

Librarians need to think about how to add value to the information that they provide. Some are avoiding downsizing by expanding their jobs. Librarians at Air Products and Chemicals Inc. gather information and prepare analyses for scientists and market researchers. Their supervisor was quoted as saying "Librarians are moving toward a two-tier pay scale with those who can analyze information earning much more than those who shelve books" (Levinson, 1996, p. 43). Although his view of what librarians had been doing was incorrect, many people share his perception of what librarians do. By definition, librarians are supposed to be experts in finding information. By implication, the information that experts find should be current, complete, and as accurate as possible by a reasonable standard. This may not be a new role, but it could be one to take into the next millennium.

NOTES

[1] The *Last Chance Health Report*, published by the University of Natural Healing Inc., Charlottesville, Virginia, carries a disclaimer on the masthead: "This newsletter contains unorthodox ideas and opinions which are NOT accepted by the consensus of medical opinion…." The end of the disclaimer reminds readers that the First Amendment allows the expression of "viewpoints no matter how controversial or unaccepted they may be."

[2] "Information Services for Information Consumers" replaces "A Commitment to Information Services," adopted in 1976 and revised in 1979.

8

MISCONDUCT: MAINTAINING THE PUBLIC TRUST

Peter Hernon

> Unethical research and professional conduct occur throughout the university, in all fields....
>
> —LaFollette, 1994, p. 10

Although research misconduct could pose a problem for almost any discipline or field of study, in fact, as discussed in the first two chapters, it is more likely to do so for the sciences and behavioral sciences than for the social sciences and humanities. Clearly, excluding plagiarism, there are far fewer documented examples of misconduct in the social sciences and humanities. As the example of Maxwell A. Mega (see Chapters 4 and 5) indicates, however, misconduct could occur (and go undetected) in the social sciences, especially when researchers examine different populations and rely on survey or other types of research in which there is little or no replication and cumulation of research findings. There is no reason why research misconduct *could not* occur in library and information science, for instance. We do not know if there is a problem in library and information science or many other social science disciplines, or, if there is, how severe that problem is. As the literature on scientific fraud and research misconduct indicate, however, it is not always that difficult to fool the scholarly and academic community, because the expectation is that research is undertaken and submitted to journal and book editors in good faith. Violations of the "good faith" principle may be difficult, or in some instances, virtually impossible to detect.

As a result, it is the responsibility of the teaching faculty, editors and editorial boards, publishers, and librarians—be they in public or technical services, or in management—to understand the issues related to misconduct and determine the extent to which they believe a problem could arise and how best to cope with that possibility. At the very minimum, teaching faculty and librarians should be concerned about the extent to which students question the information that they use (see Chapter 3) and how to teach critical thinking (see Chapters 3 and 6).

When teaching faculty, such as those offering research methods courses in graduate programs of library and information science, discuss misconduct, they are perhaps most likely to focus on teaching students "to look analytically and critically at the professional literature" (Bates, 1979, p. 339). In "An Exercise in Research Evaluation: The Work of L.C. Puppybreath," Marcia Bates (1979) wrote an hypothetical article in which "Puppybreath's research skills are minimal and he makes a lot of mistakes. The paper is no joke, however. It is not at all inconceivable that such a paper could have appeared somewhere in the library literature" (p. 339). She "identified about 40…mistakes in the paper" (p. 339) and asked students to evaluate the paper. She acknowledged that the hypothetical author "has not benefited from a course in library research methods" (p. 340). The fictitious acknowledgments are far-fetched: "I wish to thank my wife... for her heroic typing and delicious meals throughout this effort" (p. 342). As is evident, the work of Mr. Puppybreath and Mr. Mega are not comparable; each was done for a different purpose and audience, and each was presented in an entirely different manner—one attempted to be more believable than the other. Furthermore, they do not share the same types of shortcomings. Readers of Puppybreath's paper know that they are reading an hypothetical work, whereas those of Mega's paper are not so informed.

Using both types of papers, as well as the other methods of data collection discussed in this book, it is possible to gain more insights into research misconduct. How might different groups cope (or not cope) with it, and what strategies for dealing with it in the most cost-beneficial manner can be developed? As focus group participants (see Chapter 5) discussed, the cure, at this time, should not paralyze or place undo hardships on the peer-reviewing process. For this reason, we recommended that journal editors and publishers require, when feasible, all contributing authors to sign a copyright form that acknowledges that the work does not represent fraud, misconduct, or a "sting" operation testing the editorial decision-making process (see Chapter 5).

As for institutions of higher education, they should review their internal documentation and how they would cope with a Maxwell A. Mega if the need ever arose. Librarians need to address the types of issues noted in Chapters 4, 5, and 7. Although the research occurred within universities within New Zealand, as well as at Tufts University, Medford, Massachusetts, the implications are far-reaching.

They apply, we believe, to all academic libraries as well as to other types of libraries in at least those countries in which instances of misconduct have been documented.

In summary, it is important for teaching faculty, librarians, editors, and publishers to plan and be prepared in case they encounter an instance of misconduct. At the same time, students should be educated to think critically and to be intelligent consumers of information, data, and publications. They should understand that the peer-reviewing process is not intended as a guarantee that published scholarship is devoid of misconduct. Teaching faculty should question the sources which students cite and their rationale for citing sources, thereby challenging students to justify their inclusion of citations and their strategies for gathering and evaluating literature and information. It is important to set standards for the proper conduct of researchers and to develop strategies for dealing effectively with allegations of research misconduct. Funding organizations, such as government agencies, will set their own procedures for investigating problems and instituting remedies.

Kenneth J. Ryan (1996), chairperson of the Commission on Research Integrity (National Institutes of Health) and Professor Emeritus of Obstetrics, Gynecology, and Reproductive Biology at Harvard Medical School, offers a chilling reminder: in spite of congressional concern about scientific fraud dating from hearings held in 1981, scientists have failed to cope successfully with allegations of misconduct. Furthermore, the Office of Research Integrity (ORI), Department of Health and Human Services, "has had little success in resolving the misconduct cases that it has investigated" (p. B1). Yet, "the problems will not go away by themselves, and both the government and the public will continue to expect scientists to be accountable for the federal money they receive" (p. B2). Ryan concludes that "The more scientists do to regulate their own conduct, the less intrusive government oversight will be" (p. B2). As already noted, coping with scientific misconduct, and the broader concept of research misconduct, should not be cast solely in the context of a threat: deal with it or else the government will intervene. The problem, or the possibility of one, should not be one only for scientists. There are implications for all disciplines, the management and credibility of peer-reviewed journals, funding organizations, promotion and tenure reviews, codes of professional conduct, internal policies of universities, and so forth.

Table 8.1, which identifies journals that have devoted entire issues to research misconduct and ethics, reinforces the conclusion that there is now broad interest in research ethics and misconduct.[1] There is increased recognition that, although there might not yet be a problem in some disciplines or fields of study, the possibility is always present. It is only prudent planning to prepare for that eventuality in the hope that it will not materialize, but that if it ever does, appropriate policies and procedures already exist.

**TABLE 8.1   Journal Issues Devoted to Research Misconduct and Ethics:
A Selected List***

Academic Medicine (September 1993, supplement entitled "Integrity in Biomedical Research,"
Volume 68, No. 9):
- "Introduction"
  - "Research Integrity."
- "Part I: Responsibilities and Responses of Academic Institutions:"
  - "Studying Science in the Context of Ethics;"
  - "Ethical Considerations in Planning and Conducting Research;"
  - "Integrity in the Education of Researchers;"
  - "Conflicts of Interest and Commercialization of Research;" and
- "Part II: Dealing with Misconduct in Theory and Practice:"
  - "Institutional Structures to Ensure Research Integrity;"
  - "Sanctions for Research Misconduct: A Legal Perspective;" and
  - "Sanctions and Remediation for Research Misconduct: A Legal Perspective;" and
  - "Sanctions and Remediation for Research Misconduct: Differential Diagnosis, Treatment, and Prevention."
- "Part III: Governmental Policies and Practices:"
  - "Policy Development Lessons from Two Federal Initiatives: Protecting Human Research Subjects and Handling Misconduct in Science;"
  - "Should the Government Assure Scientific Integrity?;" and
  - "Problems in Research Integrity Arising from Misconceptions about the Ownership of Research."
- "Part IV: Understanding Scientific Misconduct and Research Integrity:"
  - "Integrity Versus Misconduct: Learning the Difference between Right and Wrong;"
  - "A New Perspective on Scientific Misconduct;"
  - "Deviance in the Practice of Science;"
  - "Overlooking Ethics in the Search for Objectivity and Misconduct in Science;"
  - "Intellectual Property and Control;" and
  - "Innovation and Integrity in Biomedical Research."
- "Afterword."
- "Appendix:"
  - "Background and Advice to Faculty Serving on Ad Hoc Committees of Inquiry Concerning Questions of Research Integrity."

Annals of Internal Medicine (February 1986, Volume 104, No. 2): "Perspective:" "Fraud, Irresponsible Authorship, and Their Causes"
- "The Pathogenesis of Fraud in Medical Science;"
- "Pressure to Publish and Fraud in Science;"
- "Irresponsible Authorship and Wasteful Publication;"
- "Science, Statistics, and Deception;" and
- "Publish or Perish! A Proposal."

Journal of Higher Education (Spring 1994, Volume 65, No. 3):
- "Introduction;"
- "A Social Control Perspective on Scientific Misconduct;"
- "The Politics of Research Misconduct: Congressional Oversight, Universities, and Science;"
- "Definitions and Boundaries of Research Misconduct: Perspectives from a Federal Government Viewpoint;"
- "Scientific Misconduct and Editorial and Peer Review Processes;"
- "Research Universities and Scientific Misconduct: History, Policies, and the Future;"

TABLE 8.1   (Continued)

- "Disciplinary and Departmental Effects on Observations of Faculty and Graduate Student Misconduct;"
- "Perceptions of Research Misconduct and an Analysis of Their Correlates;"
- "Misconduct and Social Control in Science: Issues, Problems, Solutions;" and
- "Investigating Misconduct in Science: The national Science Foundation Model."

Journal of Information Ethics:

A. Spring 1994 (Volume 3, No. 1):
- "Readings between Texts: Benjamin Thomas's *Abraham Lincoln* and Stephen Oates's *With Malice Toward None*;"
- "'A Horse Chestnut Is Not a Chestnut Horse': A Refutation of Bray, Davis, MacGregor, and Wollan;"
- "Sharing and Stealing: Persistent Ambiguities;"
- "'A Sin against Scholarship': Some Examples of Plagiarism in Stephen B. Oates's Biographies of Abraham Lincoln, Martin Luther King, Jr., and William Faulkner;"
- "Plagiarism and the Art of Copying;"
- "A Crying Need for Discourse;"
- "Towards a Definition of Plagiarism: The Bray/Oates Controversy Revisited;"
- "The Oates Case;"
- "Concerning the Charge of Plagiarism against Stephen B. Oates;"
- "Popular Biography, Plagiarism, and Persecution;" and
- "When the Trial Is the Punishment: The Ethics of Plagiarism Accusations."

B. Fall 1994 (Volume 3, No. 2):
- "Plagiarism: For Accusers and the Accused;"
- "Avoiding Plagiarism: Some Thoughts on Use, Attribution, and Acknowledgment;"
- "Plagiarism: A Misplaced Emphasis;"
- "Plagiarism: A Tale of Telltale Words;"
- "Kidnapping;"
- "The 1993 ORI/AAAS Conference on Plagiarism and Theft of Ideas:" and
- "Fraud in Research (1986-1992): An Annotated Bibliography."

C. Spring 1996 (Volume 5, No. 1):
- "Editorial: Rampant Misconduct;"
- "Publisher's Comments;"
- "Information Ethis in the Workplace;"
- "Misconduct and Departmental Context;"
- "Federal Actions against Plagiarism in Research;"
- "Scientific Misconduct;"
- "Glory Days or the Lure of Scientific Misconduct;"
- "Digital Imaging;" and

Science and Engineering Ethics:

A. January 1995 (Volume 1, No. 1):
- "(Not) Giving Credit Where Credit Is Due: Citation of Data Sets;"
- "On the Assessment of Genetic Technology: Reaching Ethical Judgments in the Light of Modern Technology;"
- "An Historical Preface to Engineering Ethics;"
- "Honest Research;"
- "Guidelines for Training in the Ethical Conduct of Scientific Research;" and
- "Convention on Scientific Conduct, National Academy of Sciences."

B. October 1995 (Volume 1, No. 4):
- "Editorial: Trustworthy Research—Ediorial Introduction;"

TABLE 8.1   (Continued)

- "On the Hazards of Whistleblowers and on Some Problems of Young Biomedical Scientists in Our Time;"
- "Commentary: 'On the Hazards of Whistleblowers...';"
- "Commentary: 'On the Hazards of Whistleblowers...';"
- "How Are Scientific Corrections Made?;"
- "Commentary on: 'How Are Scientific Corrections Made?';"
- "Policies and Perspectives on Authorship;"
- "Trust and the Collection, Selection, Analysis and Interpretation of Data: A Scientist' View;"
- "Effectiveness of Research Guidelines in Prevention of Scientific Misconduct:
- "The Ombudsman for Research Guidelines in Prevention of Scientific Misconduct;"
- "Truth and Trustworthiness in Research;" and
- "Reaching for the 'Low Hanging Fuit': The Pressue for Results in Scientific Research."

Society (March/April 1994, Volume 31, No. 3):

- "Introduction;"
- "Research Misconduct;"
- "Benevolent Misdiagnosis;"
- "Miscounting Social Ills;"
- "The Myth of a 'Stole Legacy';"
- "Did Freud Commit Graud?;"
- "Victim of Scientific Hoax;"
- "Fallible Judgments;"
- "Egalitarian Fiction and Collective Fraud;" and
- "Investigating Sexual Coercion."

*This *Journal of Business Ethics*, in 1991, published various papers on this and related topics, as has the *Journal of the American Medical Association* in 1990, 1991, 1993, 1994, and 1996; and *Knowledge: Creation, Diffusion, Utilization* in December 1992.

DEFINITION

The Commission on Research Integrity, which was created as part of the National Institutes of Health Revitalization Act of 1993, proposed new procedures for addressing scientific misconduct "because, beyond the high-profile cases, widespread problems in the conduct of research remain" (Ryan, 1996, p. B1). The Commission's report "proposed a new definition of scientific misconduct, which we believe describes the types of violations that occur far more precisely than the current federal definition does" (Ryan, 1996, p. B1). Misconduct was defined as:

> significant misbehavior that improperly appropriates intellectual property or contributions of others, that intentionally impedes the progress of research, or that risks corrupting the scientific record or compromising the integrity of scientific practices. (p. B2)

As Ryan explains,

> Instead of relying on the current federal categories of misconduct—falsification, fabrication, and plagiarism—the commission proposed new categories that it con-

sidered more specific: *misappropriation*, which includes plagiarism as well as peer reviewers' unauthorized use of confidential information in grant applications and manuscripts; *interference*, which occurs when one researcher physically takes or damages the writings or materials of another investigator; and *misrepresentation*, which covers not only falsification and fabrication, but also omissions from research reports that would render them false. (p. B2)

Ryan correctly notes that some scientists have rejected the Commission's definition because it "covers new ground, such as actions that interfere with research" (p. B). A misperception, according to him, is that some scientists conclude that the definition applies to "all cases of omissions of data, when in fact the commission included only omissions that would falsify a researcher's conclusion" (p. B2). The Commission's report

proposed additional protections for whistle blowers who expose research misconduct, as the legislation establishing the commission directed us to do. And further, as directed, we suggested improvements in the administrative practices that both research institutions and the federal government follow in handling allegations of misconduct. (p. B1)

According to Ryan, there is the

need to create guidelines for educating scientists in how to collect and handle data, to assign authorship in an equitable way, to treat intellectual property with confidentiality and respect during peer review of journal articles and grant proposals, to supervise colleagues and students involved in research projects, and to protect whistle blowers who come forward in good faith. (p. B1)

The definition deserves widespread examination and review. At the same time, there should be increased recognition that problems of misconduct may apply to *misappropriation* and *misrepresentation*. The latter includes those instances in which researchers or students falsify an answer on a questionnaire or a set of questionnaires for the dataset which will form the basis for their report, article, or thesis or dissertation.

Donald E. Buzzelli (1996), Deputy Assistant Inspector General for Oversight at the National Science Foundation, Arlington, Virginia, offers an important reminder:

There seems to be a widespread misconception that revising the definition will correct whatever is wrong in agency handling of misconduct cases. The real problems, where they exist, are about organization and processes. It is easier to propose changes in the definition than to address matters of organization and process, but ill-considered changes in the definition would only make things worse. (p. B4)

The extent to which academic institutions would and could cope with a Maxwell A. Mega also relates to issues of organization and processes. Clearly, librarians and others should be aware of the debate over the Commission's definition and recommendations. They should also be aware of the types of sources identified in Appendices F and G. Greater awareness of the issues is important; however, to maintain the public trust will require a concerted effort along the lines presented in the previous two chapters.

THE PUBLIC TRUST

Research misconduct, whether practiced by faculty members, students, or others, appears to be a part of a larger societal problem: the perceived increase (or at least broad acceptance) of academic dishonesty. An internal survey at one state university showed that "59 percent of the 17,000-strong student body...[admitted] to some form of cheating during the last school year. Seventy-two percent said a friend had been academically dishonest" ("UMass, Be Not Proud," 1996, p. A22). It would seem that maintaining the public trust requires the linkage of cheating to research misconduct and the implementation of an education program targeted at undergraduate and graduate students, as well as junior faculty members. Mentors should be reminded to spend more time addressing ethical issues and career advancement based on honesty.

The recommendations of Ryan and the Commission, as well as those contained in this book, for coping with misconduct, either real or potential, are intended to maintain and heighten the public trust in higher education, research which is funded and reported, disciplines, and service organizations such as libraries. The need for educating graduate students in how to collect and handle data extends beyond the sciences. As discussed in connection with the Maxwell A. Mega paper (see Chapters 4 and 5), focus group participants emphasized the need for better mentoring. In effect, they believed that mentors should be responsible for current and subsequent actions of those whom they supervise. It is important that both the established and fledgling researchers share a personal stake in research ethics. Students should realize that they have a responsibility not to invent or distort (fudge) data. As well, "universities need to rethink their own commitment to ethical standards and the role they can play in engendering respect for those standards among students" (McGee, 1996, p. B3).

The assignment of authorship does not present a problem for all disciplines. It is probably more of an issue in the sciences where the list of co-authors is long and does not necessarily guarantee involvement in setting up and conducting the research. In the social sciences, such as library and information science, the typical research paper has one or two authors. As well, there is no indication in some social sciences, such as library and information science, that reviewers fail to treat the intellectual property of those whose papers and proposals they are critiquing with other than confidentiality and respect. Nonetheless, David Goodstein (1996), Vice Provost and Professor of Physics and Applied Physics at the California Institute of Technology, indirectly issues an important reminder or challenge to journal editors. He states that:

> every scientist I know has stories of being treated unfairly by anonymous referees when they themselves were authors. That kind of experience erodes your ethical standards, until you get to the point where you say, "Why should I be the only good guy?" When that happens, the whole system crashes, which places peer review…in severe difficulties. (p. B5)

It would seem, therefore, that to maintain the public trust and the continued support of authors, journal editors should screen reviewer comments shared with authors, and they should not accept all reviewer comment at face value. In letters of rejection or requests for revision, editors might unintentionally send an incorrect message. They could conceivably produce an environment in which editorial decisions are viewed as arbitrary, and some individuals might even want to extract revenge, through a "sting" operation unknown to the editor.

Public trust also extends to publishers and the publications which they offer. As noted in Chapter 4, some librarians participating in focus groups expressed a willingness to discontinue subscriptions to journals that carried the results of misconduct. They equated prestige with never or perhaps seldom carrying fabricated or falsified information within their pages. Assuming that the fraud was later detected, what would have happened to a journal that published Maxwell A. Mega's paper without knowing about its deception? Presumably the answer would depend on how long ago the fraud was detected, how the journal responded, whether there were other incidents of misconduct known to have appeared in that journal, the level of prestige which librarians and library users attached to the journal, and so forth. In today's environment of financial stringencies, publishers should be very concerned about the misuse of their journals and any decline in journal prestige.

Other elements of public trust extend to whether the researcher used taxpayer funds, the trustworthiness of a discipline's or field's base of knowledge, and the extent to which government officials, governing boards, and taxpayers believe that academic faculty work long enough hours to justify sufficiently the salaries that they receive. In other words, state legislators and others have asked, "What do teaching faculty do?" The popular misperception is that many of them spend little time in the classroom each week, have large blocks of time during the year in which classes do not meet, and have minimal outside responsibilities; yet, they earn generous salaries. Re-examination of the ways in which faculty use their time could result if the perception is that they have lots of "free or extra time" and they spend that time engaged in research misconduct. In effect, as we all know, critics only need a few isolated examples to make their charges seem credible.

The public also places trust in library collections and services. Librarians do not want to jeopardize this trust. Thus, the type of research reported in Chapter 4 has broad implications for librarians, whatever the findings. We do not advocate blind acceptance of any findings, but do suggest that there might be a need for educational programs to attack and correct misperceptions.

In conclusion, to maintain the public trust, to create a better understanding of the role and nature of library collections, and to perfect the internal policies and procedures of peer-reviewed journals and colleges and universities, there is need for librarians, social scientists, college and university administrators, and others to realize that government regulation and other remedies may affect all disciplines, "even those in which instances of fraud and fakery have been 'rare'"[2] (LaFollette, 1994, p. 10). Controls enacted to cope with problems in the sciences may have broader ramifications. Clearly, research misconduct is a problem not limited to the behaviorial, medical, and natural sciences; it is also a social science problem, and there are implications for the humanities, as well. Addressing the problem outlined in this book is not an option for librarians, social scientists, and others; rather, it is "a social obligation" (p. 10).

NOTES

[1] The American Association for the Advancement of Science offers a video series on integrity in scientific research (1996, $79.75).

[2] "For every assertion that scientists are 99.99999 percent honest, or that only a tiny fraction of articles in the Medline data base have ever been formally retracted and hence fraud is rare and attention to it irrelevant, there have been social surveys that point to a quite different conclusion" (LaFollette, 1994, p. 8).

Appendix A

SOME PUBLICLY-
DISCUSSED CASES
INVOLVING SCIENTIFIC
MISCONDUCT AND THE
RESEARCH LITERATURE

The cases presented here are only a fraction of those in which scientific misconduct was determined either by an investigation conducted by the employing institution, by the funding agency, by a court decision, or by the perpetrator admitting guilt. Only cases involving research literature that was fabricated, falsified, or plagiarized are included. In a few instances, cases uncovered by the journals in which the work was published are presented along with evidence for the decision of the journals' editors. Cases involving plagiarism in grant applications to the federal government, of which there are many, are excluded.

A short section at the end describes cases in which the misconduct was discovered after manuscripts had been submitted, but the articles on which they were based were never published.

The *Newsletter* from the Office of Research Integrity (ORI) and its annual reports were primary sources used to compile these data. The federal government, however, did not release the names of individuals found guilty of scientific misconduct involving federally-funded grants until 1993. Other published sources, such as reports in the journals *Science* and *Nature*, and some newspaper accounts, were also used to identify cases involving misconduct affecting the research literature. Sources of documentation are cited at the end of each case.

James Abbs, Ph.D., University of Wisconsin, Madison. In April 1996, the ORI overturned four previous "not guilty" findings done since 1987. Abbs served as thesis advisor for Steven Barlow, who noticed that a figure included in an article by Abbs published in *Neurology* was strikingly similar to a figure published in another article by Abbs and Barlow four years earlier. Barlow notified officials at the university and at the National Institutes of Health (NIH). In a settlement agreement, Abbs will voluntarily exclude himself from serving on Public Health Service panels for three years, and the University of Wisconsin is to ensure the scientific integrity of his grants. The agreement also required a notification to *Neurology*, but not retraction. Robert Daroff, the journal's editor, however, said: "If Abbs doesn't, I will retract."

Source: Jock Friendly, "After 9 Years, a Tangled Case Lurches toward a Close," *Science*, 272 (May 17, 1996): 947-948.

Andrew Friedman, M.D., Harvard Medical School and Brigham and Women's Hospital. According to an ORI statement, Dr. Friedman altered and fabricated information in permanent patient medical records. He admitted to falsifying and fabricating approximately 80% of the data in two published articles.

- "Gonadotrophic-Releasing Hormone Agonist Plus Estrogen-Progestin 'Add-Back' Therapy for Endometriosis-Related Pelvic Pain," *Fertility and Sterility*, 60 (1993): 236-241; Retracted 65 (1996): 211.
- "Does Low-Dose Combination Oral Contraceptive Use Affect Uterine Size or Menstrual Flow in Premenopausal Women with Leiomyomas?," *Obstetrics and Gynecology*, 85 (1995): 631-635; Retracted 86 (1996): 728.

Source: *NIH Guide*, 25 (15) (May 10, 1996).

Weishu Y. Weiser, Ph.D., Brigham and Women's Hospital/Harvard Medical School. ORI determined that she committed scientific misconduct by falsifying data in biomedical research. She has agreed to retract articles:

- "Human Recombinant Migration Inhibitory Factor Activates Human Macrophases to Kill Leishmania Donovani," *Journal of Immunology*, 147 (1991): 2006-2011.
- "Recombinant Migration Inhibitory Factor Induces Nitric Oxide Synthase in Murine Macrophages," *Journal of Immunology*, 150 (1993): 1908-1912.
- "Recombinant Human Migration Inhibitory Factor Has Adjuvant Activity," *Proceedings of the National Academy of Sciences*, 89 (1992): 8049-8052.

Source: *ORI Newsletter*, 4 (March 1996): 6-7.

Amitov Hajra, graduate student at the University of Michigan. The University is currently investigating the matter. However, Dr. Francis S. Collins, the head of

NIH's project to map all human genes, "…[is] retracting five research papers on leukemia in leading scientific journals because a junior colleague had fabricated data. The flawed papers involved laboratory research on the role of a defective gene in producing acute leukemia, The research did not involve patients or treatment of the disease" (pp. 1-2).

Source: Lawrence K. Altman. "Fraud Leads Scientist to Withdraw Research Papers on Leukemia" (http://www.nytimes.com/yr/mo/day/news/national/ leukemia-fraud.html) (October 30, 1996).

Tetsuya Matsuguchi, M.D., Ph.D., Dana-Farber Cancer Institute/Harvard Medical School. Based on an investigation conducted by his employer, ORI found that Dr. Matsuguchi, formerly a research fellow, committed scientific misconduct "by intentionally falsifying data by artificially darkening one band each on two autoradiographs in figures that he had prepared for a presentation…and by altering three bands on the print of an immunoblot included in Figure 2A of:"

- "Tyrosine Phosphorylation of P85 Vav in Myeloid Cells Is Regulated by GM-CSF, IL-3 and Steel Factor…," *EMBO Journal,* 14 (1995): 257-265.

Source: *ORI Newsletter*, 4 (March 1996): 5-6.

Cathy Q. Lee, Ph.D., Postdoctoral Fellow, Molecular Endocrinology Laboratory, Massachusetts General Hospital. She engaged in falsification and fabrication of research data in two papers, one of which was not published; the other involved improper data selection and falsification of data published in:

- "Cyclic-AMP Responsive Transcriptional Activation of CREB-327 Involves Interdependent Phosphorylated Subdomains," *EMBO Journal,* 9 (1990): 4455-4465. Retracted 13 (1994): 2736.

Source: *NIH Guide*, 25 (10) (March 29, 1996.

Aws S. Salim, Ph.D., published over 50 articles within five years. The *Journal of Laboratory and Clinical Medicine* investigated his work after questions and concerns had been raised about the legitimacy of his papers. As a result of its investigation, which allowed Dr. Salim to respond to the charges, the journal withdrew its aegis from:

- "Role of Oxygen-Derived Free Radical Scavengers in the Management of Recurrent Attacks of Ulcerative Colitis: A New Approach," *Journal of Laboratory & Clinical Medicine*, 119 (June 1991): 710-717.

Source: Dale E. Hammerschmidt & Alan G. Gross, "The Problem of Bio-medical Fraud: A Model for Retrospective and Prospective Action," *Journal of Scholarly Publishing*, 27 (October 1995): 3-11.

J.M. Pearce, M.D., St. George's Hospital, London, removed from the Medical Register for publishing of false data in the *British Journal of Obstetrics and Gynaecology*. Pearce was an editor of the journal, and the editor-in-chief was head of his medical department. The journal did not review case reports, and the review of the clinical trial was inadequate. "Gift authorship" was also involved. Two junior people were added as authors and claimed that when they questioned points about the article "they were made to feel small." See:

- "Low Dose Aspirin in Women with Raised Maternal Serum Alpha-Fetoprotein and Abnormal Doppler Wave-Form Pattern from the Uteroplacental Circulation," *British Journal of Obstetrics and Gynaecology,* 101 (1994): 481. Retracted 102 (1995): 853.
- "A Randomized Controlled Trial of the Use of Human Chorionic-Gonadotropin in Recurrent Miscarriages Associated with Polycystic Ovaries," *British Journal of Obstetrics and Gynaecology,* 101 (1994): 685. Retracted 102 (1995): 853.
- "Term Delivery after Intrauterine Relocation of an Ectopic Pregnancy," *British Journal of Obstetrics and Gynaecology,* 101 (1994): 716. Retracted 102 (1995): 853.
- "Doppler Ultrasound of the Uteroplacental Circulation in the Prediction of Pregnancy Outcome in Women with Raised Maternal Serum Alpha-Fetoprotein," *British Journal of Obstetrics and Gynaecology,* 101 (1994): 477. Retracted 102 (1995): 853.

Source: Sara Abdulla, "UK Fraud Verdict Prompts Moves on Ethics," *Nature*, 375 (June 15, 1995): 529; Stephen Lock, "Lessons from the Pearce Affair: Handling Scientific Fraud," *British Medical Journal*, 310 (17 June 1995): 1547-1548.

Anand Tewari, M.D., Post Doctoral Fellow, Department of Surgery, Stanford University, found guilty by the ORI for fabricating opthalmologic examination results; fabricating and falsifying blood gas data and values for glycerol determinations; falsifying standard errors; and including fabricated data on platelet counts. See:

- "Effects of Interleukin-1 on Platelet Counts," *The Lancet*, 336 (1990): 712-714. Retracted 340 (1992): 496.

Source: "Washington Update," *Chronicle of Higher Education*, 40 (49) (August 10, 1994), p. A26; *ORI Newsletter*, 2 (September 1994): 3-4.

Guido Zadel, Ph.D., University of Bonn, Germany. Zadel was a post doctoral candidate whose thesis was the basis for the retracted article. He worked in the lab, but was not listed as an author on the paper hailed as a startling new discovery on the "handedness of biomolecules and DNA." Suspicions arose when other teams could not duplicate the results. The lab chief, one of the co-authors of the paper, then assigned other experienced workers who had not participated in the original research to redo the work. They found that an additive had biased the reaction. Zadel admitted his deception and the university is conducting an investigation. See:

- "New Porphyrinoid Macrocycles Containing Pyridine," *Angewandte Chemie*, International Edition. English, 33 (2) (1994): 219-220.

Source: Daniel Clery & David Bradley, "Underhanded 'Breakthrough' Revealed," *Science*, 265 (July 1, 1994): 21.

John L. Ninnemann, Ph.D., Professor of Biology, Adams State College. "The Justice Department announced that the University of California system and the University of Utah would pay nearly $1.6 million to settle all claims raised by the government against the universities and their former employee John L. Ninnemann." "Ninnemann has reached a separate agreement with the Research Integrity Office. It states that he has agreed not to seek Federal grants for 3 years." J. Thomas Condie, his former lab assistant, was awarded $311,000 plus $225,000 for legal costs for turning Ninnemann in.

"Although Dr. Ninnemann has not admitted that he falsified and misrepresented scientific experiments...he agreed to submit letters of retraction for five scientific articles and letters of correction for four additional...articles" (*ORI Annual Report* (1994): 17-18). Articles to be retracted as part of Ninnemann's agreement with the ORI:

- "Melanoma-Associated Immunosuppression through B. Cell Activation of Suppressor T. Cells," *Journal of Immunology*, 120 (1978):1573-1579.
- "Induction of Prostaglandin Synthesis-Dependent Suppressor Cells with Endotoxin," *Journal of Clinical Immunology*, 3 (1983): 142-150.
- "Immunosuppression Following Thermal Injury through B Cell Activation of Suppressor T. Cells," *Journal of Trauma*, 20 (1980): 206-213.
- "Isolation of Immunosuppressive Serum Components Following Thermal Injury," *Journal of Trauma*, 22 (1982): 837-844.
- "Participation of Prostaglandin E. in Immunosuppression Following Thermal Injury," *Journal of Trauma*, 24 (1984): 201-207.

The following articles were corrected by letters from Dr. Ninnemann:

- "Hemolysis and Suppression of Neutrophil Chemotaxis by a Low Molecular Weight Component of Human Burn Patient Sera," *Immunology Letters,* 10 (1985): 63-69.
- "Reversal of SAP-Induced Immunosuppression and SAP Detection by a Monoclonal Antibody," *Journal of Trauma,* 27 (1987): 123-127.
- "Definition of a Burn Injury-Induced Immunosuppressive Serum Component," *Journal of Trauma,* 25 (1985): 113-117.
- "Immunosuppression Activity of CIQ Degradation Peptides," *Journal of Trauma,* 27 (1987): 119-122.

Source: *NIH Guide,* 23 (45) (December 23, 1994); *ORI Annual Report* (1994), pp. 17-18.

Tian-Shing Lee, M.D., Post Doctoral Fellow, Joslin Diabetes Center, Harvard Medical School. Dr. Lee was barred from receiving federal grants or contracts and from service on any Public Health Service panels for five years. Harvard notified the four scientific journals that had published papers containing data fabricated or falsified by Dr. Lee that the papers should be retracted. The papers were:

- "Differential Regulation of Protein Kinase C and (NaK)-Adenosine Triphosphatase Activities by Elevated Glucose Level in Retinal Capillary Endothelial Cell," *Journal of Clinical Investigation,* 83 (1989): 90-94.
- "Endothelin Stimulates a Sustained 1,2-Diacylglycerol Increase and Protein Kinase C Activation in Bovine Aortic Smooth Muscle Cells," *Biochemical and Biophysical Research Communications,* 162 (1989): 381-386.
- "Characterization of Endothelin Receptors and Effects of Endothelin on Diacylglycerol and Protein Kinase C in Retinal Capillary Pericytes," *Diabetes,* 38 (1989): 1642-1646.
- "Activation of Protein Kinase C by Elevation of Glucose Concentration: Proposal for a Mechanism in the Development of Diabetic Vascular Complications," *Proceedings of the National Academy of Sciences,* 86 (1989): 5141-5145.

Source: *Federal Register,* 58 (117) (June 21, 1993): 33831; *ORI Newsletter,* 1 (June 1993): 6.

David F. Eierman, Ph.D., University of North Carolina, Chapel Hill. The university conducted an investigation; "based, in part, on Dr. Eierman's admission, the university concluded that he committed scientific misconduct by falsifying or fabricating data...." ORI accepted these findings. Two manuscripts containing false data were not published, but one figure was included in:

- "Cellular and Cytokine Networks in Tissue Immunity," *Proceedings of the 12th International Reticuloendothelial Societies Congress and the 27th*

Annual Meeting of the Society for Leukocyte Biology Held in Heraklion, Crete, Greece, October 14-18, 1990, edited by Monte S. Meltzer & Alberto Mantovani (New York: Wiley-Liss, 1991).

Source: *ORI Annual Report* (1994), pp. 19-20.

Anthony A. Paparo, Ph.D., Southern Illinois University. He was barred from receiving federal grants or contracts for three years and from service on panels for the same period. "He used the same micrograph in two papers, while stating that the micrographs had been obtained from two different biological species of mussel. Multiple instances were found of other such falsifications of micrographs and radioisotope data in published scientific articles which were not supported by the PHS." Southern Illinois University notified the journal and other journals "about the problems identified in the investigation." See:

- "The Effect of STH and 6-OH-DOPA on the SEM of the Branchial Nerve and Visceral Ganglion of the Bivalve *Elliptio Companata* as it Relates to Ciliary Activity," *Comparative Biochemistry and Physiology,* 51 (1975): 169-173.
- "The Effect of STH on the SEM and Frequency Response of the Branchial Nerve in *Mytilus Edulis* as it Relates to Ciliary Activity," *Comparative Biochemistry and Physiology,* 51 (1975): 165-168.

Source: *Federal Register*, 58 (117) (June 21, 1993): 33831; *ORI Newsletter*, 1 (June 1993): 6.

Prem Fry, Ph.D., University of Calgary. An investigation conducted by the university concluded that she was guilty of publishing false research. Although the committee recommended dismissal, Dr. Fry was subsequently allowed to retire from the university and then obtained a non-teaching post at Victoria University in British Columbia. Two articles "at the heart of the investigation" are:

- "Children's Perceptions of Major Positive and Negative Events and Factors in Single-Parent Families," *Journal of Applied Developmental Psychology,* 4 (1983): 371-388. The co-author of this paper, who was a graduate student at the time, said that she neither collected data nor participated in writing this article.
- "The Relationship between Father Absence and Children's Social Problem Solving Competencies," *Journal of Applied and Developmental Psychology,* 3 (1982): 105-120.

Source: Paul Kaihla, "Academe on Trial," *Maclean's*, 107 (December 19, 1994): 142-146.

Mitchell H. Rosner, NIH scholar in residence at National Cancer Institute. He falsified research on embryonic development in mice. He admitted to these acts and signed an agreement with ORI to exclude himself for a five-year period from any federal grants or contracts or from serving on any review panels. See:

- "Oct-3 Is a Maternal Factor Required for the First Mouse Embryonic Division," *Cell*, 64 (1991): 1103-1110. Retracted by co-authors who explicitly stated that experimental evidence was fabricated by Rosner, *Cell*, 69 (May 1992): 724.

Source: *Federal Register*, 58 (117) (June 21, 1993): 33832; *ORI Newsletter*, 1 (June 1993): 7.

Michael A. Sherer, M.D., Addiction Research Center, National Institute on Drug Abuse. The Office of Scientific Integrity (OSI) found that Dr. Sherer had falsified the nature, quality, and methodology for data collection and behavioral ratings as well as the descriptions in two publications. He was barred from Public Health Service (PHS) panels. His work must be closely supervised. He was required to submit a retraction and a letter of correction for:

- "Suspiciousness Induced by Four-Hour Intravenous Infusions of Cocaine," *Archives of General Psychiatry*, 45 (1988): 673-677.
- "Intravenous Cocaine: Psychiatric Effects," *Biological Psychiatry*, 24 (1988): 865-885.

Source: *Federal Register*, 58 (117) (June 21, 1993): 33832; *ORI Newsletter*, 1 (June 1993): 7.

Raphael B. Stricker, M.D., University of California at San Francisco. He falsified data for research on AIDS. Dr. Stricker executed a agreement in which he agreed neither to apply for federal grants or contracts nor to serve on PHS panels for three years. See:

- "Target Platelet Antigen in Homosexual Men with Immune Thrombocytopenia," *New England Journal of Medicine*, 313 (1985): 1315-1380. Retracted 325 (1991): 1487.

Source: *Federal Register*, 58 (117) (June 21, 1993); *ORI Newsletter*, 1 (June 1993): 7.

Charles J. Glueck, M.D., University of Cincinnati, Head of the General Clinical Research Center and its Lipid Research Center. "An internal university committee…has concluded that…because of 'arbitrary' data selection as well as internal inconsistencies and inaccuracies 'no meaningful interpretation of the results of [the following article] can be made':"

- "Safety and Efficacy of Long-term Diet and Diet Plus Bile Acid Binding Resin Cholesterol Lowering Therapy in 73 Children Heterozygous for Familial Hypercholesterolemia," *Pediatrics*, 78 (August 1986): 338-348.

"According to the NIH committee that reviewed the university's findings...the manner in which the study was conducted and reported is 'unacceptable by any scientific standard known to the NIH.'" Barred from federal funding for two years. In addition NIH "recommended...that he 'immediately retract or issue a clarification' of the *Pediatrics* paper. It also said that notification of the investigation should be sent to editors at Elsevier-Australia which has a manuscript based on the study; *Pediatric Research*, where Glueck submitted a paper based on the reanalyzed data; and the *New England Journal of Medicine*, where he published a letter referring to the study."

Source: Constance Holden, "NIH Moves to Debar Cholesterol Researcher," *Science*, 237 (August 14, 1987): 718-719.

C. David Bridges, Ph.D., Professor of Biological Sciences, Purdue University. "In June 1987, Bridges, then at Baylor College of Medicine in Houston published news of the discovery of an enzyme in the eye." *Chemical & Engineering News* [(June 29, 1987): 22] cited the Bridges paper in *Science* as a "significant discovery in the chemistry of vision."

NIH stripped him of his funding after an NIH investigatory panel concluded that he plagiarized a scientific manuscript that he had been asked to review for the *Proceedings of the National Academy of Sciences*. The article supposedly resulting is:

- "Visual Cycle Operates Via an Isomerase Acting on All-trans Retina in the Pigment Epithelium," *Science*, 236 (1987): 1678-1680.

The NIH report says that "the panel concluded that the *Science* paper was seriously flawed, that the research records were not substantiating, and that no evolution of experimentation existed that would have permitted Dr. Bridges to have conducted the experiments he reported without the aid of the privileged information that became available to him in his capacity as a potential reviewer of the Bernstein-Law-Rando manuscript."

Source: Pamela S. Zurer, "NIH Panel Strips Researcher of Funding after Plagiarism Review," *Chemical & Engineering News* (August 7, 1989), pp. 24-25.

Vipin Kumar, Ph. D., research fellow, Biology, Caltech. A university committee concluded and notified NIH that Dr. Kumar falsified data in:

- "In Individual T Cells One Productive, Rearrangement Does Not Appear to Block Rearrangement at the Second Allele," *Journal of Experimental Medicine*, 170 (December 1989): 2183.

Lab chief Leroy Hood retracted that paper and another paper because all the data were missing:

- "Amino Acid Variations at a Single Residue in an Autoimmune Peptide Profoundly Affect Its Properties…," *Proceedings of the National Academy of Sciences*, 87 (February 1990): 1337. Retracted by Hood (August 1991), p. 6899.

(Kumar's appointment with Caltech was terminated on March 31, 1991.)

Source: Leslie Roberts, "Misconduct: Caltech's Trial by Fire," *Science*, 253 (September 20, 1991): 1344-1347.

James Urban, M.D., Ph.D., research fellow, Biology, Caltech. A university committee concluded that data in an article in *Cell* had been fabricated—"a charge that Urban reportedly did not deny." He was found guilty of misconduct in:

- "Autoimmune T Cells: Immune Recognition of Normal and Variant Peptide Epitopes and Peptide-based Therapy," *Cell,* 59 (1989): 257-271.

He was also found guilty of misconduct for:

- "Restricted Use of T-Cell Receptor V Genes on Murine Autoimmune Encephalomyelitis Raises Possibilities for Antibody Therapy," *Cell,* 54 (1988): 577-592. Retracted (January 25, 1991).

Source: Leslie Roberts, "Misconduct: Caltech's Trial by Fire," *Science*, 253 (September 20, 1991): 1344-1347; *ORI Newsletter*, 3 (September 1995): 6-7.

Viswa Jit Gupta, paleontologist, Panjab University, Chandigarh, India. He was accused of seeding his fossil finds. John Talent, an Australian paleontologist, and three others examined more than 300 papers by Gupta. They claim in a *Nature* article (April 1989) that the review found 100 discrepancies in Gupta's data. "A leading scientific journal in India [*The Journal of the Geological Society of India*] has advised its readers to ignore all the research papers it has published over the past 21 years by a leading Indian paleontologist…." The Geological Survey of India and Panjab University both found Gupta had fabricated and falsified fossil findings. The university tried to dismiss him. He, however, took his case to the courts. In 1996, a court ruled that Gupta would have to be reinstated as a professor at Panjab University.

Source: Ian Anderson, "Himalayan Scandal Rocks Indian Science," *New Scientist*, 129 (February 9, 1991): 17; K. S. Jayaraman, "Court Allows Fossil Fraudster to Return," *Nature*, 380 (April 18, 1996): 570.

Isidro Ballart, graduate student, University of Zurich. "...Shortly before evidence of the fraud began to emerge, the student was found dead in his laboratory." A suicide. Ballart had published claims based on fraudulent data in two articles:

- "Infectious Measles Virus from Cloned cDNA," *EMBO Journal,* 9 (1990): 385.
- "Functional and Nonfunctional Measles Virus Matrix Genes from Lethal Human Brain Infection," *Journal of Virology,* 65 (1990): 5656.

Martin Billeter, the leader of the research group involved, retracted both articles in 1991.

Source: Peter Aldhous, "Tragedy Revealed in Zurich," *Nature*, 355 (February 13, 1992): 577.

Bhusnan Kumar, M.D., Chandigarh Postgraduate Institute for Medical Research, India. The dermatologist coauthored a paper "claiming that the herpes zoster virus had been cultured in egg yoke." A nine-member ethics committee investigated and declared that the data reported were not based on facts. "Kumar confessed...that the culture results...cannot be substantiated." See *Indian Journal of Dermatology Venereology and Leprology.*

Source: K. S. Jayaraman, "Politics Alleged in Indian Fraud," *Nature*, 360 (December 17, 1992): 614.

Philip Berger, M.D., psychiatrist, Stanford University. Dr. Berger was found guilty of "deviations from accepted practices in the conduct and reporting of science" by the U.S. OSI Review. He was barred from grants or contracts for three years. Dr. Berger resigned from Stanford in May 1987. One article says that an inquiry at Stanford cast doubt on 11 papers; however, the names of the journals were not given.

Source: Colin Norman, "Stanford Inquiry Casts Doubt on 11 Papers," *Science*, 242 (November 4, 1988): 659-661.

Barry Garfinkel, M.D., Professor of Psychiatry, University of Minnesota. He was found guilty in court of federal charges that he faked research on a drug used to treat obsessive-compulsive patients. The drug was Anafranil and the manufacturer is Ciba-Geigy. "A former assistant testified that he had told her to 'make up' data. He is one of the few U.S. scientists ever convicted of a crime involving a study of a drug regulated by the Food and Drug Administration." No specific article was mentioned, but Dr. Garfinkel has written a number of articles on attention deficit disorder.

Source: *Arizona Republic* (August 8, 1993), p. A4; *Chronicle of Higher Education* (February 24, 1993): A4.

Leonard Freeman, M.D., Professor, Albert Einstein College of Medicine, Yeshiva University. He was found guilty of plagiarism in a federal court suit brought by Dr. Heidi Weissman, a specialist in gall bladder disease at Montefiore Medical Center, the teaching hospital for Yeshiva. Dr. Weissman claimed that Dr. Freeman, chief of her division at the center, had plagiarized a book chapter that she had already published. She was dismissed from Albert Einstein College of Medicine and the hospital the day after filing suit. The university settled with Weissman for $900,000. Freeman supposedly whited out her name and submitted the paper as his own.

Source: Heidi A. Weissman, "The Freeman Case: Plagiarism at the Albert Einstein College of Medicine of Yeshiva University (AECOM): Montefiore Medical Center (MMC)," *Abstracts of the American Chemical Society*, 202 (1994): vol. 2, Prof 0004; *Insight*, 10 (18) (May 2, 1994), pp. 6-11.

Monica P. Mehta, graduate research assistant, Chemistry, Columbia University. Co-author Ronald Breslow, professor of chemistry at Columbia, withdrew three communications published in 1986 in the *Journal of the American Chemical Society* (108, communications 2485, 6417, and 6418). "Breslow stresses that major elements of the work are valid....However, co-workers in Breslow's laboratory and an industrial chemist collaborating with Breslow have been unable to duplicate parts of it...." Mehta resigned because she "was advised that resignation was the course of action least damaging to her career," according to the head of the chemistry department.

Source: "Research Results to Be Withdrawn from JACS," *Chemical & Engineering News* (December 8, 1986): 6.

Jeffery S. Borer, M.D., Cornell University Medical College. NIH "has chastised [him] for carelessness in the conduct of two studies...'lack of attention to study requirements and generally accepted standards of record-keeping' but it found no evidence of intentional misconduct." "It told Borer to issue a clarification of a study of heart function under stress:"

- "Exercise Versus Cold Temperature Stimulation During Radionuclide Cineangiography: Diagnostic Accuracy in Coronary Artery Disease," *American Journal of Cardiology*, 51 (1983): 1091-1097.

"NIH report said that, for the next 3 years, copies of its report should be given to anyone at NIH who is considering putting him on a peer review panel or giving him research money."

Source: Constance Holden, "NIH Finally Reserves a 7-Year Dispute," *Science* (October 9, 1987), p. 151.

Scheffer Tseng, M.D., Ph.D., Harvard and Massachusetts Eye and Ear Infirmary. He was heavily subsidized by federal grants; he tested vitamin A drops for an eye ointment. He and others formed a company to take advantage of the treatment and sold stock in which he had a financial interest, and earned more than $1 million while misrepresenting his research results. A lawsuit was filed by stockholders changing deception in 1990.

Source: Jeff Hecht, "Research 'Fraud' Puts Poison into the Ivy League," *New Scientist*, 120 (December 10, 1988): 18.

Torrey Johnson, predoctoral graduate student, Tufts University. He worked on a grant from the National Institute of Child Health and Human Development. A university investigation concluded that Johnson's reports that he had extracted, purified, and characterized a transcription factor protein were fabricated. See:

- "Protein Binding to a Conserved Promoter Element of the Male Germ Cell Specific Mouse Protamine 1 and 2 Genes Suppresses Transcription in Vitro in Non-Expressing Tissues," *Journal of Cell Biology Abstracts*, 115 (1991): 48a.

Source: *ORI Newsletter*, 1 (September 1993): 4.

Pantelis Constantoulakis, Advanced Bio Science Laboratories. He committed scientific misconduct by falsifying and fabricating data in biomedical research supported by a contract with the National Cancer Institute and by misrepresenting his academic credentials for purposes of his employment under the contract. See:

- "Inhibition of Rev-Mediated HIV-1 Expression by an RNA Binding Protein Encoded by the Interferon-Inducible 9-27 Gene," *Science*, 259 (1993): 1314-1318. Retracted 264 (1994): 492.

Source: *ORI Newsletter*, 2 (September 1994): 3.

Terence S. Herman, M.D., Harvard Medical School. He "committed scientific misconduct by falsely reporting in a published article that research had been conducted according to a stated protocol, when, in fact, Dr. Herman knew at the time that the protocol for tumor measurements had not been carried out as described." The research was supported by grant awards from the National Cancer Institute and the National Center for Research Resources, NIH. He agreed to submit a retraction for:

- "A Phase I-II Trial of Cisplantin, Hyperthermia and Radiation in Patients with Locally Advanced Malignancies," *International Journal of Radiation Oncology, Biology, Physics,* 17 (1989): 1273-1278.

Source: *ORI Newsletter*, 3 (September 1995): 6.

Farooq A. Siddiqui, Ph.D., Roswell Park Cancer Institute. Dr. Siddiqui committed scientific misconduct by misrepresenting data in a published article. The research was supported by a grant award from the National Cancer Institute, NIH. He agreed to submit a letter to retract the article:

- "Purification and Immunological Characterization of DNA Polymerase-Alpha from Human Acute Lymphoblastic Leukemia Cells," *Biochemica et Biophysica Acta (BBA),* 745 (1983): 154-161.

Source: *ORI Newsletter*, 3 (September 1995): 6.

Mark Spector, Ph.D. candidate at Cornell University. So brilliant was Spector that he got accepted and functioned successfully in a leading biomedical research laboratory with no bachelor's or master's degree. He had falsified his credentials to obtain admission. The work he did with Professor Efrim Racker on the origin of cancer cells attracted much national attention. Many laboratories bought chemical compounds that Spector developed for use in their own research. See:

- "A Mouse Homolog of the Avian Sarcoma Virus SRC Protein in a Member of a Protein Kinase Cascade," *Cell,* 25 (1981): 9.
- "Regulation of Phosporylation of the -Subunit of the Erlish Asices Tumor Na+/ K+ATPase by a Protein Kinase Cascade," *Journal of Biological Chemistry,* 256 (1981): 4219-4227.

Source: Nicholas Wade, "The Rise and Fall of a Scientific Superstar," *New Scientist*, 91 (September 24, 1981): 781-782.

John C. Hiserodt, M.D., Ph.D., former assistant professor and researcher at the Pittsburgh Cancer Institute. He was found to have falsified critical data and fabricated experimental results in two grant applications to NIH. "Had he succeeded in his deception, he would have obtained more than $1 million of public funds." His request for dismissal of summary judgment and injunctive relief from ORI investigation and finding was rejected by Third Circuit Court of Appeals for the Western District of Pennsylvania, July 5, 1995. See:

- "The Expression and Functional Involvement of Laminim-Like Molecules in Non-MCH Restricted Cytotoxicity by Human Leu-19+/CD3-Natural Killer Lymphocytes," *Journal of Immunology*, 141 (1988): 3318-3323.

Source: *ORI Annual Report* (1994), p. 20.

Gloria Clayton, professor of adult nursing, Medical College of Georgia. She admitted fabricating the existence of subjects and associated data under a subcontract with the Gerontology Center at the University of Georgia. She agreed to submit letters of correction to appropriate journals for publications shown to contain the fabricated data.

Source: *ORI Newsletter*, 3 (September 1995): 5.

Thereza Imanishi-Kari, Ph.D., Tufts and MIT. She was accused of altering lab notebooks. She was principal investigator on the infamous Baltimore article. See:

- "Altered Repertoire of Endogenous Immunoglobin Gene in Transgenic Mice Containing a Rearranged Mu Heavy Chain Gene," *Cell* (April 25, 1986). Retracted by co-authors, including Baltimore (*Cell*, 65 (May 17, 1991): 536); the retraction specifically noted that Imanishi-Kari and Moema H. Reis were not parties to the retraction.

Both MIT and Tufts claimed to have investigated with no finding of misconduct. The case, however, came to the attention of the Commerce Committee in the House of Representatives. That caused the Secret Service to do forensic analysis, which the Service said proved the notebook data was fabricated. Baltimore retracted the paper some years later. Imanishi-Kari appealed this decision to the next level within the Department of Health and Human Services. In June 1996, the Research Integrity Adjudications Panel decided in her favor and criticized the ORI for its handling of the case.

Source: *ORI Newsletter*, 3 (December 1994): 1; Judy Foreman & Peter J. Howe, "Ex-MIT Scientist Is Cleared of Fraud," *Boston Globe* (June 21, 1996), pp. 1, 7.

Alan L. Landay, Ph.D., Rush-Presbyterian, St. Luke's Medical Center. ORI found that Landay engaged in scientific misconduct involving two instances of plagiarism in publications related to PHS grants. In addition he was to correct the literature regarding the following publications:

- "Advances in Flow Cytometry for Diagnostic Pathology," *Laboratory Investigations,* 57 (1987): 453-479. Corrected: 70 (1994): 134.
- "Whole Blood Methods for Simultaneous Detection of Surface and Cytoplasmic Antigens by Flow Cytometry," *Cytometry,* 14 (1993): 433-440. Corrected: 14 (1993): 698.

Source: *ORI Newsletter,* 4 (December 1995): 5-6.

Mark Hofmann, document dealer, Salt Lake City, Utah. He forged many broadsides and letters that he sold to the Mormon Church, private collectors, galleries, autograph dealers, and libraries. He claimed that a poem that he "made up...and signed" as Emily Dickinson was later published in a magazine as a "newly discovered poem." At his trial for murder, forensic evidence was presented showing that the documents were forged. Hofmann, who has admitted his guilt to both forgery and murder, is currently serving a life sentence.

Source: Robert Lindsey, *A Gathering of Saints* (New York: Simon & Schuster, 1988), p. 377.

Michael Briggs, D. Sc., found to be bogus. Biologist, Deakin University, Australia. He forged data on oral contraceptives, 1981-1987. As a result of an investigation, the following publications were determined to have been the results of misconduct:

- "Oral Contraceptives and Plasma Protein Metabolism," *Journal of Steroid Biochemistry,* 2 (1979): 425-428.
- "Progestogens and Mammary-Tumors in the Beagle Bitch," *Research in Veterinary Sciences,* 28 (1980): 199-202.
- "The Development of a New Triphasic Oral Contraceptive," in *Proceedings of the 10th World Congress on Fertility and Sterility Symposium,* July 1980, edited by R. B. Greenblatt (M.T.P. Press Ltd, n.d.).

Source: E. J. R. Rossiter, "Reflections of a Whistle-Blower," *Nature,* 357 (June 11, 1992): 434-436.

Ashoka Prasad, Psychiatrist, Victoria Mental Health Institute, Australia. A committee of inquiry determined that he had fabricated data on 1,000 patients with schizophrenia, showing higher incidence of birth in winter, 1988. The committee also established that Prasad claimed academic credentials that he did not have.

Source: Stephen Lock, "Misconduct in Medical Research: Does It Exist in Britain?," *British Medical Journal*, 297 (December 10, 1988): 1531-1535; Ian Anderson, "A Question of Fraud," *New Scientist*, 128 (April 28, 1990): 87-88.

William McBride, M.D., Foundation 41, University of New South Wales, Australia. He exposed the danger of birth defects from pregnant women taking the drug thalidomide. In the 1980s, he forged data on studies of action of hyoscine on fetal rabbit. The *Australian Journal of Biological Research* published the tainted work. It was never retracted. "Instead he wrote a letter to the editor saying that there had been errors and part of the experiment was to be repeated. But it never was." Meantime, his co-author, Phil Vardy, wrote to the editor to disassociate himself from the article because the paper had been submitted and published without his knowledge. The editor never published Vardy's letter on the grounds that the journal did not have a letter page.

Source: Norman Swan, "The Exposure of a Scientific Fraud," *New Scientist*, 120 (December 3, 1988): 30-31.

Ronald Wild, professor and dean of social science, LaTrobe University, Australia. His fifth book contained large-scale plagiarism from 10 different sources. In 1985, he resigned after difficulties with the initial inquiry.

Source: Stephen Lock, "Misconduct in Medical Research: Does It Exist in Britain?," *British Medical Journal*, 297 (December 10, 1988): 1531-1535.

M. J. Purves, Department of Physiology, University of Bristol. In a letter to *Nature*, he admitted that false data had been published in:

- "Cerebral Blood Flow and Metabolism in the Sheep Fetus," *Advances in Physiological Sciences*, 9 (1981): 199,126.

Junior colleagues could not reproduce the work and reported their suspicions. The work was supported, in part, by a (United States) PHS grant.

Source: "Scientific Fraud in Bristol Now," *Nature*, 294 (December 10, 1981): 509.

Robert J. Gullis, Ph.D., Max Planck Institute for Biochemistry in West Germany. "Three competent biochemists spent four man years trying to repeat this exciting work of a Ph. D. student." He published a retraction in the Statement section of *Nature*, 265 (1977): 764, admitting that he had faked certain results. See:

- "Pharmacological Studies on the Stimulation of the Phospholipase A2-acylation System of Synaptic Membranes or Brain by Neurotransmitters and Other Agonists," *Journal of Neuro-chemistry,* 26 (1976): 1217-1230.

Source: Mike Muller, " Why Scientists Don't Cheat," *New Scientist,* 74 (June 2, 1977): 522-523; Mark Pfiefer & Gwendolyn L. Snodgrass, "The Continued Use of Retracted, Invalid Scientific Literature," *Journal of the American Medical Association,* 263 (March 9, 1990): 1423.

Jayme Sokolow, Ph.D., Assistant Professor of History, Texas Tech University. He resigned when the Promotion and Tenure committee assembled copies of his publications and those of remarkably similar ones that had been published previous to his. Stephen Nissenbaum, a professor at the University of Massachusetts, requested the American Historical Association to investigate what he considered the plagiarism of large parts of his doctoral dissertation in Sokolow's book, *Eros and Modernization: Sylvester Graham, Health Reform, and the Origins of Victorian Sexuality in America* (Rutherford, NJ: Fairleigh Dickinson University Press, 1983). As part of the settlement, Sokolow was to send letters to the *American Historical Review* and the *Journal of American History* acknowledging that an Errata now accompanies the book and further that he apologized to Professor Nissenbaum. The letter appeared with the notice "The following communication is published at the direction of the American Historical Association."

Source: Thomas Mallon, *Stolen Words* (New York: Ticknor & Fields, 1989).

E. A. K. Alsabti, M.D., Jordanian national. He was at Temple University, the University of Virginia, Jefferson Medical College, and Anderson Hospital in Houston. Dr. Alsabti published three identical articles from grant application and manuscripts actually written by his lab director at Jefferson, Dr. Frederick Wheelock. These appeared in:

- "Tumor Dormancy: A Review," *Neoplasma,* 26 (1979): 351-361.
- "Tumor Dormancy: A Review," *Tumor Research,* 13 (1978): 1-13.
- "Tumor Dormancy: A Review," *Journal of Cancer Research and Clinical Oncology,* 95 (1979): 209-220.
- "Serum Lipids in Hepatoma," *Oncology,* 36 (1979): 11-14. The paper was copied from Takanobu Yoshide et al., "Diagnostic Evaluation of Serum Lipids in Patients with Hepatocelular Carcinoma," *Japanese Journal of Clinical Oncology,* 7 (1977): 15-20.

Other plagarized works were published as:

- "Serum Immunoglobins in Breast Cancer," *Journal of Surgical Oncology*, 11 (1979): 129-133.
- "Serum Proteins in Breast Cancer," *Japanese Journal of Experimental Medicine*, 49 (1979): 235-240.
- "Lymphocyte Transformation in Patients with Breast Cancer," *Japanese Journal of Experimental Medicine*, 49 (1979): 101.
- "Effect of Platinum Compounds of Murine Lymphocyte Mitogenesis," *Japanese Journal of Medical Science and Biology*, 32 (1979): 53-65. The original paper appeared in *European Journal of Cancer*.

Source: William Broad & Nicholas Wade, Betrayers of the Truth (New York: Simon and Schuster, 1982), p. 236; Allan Mazur, "Allegations of Dishonesty in Research and Their Treatment by American Universities," *Minerva*, 27 (1989): 177-194.

Vijay Soman, M.D., Yale University. Dr. Soman was accused of plagiarizing from a manuscript sent to his supervisor, Dr. Philip Felig, for peer review in 1979. He published an article co-authored with his supervisor in which he later admitted that he had falsified some of the data. Based on findings of an investigation by the university, an outside auditor examined Dr. Soman's other work. "Dr. Felig withdrew 12 of Soman's publications, including eight of which he was co-author." For a complete list of the retracted papers, see *American Journal of Medicine*, 69 (1980): 38-39.

Source: William Broad, "Imbroglio at Yale: Emergence of a Fraud," *Science*, 210 (October 3, 1980): 38-39.

Philip Lambert, M.D., Case Western Reserve University. Bruce Hollis, a postdoctoral fellow, worked with Lambert, who is an endocrinologist. Hollis became suspicious of Lambert's research and reported his suspicions; no investigation, however, was begun. Later, Hollis, who had found another position at the university, noted that Lambert was publishing research, supposedly co-authored with Hollis, on which Hollis had not worked. The NIH, which finally began an investigation some three years later, criticized the university's investigation and debarred Dr. Lambert from the receipt of federal grants.

Source: Allan Mazur, "Allegations of Dishonesty in Research and Their Treatment by American Universities," *Minerva*, 27 (1989): 177-194; Bruce Hollis, "I Turned in My Mentor," *The Scientist*, 1 (December 14, 1987): 11.

Stephen Breuning, University of Pittsburgh. Psychologist Breuning achieved a national reputation for his published studies of the effects of behavior-controlling drugs on severely retarded, institutionalized persons. These studies, now regarded as mostly fabricated, influenced the way severely retarded patients with serious problems of behaviors were treated. Breuning's deception was uncovered by his former professor at the University of Illinois, Dr. Robert Sprague, who brought the case to the attention of the National Institute of Mental Health in 1983. In 1987, Breuning was found guilty and subsequently pleaded guilty to criminal charges of falsifying medical research. A complete listing of Breuning's publications can be found in:

Source: Eugene Garfield & Alfred Welljams-Dorof, "The Impact of Fraudulent Research on the Scientific Literature," *Journal of the American Medical Association*, 263 (March 9, 1990): 1424-1426.

John Darsee, M.D., Harvard University and Emory University, specialized in cardiology. He wrote 116 articles and abstracts. Emory University Medical School conducted its own investigation of the writing produced while Darsee was employed there. The committee evaluating the matter found "overwhelming direct and circumstantial evidence of flagrant and extensive fraud in his research…seven of nine full papers and many of the abstracts must be considered to be invalid." The evidence for the committee decisions regarding each writing is detailed in:

Source: "Report of Ad Hoc Committee to Evaluate Research of Dr. John Darsee at Emory University," *Minerva*, 23 (1985): 276-305.

Robert Slutsky, M.D., University of California, San Diego. He published 137 articles during a seven-year period. All these publications were evaluated by a university committee. "Seventy-seven (including four reviews) were judged as valid, 48 were judged as questionable and 12 were deemed fraudulent." Most of the tainted work had been fabricated. A complete list of Slutsky's publications along with the committee's evaluation of the validity of each is given in:

Source: Robert L. Engler, James W. Covell, Paul J. Friedman, Philip S., Kitcher, and Richard M Peters, "Misrepresentation and Responsibility in Medical Research," *New England Journal of Medicine*, 317 (November 26, 1987): 1383-1389.

Steven Derr, Ph. D., chemist, Hope College, Michigan. He supposedly discovered a method for removing the toxic metals, cadmium and plutonium, from mice. The discovery had implications for treating workers exposed to these metals. Jack Schubert, the senior member of the team, sent a letter to *Nature* confessing that the results were invalid. See:

- "Mixed Legand Chelate Therapy for Plutonium and Cadmium Poisoning," *Nature*, 275 (1978): 311-313.

Source: Lawrence McGinty, "Researcher Retracts Claims on Plutonium Treatment," *New Scientist*, 84 (October 4, 1979): 3-4.

Shervant H. Frazier, M.D., Harvard University and McLean Hospital in Belmont, MA. Dr. Frazier was found to have plagiarized material in four papers published between 1966 and 1975. The plagiarism did not come to light until the late 1980s. Harvard fired him, but he subsequently regained his position at McLean. He was honored for his work by the American Psychiatric Association shortly after the plagiarism became known. The following was found to contain passages previously published by another author:

- "Complex Problems of Pain as Seen in Headache, Painful Phantom, and Other States," in *American Handbook of Psychiatry* (1975).

Source: Jeff Hecht, "Research 'Fraud' Puts Poison into the Ivy League," *New Scientist* (December 10, 1988), p. 18; Alison Bass, "Plagiarism Topples Leading Psychiatrist," *Boston Globe* (November 29, 1988), pp. A1, 31.

Joseph Cort, M. D., an employee of Vega Biochemicals in Tucson, AZ, also a part-time faculty member at the Mt. Sinai Medical School, New York City. He "admitted fabricating data that appeared in two scientific papers, a patent application that was granted and a National Institutes of Health grant application and progress report," after an investigation by Mt. Sinai Medical School. The fabricated data appeared in articles published in *International Journal of Peptide and Protein Research* and *Advances in Physiological Sciences*.

Source: Stephen Budiansky, "False Data Confessed," *Nature*, 301 (January 13, 1983): 101.

John C. Long, M.D., Massachusetts General Hospital. He received over $750,000 from NIH for study of Hodgkin's disease. It was determined that a cell line that he had cultured, supposedly taken from patients suffering from Hodgkin's disease, was from monkeys, not from humans. Long admitted fabricating data for:

- "Reaction of Immune Complexes with Hodgkin's Disease Tissue Cultures: Radioimmune Assay and Immunoferritin Electron Microscopy," *Journal of the National Cancer Institute*, 62 (1979): 787-795.

Suspicions about the veracity of his other papers have come up as a result of other further investigation by his former colleagues.

Source: Nicholas Wade, "A Diversion of the Quest for Truth," *Science*, 211 (March 6, 1981): 1022-1025.

Claudio Milanese, Italian scientist visiting at Harvard and Dana Farber Cancer Center Institute. He "reported the discovery of a new molecule that would stimulate the development of T-cells in the immune system. The discovery would have been useful in the treatment of both cancer and AIDS." After he returned to Italy, others in the lab could not continue his experiments. Milanese admitted manipulating the data and retracted the article he had published with the head of the lab, Ellis Reinherz, and a graduate student. He and co-authors retracted the following:

- "Identification of T Helper Cell-Derived Lymphokine That Activates Resting T Lymphocytes," *Science*, 231 (1986): 1118-1122.
- "A Lymphokine that Activates the Cytolytic Program of Both Cytotoxic T Lymphocyte and Natural Killer Clones," *Journal of Experimental Medicine*, 163 (1986): 1583.

Source: James R. Wible, "Fraud in Science: An Economic Approach," *Philosophy of the Social Sciences*, 22 (1) (March 1992): 5-27; "Retraction of Data," Science, 234 (November 28, 1987): 1036.

David Van Theil, M. D., Department of Surgery, University of Pittsburgh. He was found guilty in an institutional investigation of plagiarizing three chapters of a book by three different authors and using the materials in subsequent articles. The OSI accepted those findings and barred Van Theil from receiving federal grants or serving on federal grant committees for three years.

Source: Alan R. Price, "Federal Actions against Plagiarism in Research," *Journal of Information Ethics*, 5 (1) (Spring 1996): 34-51.

SOME CASES INVOLVING MISCONDUCT IN RESEARCH SUBMITTED BUT NOT PUBLISHED

James T. Kurtzman, M. D., Resident Fellow in the Department of Obstetrics, Gynecology and Reproductive Sciences, University of California, San Francisco. He falsified results on research on the kinetics of nitric oxide synthase cells and homogenates of human nyometrial tissue in pregnant women. His paper was submitted to *Journal of Clinical Investigation*, but not published. Kurtzman admitted his guilt and agreed to debarment from federally-funded research for three years. A fuss has arisen over the agreement that his exclusion "shall not apply to his future training or practice of clinical medicine whether as a resident, fellow, or licensed practitioner unless that practice involved federally-funded research."

Source: *ORI Newsletter*, 3 (June 1995): 3.

Daniel P. Bednarik, Ph. D., Center for Disease Control and Prevention. Based on an investigation conducted by ORI it was found that Bednarik engaged in misconduct by falsifying and fabricating research data in two manuscripts sent to the journal *Nucleic Acids Research* and to the journal AIDS. The first paper was not accepted and the second for AIDS was withdrawn before review. Dr. Bednarik has agreed not to appeal ORI's jurisdiction or its findings.

Source: *NIH Guide*, 24 (42) (December 8, 1995).

Alok Bandyopadhyay, Laboratory of Developmental Pharmacology at the National Institute of Child Health and Human Development, NIH, was first author on "Analysis of Mammalian P450 Catalytic Activities by Genetic Engineering and Expressions in Yeast." "The paper was intended for publication in the *Proceedings of the National Academy of Sciences*, but certain inconsistencies in the data were detected before it was actually submitted...." An investigation was begun at NIH. Bandyopadhyay was dismissed in November and in the following February, 1987, Howard Eisen, head of the lab, committed suicide "10 days after appearing before a panel looking into the affair."

Source: Joseph Palaca, "Investigations into NIH Fraud Allegations End with Suicide," *Nature*, 325 (February 19, 1987): 652.

PUBLICIZED CASES IN WHICH MISCONDUCT WAS NOT FOUND

Herbert Needleman, Professor, University of Pittsburgh. ORI accepted the university's finding that his reports on the effects of low levels of lead on the intellectual abilities of children did not constitute misconduct in science as defined in the federal regulation. Both the university and ORI, however, found numerous problems, errors, and inaccuracies in Dr. Needleman's reports and presentations of his research. Because of the number and magnitude of these problems, ORI notified NIH (the funding agency), the Centers for Disease Control and Prevention (involved in lead poisoning issues), and the Environmental Protection Agency (set lead standards based, in part, on Needleman's data).

ORI concurred with the university's proposed actions, in particular that Dr. Needleman correct the scientific literature and allow researchers access to the data that support his reports so that they may be independently assessed. ORI released its report because the research affected significant public issues and ORI strongly believes that the public has a right to know the results of the investigation.

Source: *ORI Newsletter*, 2 (June 1994): 3.

Appendix B

SOME JOURNALS AND MONOGRAPHS IN WHICH THOSE IMPLICATED IN MISCONDUCT HAVE BEEN PUBLISHED[1]

JOURNALS

Advances in Experimental Medicine and Biology (Lucas)
Advances in Physiological Sciences (Cort)
American Heart Journal (Slutsky 9)
American Journal of Cardiology (Darsee 2, Borer, Slutksy 6)
American Journal of Medicine (Soman)
American Journal of Mental Deficiency (Breuning 3)
American Journal of Physiology (Darsee)
American Journal of Psychiatry (Breuning)
American Journal of Radiology (Darsee)
Annals of Internal Medicine (Darsee 2)
Applied Research in Mental Retardation (Breuning 2)
Archives of General Psychiatry (Breuning, Sherer)
Australian Journal of Biological Sciences (McBride)
Biochemica et Biophysica Acta (Siddiqui)
Biochemical & Biophysical Research Communications (Lee, T. S.)
Biological Psychiatry (Sherer)
British Journal of Obstetrics and Gynaecology (Pearce 4)
Cardiovascular and Interventional Radiology (Slutsky 4)
Cardiovascular Research (Slutsky)

Cell (Imanishi-Kari, Rosner, Urban, Illmensee, Spector)
Chest (Darsee 2, Slutsky 3)
Circulation (Darsee 11, Slutsky 3)
Circulation Research (Darsee)
Circulation Shock (Slutsky)
Clinical Cardiology (Slutsky)
Clinical Psychology Review (Breuning)
Clinical Research (Darsee 10)
Comparative Biochemistry and Physiology (Paparo 2)
Computers in Biomedical Research (Slutsky)
Critical Care Medicine (Slutsky)
Cytometry (Landay)
Diabetes (Lee, T. S., Soman)
Diseases of the Nervous System (Frazier)
Education and Training of the Mentally Retarded (Breuning)
Eighteenth Century (Sokolow)
EMBO Journal (Lee, C. Q., Matsuguchi, Ballart)
European Journal of Nuclear Medicine (Slutsky)
Fertility and Sterility (Friedman, A. J.)
Genes, Chromosomes and Cancer (Hajra)
Genomics (Hajra)
International Journal of Peptide and Protein Research (Cort)
International Journal of Radiation, Oncology, Biology, Physics (Herman)
Investigative Radiology (Slutsky 11)
Japanese Journal of Experimental Medicine (Alsabti 2)
Japanese Journal of Medical Science and Biology (Alsabti)
Journal of Applied Developmental Psychology (Fry 2)
Journal of Biological Chemistry (Spector)
Journal of Cancer Research and Clinical Oncology (Alsabti)
Journal of Cardiology (Darsee)
Journal of Cell Biology Abstracts (Johnson, T.)
Journal of Clinical Immunology (Ninnemann)
Journal of Clinical Investigation (Lee, T. S.)
Journal of Experimental Medicine (Kumar, Long, Milanese)
Journal of Immunology (Weiser, Lucas, Hiserodt, Ninnemann)
Journal of Laboratory and Clinical Medicine (Salim)
Journal of Nervous and Mental Disorders (Breuning)
Journal of Neuro-Chemistry (Gullis)
Journal of Nuclear Medicine (Slutsky)
Journal of Surgical Oncology (Alsabti)
Journal of Surgical Research (Slutsky)
Journal of the American Chemical Society (Mehta)
Journal of the American College of Cardiology (Slutsky 4)

Journal of the Geological Society of India (Gupta)[2]
Journal of the National Cancer Institute (Long)
Journal of Trauma (Ninnemann 3)
Journal of Virology (Ballart)
Laboratory Investigations (Landay)
The Lancet (Tewari)
Molecular and Cellular Biology (Hajra)
National Academy of Sciences, Proceedings (Weiser, Long 2, Spector, Illmensee, Kumar, Lee, T. S.)
Nature (Derr, Beneveniste, Purves)
Neoplasma (Alsabati)
Neurology (Abbs)
New England Journal of Medicine (Darsee, Long, Stricker)
Obstetrics and Gynecology (Friedman, A. J.)
Oncology (Alsabti)
Pediatrics (Glueck)
Pharmacology Biochemistry and Behavior (Breuning)
Plant Physiology (unnamed, but official investigation convened by the University of Illinois)
Psychopharmacology Bulletin (Breuning)
Radiology (Slutsky 8)
Research in Developmental Disabilities (Breuning)
Science (Milanese, Bridges, Constantaulakis)
Surgery Forum (Lucas)
Tumor Research (Alsabati)

NOTES

[1] Numbers after the names indicate two or more articles.
[2] In 1991, the journal itself advised readers to ignore all the papers that it had published by Viswa Jit Gupta over the past 21 years.

MONOGRAPHS

Assessing the Mentally Retarded, edited by J. L. Matson and S. E. Breuning. New York: Grune and Stratton, 1983. (Breuning)
Drugs and Mental Retardation, edited by S. E. Breuning and Allan Poling. Springfield, IL: Charles C. Thomas, 1982.
Eros and Modernization: Sylvester Graham, Health Reform and the Origins of Victorian Sexuality in America. Rutherford, NJ: Fairleigh-Dickinson University Press, 1983. (Sokolow)
The Heart. Update III, edited by J. W. Hurst. New York: McGraw Hill, 1980 ; Update IV, 1981. (Darsee)
International Congress of Psychological Sciences, 28th. (Purves)

Psychopathology in the Mentally Retarded, edited by J. L. Matson & R. P. Barrett. New York: Grune and Stratton, 1982. (Breuning)

Appendix C

RESEARCH MISCONDUCT (FACULTY SURVEY)

There is increased discussion about the extent to which research and scholarship have been subject to fraud, fabrication, plagiarism, and conflicts of interest between funding source and research findings. Given that discussion, we would appreciate your taking a few minutes to complete and return the brief survey. The information you supply will be useful for a research project that examines the roles of instructors and librarians.

1. When you find information or a source in the library which might be useful, do you ever wonder if the content might be falsified or fabricated? **(Please circle your response)**

1　2　3　4　5

Never......................Always

If you checked "1," in question 1, skip to question 3.

2. If you had questions about whether or not a work might be falsified or fabricated, what would you do? (Check all that apply)
   a. ___Ask a colleague
   b. ___Ask a librarian
   c. ___Check for notices of retraction and letters to the editor in journals
   d. ___Check the reputation of the author(s)
   e. ___Check the reputation of the book publisher or journal
   f. ___Check the reputation of the source of funding
   g. ___Other (specify):_____

3. When students find information or a source in the library which might be useful to them for completion of a class assignment, do they ever question the content as falsified or fabricated? **(Circle the appropriate response)**

$$1 \quad 2 \quad 3 \quad 4 \quad 5$$
Never........................**Always**

4. If students question whether or not a work has been falsified or fabricated, what should they do? (**Check all that apply**)
   a. ___Ask you
   b ___Ask a librarian
   c. ___Check for notices of retraction and letters to the editor in journals
   d. ___Check the reputation of the author(s)
   e. ___Check the reputation of the book publisher or journal
   f. ___Check the reputation of the source of funding
   g. ___Other (specify):_____

5. Who should have the major responsibility to teach students to evaluate published sources in order to avoid using falsified, fraudulent work?
   a. ___Instructors
   b. ___Librarians
   c. ___Both instructors and librarians
   d. ___Neither
   Please briefly explain your preference.

6. Should library indexes and catalogs forewarn library users about material known to come from falsified or fraudulent work?
   a. ___Yes   b. ___No
   Please briefly explain your answer.

7. Do you use the Internet or the World Wide Web?
   a. ___Yes   b. ___No
   If you answered "no," please skip to question 10.

8. If you answered "yes," for what purposes do you use them?

9. If you answered "yes" to question 7, are you concerned that information you find might result from falsified or fraudulent work?
   $$1 \quad 2 \quad 3 \quad 4 \quad 5$$
   Never........................**Always**

   Please briefly explain your response.

10. Should libraries guarantee the accuracy of information contained in their collections?
    a. ___Yes   b. ___No. Briefly explain.

11. Should libraries attempt to identify as such, articles or books known to be based on fraudulent data or information?
    a. ___Yes   b.   ___No. Briefly explain.

12. Please specify your department:_____.

Thank you for your cooperation.

Appendix D

RESEARCH MISCONDUCT (STUDENT SURVEY)

There is increased discussion about the extent to which research and scholarship have been subject to fraud, fabrication, plagiarism, and conflicts of interest between funding source and research findings. Given that discussion, we would appreciate your taking a few minutes to complete and return the brief survey. The information you supply will be useful for a research project that examines the roles of instructors and librarians.

1. When you find information or a source in the library which might be useful, do you ever wonder if the content might be falsified or fabricated? (**Please circle your response**)

1   2   3   4   5
Never........................Always

   If you checked "1" in question 1, skip to question 3.

2. If you had questions about whether or not a work might be falsified or fabricated, what do you do? (Check all that apply)
   a. ___Ask a friend
   b. ___Ask a librarian
   c. ___Check for notices of retraction and letters to the editor in journals
   d. ___Check the reputation of the author(s)
   e. ___Check the reputation of the book publisher or journal
   f. ___Check the reputation of the source of funding
   g. ___Consult course instructor
   h. ___Other (specify):_____

3. Who should have the major responsibility to teach students to evaluate published sources in order to avoid using falsified, fraudulent work?
   a. ___Instructors
   b. ___Librarians
   c. ___Both instructors and librarians
   d. ___Neither
   Please briefly explain your preference.

4. Should library indexes and catalogs forewarn library users about material known to come from falsified or fraudulent work?
   a. ___Yes   b. ___No
   Please briefly explain your answer.

5. Do you use the Internet or the World Wide Web?
   a. ___Yes   b. ___No

   If you answered "no," please skip to question 8.

6. If you answered "yes" to the preceding question, for what purposes do you use them?

7. If you answered "yes" to question 5, are you concerned that information you find might result from falsified or fraudulent work? **(Circle the appropriate response)**
                    1   2   3   4   5
            Never.......................Always
   Please briefly explain your response.

8. Should libraries guarantee the accuracy of information contained in their collections?
   a. ___Yes   b. ___No. Briefly explain.

9. Should libraries attempt to identify as such, articles or books known to be based on fraudulent data or information?
   a. ___Yes   b. ___No. Briefly explain.

10. What is your class level?
    a. ___Freshman   d. ___Senior
    b. ___Sophomore   e. ___Graduate Student
    c. ___Junior   f. ___Unclassified

11. What is your major?

Thank you for your cooperation.

Appendix E

FALSIFIED STUDY: USE AND NONUSE OF U.S. GOVERNMENT INFORMATION ON THE INTERNET AND WORLD WIDE WEB BY ACADEMIC HISTORIANS AND POLITICAL SCIENTISTS: A CROSS-INSTITUTIONAL COMPARISON

by Maxwell A. Mega

ABSTRACT: This paper reports the findings of a survey of American historians and political scientists affiliated with academic institutions (baccalaureate, master's, and doctoral-granting) in the West South Central region of the United States. Survey findings indicate that political scientists use the Internet and World Wide Web more than historians do; nonetheless, use is limited to master's and doctoral-granting institutions and to selected resources. Telephone interviews expand on selected findings, and the paper explores the implications of study findings for library services.

During the 1970s and 1980s there were numerous studies on the use and nonuse of U.S. government publications by faculty members in social sciences, sciences, and humanities. The studies tended to involve surveys mailed to faculty members at one institution; however, one study did compare reasons and patterns of use and nonuse among social scientists in baccalaureate, master's, and doctoral-granting institutions in four Midwestern states.[1] Since the 1980s, there have been no published studies on faculty use and nonuse of government information[2] at a time when the information superhighway is under construction. Both the Clinton administration and Congress support and expect agencies to be involved in electronic government and to place increasingly more resources on the Internet and World Wide Web (WWW) for public use. The Government Printing Office (GPO) has even informed its 1,400 depository libraries to expect the demise of paper distribution within the next couple of years and to regroup as an electronic depository program.[3]

Against that background, this paper examines the use and nonuse of government publications and information by two groups of academicians known for their use of government publications: historians and political scientists specializing in the United States. The purpose of the study is to investigate their reasons for use and nonuse of government publications and information, the extent to which they use the Internet and the WWW for gaining access to these publications and this information, patterns of their use of electronic government information, and their perceptions about the role which librarians can play in navigating the information superhighway to provide them with access to needed information. The paper compares use and nonuse by both groups and institutional association (baccalaureate, master's, and doctoral-granting); the null hypotheses are that there are no statistically significant differences ($p = .05$) between the groups or by institutional association.

STUDY PROCEDURES

For this research, the investigator selected the West South Central region of the United States, which the U.S. Bureau of the Census defines as comprising Arkansas, Louisiana, Oklahoma, and Texas.[4] The study population comprises the 78 academic institutions in those states with libraries having membership in GPO's depository program; nine of these institutions offer the baccalaureate as the highest degree, 32 have the master's as the terminal degree, and 37 are doctoral-granting. Omitted from the population are law school, medical, and community college libraries. Because it is not the intention of the investigator to make comparisons among the states, the sample was not selected by state.

Using a systematic sample of every fourth depository library (with the institutions arranged in alphabetical order per classification group), the investigator selected six baccalaureate-granting, six master's-granting, and six doctoral-granting institutions. The 18 institutions reflected a cross-section of institutions in the four states. Next, he contacted the history and political science departments at these institutions and obtained a list of the American historians and political scientists dealing with the United States.[5] A total of 170 academicians (see below) were surveyed from October to December, 1995.

He entered survey data into the Windows microcomputer version of the *Statistical Package for the Social Sciences* and analyzed the data using percentages and the chi-square test of independence. As internal validity checks, the investigator defined government publications, consistent with previous surveys (see note 1) as "informational matter published as an individual document at government expense, or as required by law." Furthermore, he asked respondents if they were currently engaged in, or have completed within the past year, a scholarly activity intended for publication citing a government publication. Sixteen respondents—both historians and political scientists—had. An examination of those papers actually published showed that indeed they had cited government publications. Respondents were also asked if they had made reference to electronic U.S. government information in a bibliography or footnote. None had. By conducting telephone interviews with six respondents (one historian and one political scientist from three sites—one baccalaureate, one master's, and one doctoral-granting institution), the investigator reviewed their survey responses with them as a reliability check and elicited additional information about their use or nonuse of electronic government information.

SURVEY FINDINGS

Respondents

A total of 103 of the 170 faculty members responded, for a return rate of 60.6%; 45 (43.7%) of the respondents were historians and 58 (56.3%) were political scientists. Viewed from another perspective, all but one of the historians from baccalaureate institutions responded, and 11 of the 14 (78.6%) political scientists did. From the master's-granting institutions, 17 of the 31 (54.8%) historians and 29 of the 34 (85.3%) political scientists responded. Eighteen of the 30 (60%) historians and 23 of the 32 (71.9%) political scientists at doctoral-granting institutions replied. Predominantly (86.7%), respondents held the rank of professor or associate professor. Only 12 respondents were assistant professors, with the numbers evenly distributed among baccalaureate, master's, and doctoral-granting institutions. Only one respondent, an assistant professor, was not a member of that faculty the previous academic year.

Frequency of Library and Documents Use

More than three-fourths of the respondents (77.2%), regardless of their discipline, estimated that they had used the academic library more than 25 times in 1995. Four respondents used it no more than five times, and one did not use it at all that year. When asked how many times that year they had used U.S. government pub-

lications located in the college or university library collection, the number of estimated uses dropped to a maximum of 10 times. Library use, however, was not
limited to use of the collections of U.S. government publications.

There is no statistically significant difference between historians and political
scientists regarding the frequency of use of the library's collection of U.S. government publications (chi square = 4.251, 7df, p <.05). As well, there is no significance between highest degree granted by the institution and the frequency of use
of the collection (chi square = 17.215, 14df, p <.05).

Reasons for Use of Government Publications

When asked to identify their reasons for use of government publications, historians naturally indicated the need for information of historical value, whereas the
political scientists stressed the need to monitor current events and issues of interest, to consult statistical data and/or legal material, and to obtain grant information.
Only four faculty members, all from master's-granting institutions, mentioned the
need for resources that may be of value to their students.

Reasons for Limited Use or Nonuse of Government Publications

The 46 respondents using the collection of government publications a maximum
of five times were asked to identify their reasons for limited use or nonuse. They
indicated seven reasons:

- The government publishes little or nothing of value in my field (35 respondents);
- Do not need government publications on a regular basis (32 respondents);
- The amount of time expended in trying to find relevant information in govern-
  ment publications is out of proportion to what I find (19 respondents);
- Rely on government publications located in a library other than this campus
  (10 respondents);
- Unaware of the existence of such materials at the library (9 respondents);
- Unfamiliar with the arrangement of the government publications collection (9
  respondents); and
- Obtain personal, paper copies of government publications (8 respondents).

It merits mention that no respondent listed, as reasons, problems with library
staff, reliance on secretaries and others to obtain material for them, or reliance on
the Internet for information retrieval. Only a couple of them mentioned reluctance
to use microforms.

Use of Library Staff in Seeking Government Information

Of those 57 historians and political scientists using the library's collection of government publications, even on a limited basis, 13 (22.8%) never asked library staff

members for assistance and one always requested assistance. Thirty-two (56.1%) faculty members asked for assistance "sometimes" and 11 (19.3%) did so "frequently." There is no statistically significant difference between historians and political scientists regarding the frequency with which they requested assistance (chi square = 1.89, 3df, $p < .05$).

The most frequently mentioned reasons for seeking assistance were:

- Help in locating a specific government publication (43 respondents);
- Reference assistance, i.e., aid in finding materials or information to answer a specific question or solve some problem on which they are working (35 respondents);
- Assistance in finding government publications not located on the shelf (17 respondents); and
- Help in locating electronic government information not held by the library (2 respondents).

Both respondents seeking electronic information were political scientists.

Linkage to the Internet, World Wide Web, and Library's Homepage

Sixty-three (61.2%) of the 103 respondents, all from master's and doctoral-granting institutions, indicated that their library had a WWW homepage; 15 (14.6%) mentioned that their library did not and 24 (23.3%) did not know. Only nine of those professing that the library did have a homepage mentioned that it provided some access to electronic information which the U.S. government disseminated. Almost half of the respondents (50 or 49%) had a microcomputer in their office with linkage to the Internet and WWW; these respondents are predominantly political scientists.

All of the faculty members with microcomputers in their offices used the Internet primarily for purposes of electronic mail; 35 participated in discussion groups. Thirty did use the Internet in searching for information, 20 used it for gaining access to research materials, and 20 downloaded files to paper-copy form. Although political scientists were the most likely to use the Internet for other than electronic mail, a few historians (as discussed in the next section) sought research materials and downloaded some files. Only two respondents, both political scientists, used the Internet to check the holdings of other libraries.

Use of Electronic Government Information

Of the 30 respondents who used the Internet in searching for information, 27 were political scientists. The three historians made selective use of the WWW; they either sought declassified information or the status of declassification programs, or checked on the development of electronic access to the presidential libraries they anticipated visiting. When they consulted declassified information, it was most likely that from the Department of Energy.[6]

The 27 political scientists selectively use the WWW; as one of them admitted:

> The amount of government information available through the WWW is astonishing and overwhelming. I do not have the time or desire to browse all the different sources and see which ones best meet my needs. I tend to rely on a few sources and services—ones I know to be of higher quality and to provide quick access to needed information.

These academicians consulted information from the White House, the Office of Management and Budget, the Bureau of the Census, and Congress. When they consulted congressional resources, however, they mostly relied on THOMAS—a gateway of the Library of Congress and the House of Representatives named after Thomas Jefferson—and the homepages of a few members of Congress. The 20 users of THOMAS liked its coverage of House bills and the ability to search and retrieve information from the *Congressional Record*.

Despite the availability of GPO's gateway from depository libraries, only three political scientists had used it. One political scientist had browsed FedWorld, the gateway of the National Technical Information Service, and three political scientists had tried LC Marvel, another gateway of the Library of Congress.

When asked to identify the types of electronic government information sources they seek, historians marked either reports of commissions, committees, and agencies; laws and statutes; or "no pattern: use varies." By contrast, political scientists identified:

- Bills and resolutions (23 respondents);
- Information from the *Congressional Record* (20 respondents);
- Names and addresses, including phone numbers and e-mail addresses of members of Congress and agency personnel (12 respondents);
- Speeches from key agency personnel (10 respondents);
- Press releases from agencies (8 respondents);
- Reports of commissions, committees, and agencies (8 respondents);
- Statistical reports or data (4 respondents); and
- Laws and statutes (2 respondents).

The users of the Internet and WWW were asked to characterize the overall quality of government information available through these channels. They could choose from a five-point scale ranging from 1 (poor) to 5 (excellent). One respondent marked 1, 14 checked 2, 14 marked 3, and one circled 4. In summary, 29 of the 30 respondents marked 3 as the highest characterization. Clearly, there is concern about the quality of information amidst the quantity of available information. This finding becomes more evident with the next question, "How important is government information which you identify through the Internet or World Wide Web for keeping up in your field, teaching, or research?" Respondents had four options: "little importance or do not use," "slight importance," "moderate importance," and "great importance." All respondents marked either the first or second category, thus indicating that, at most, the information obtained had slight importance.

When asked about the role of librarians, 25 (83.3%) of the 30 respondents believed that they could perform a unique and important role in providing access to electronic government information. They defined that role in terms of either selective dissemination of information or information referral. In other words, they wanted librarians to be aware of their research and teaching interests and to send, via campus mail or electronic mail, announcements and information of direct interest to them. They were also interested in librarians sending them information about new WWW sites relevant to their needs which they might browse. Ten respondents inserted a reminder to the effect that they did not want to be overwhelmed with information; they appreciated "selectivity."

TELEPHONE INTERVIEWS

In order to verify the consistency of survey responses and to elicit additional insights into the use and nonuse of electronic government information, six respondents, based on the nature of their survey responses, were interviewed by telephone in January 1996. The political scientist and historian from baccalaureate institutions consider themselves to be generalists and do not need the type of detailed information which they suspect the Internet provides. The two political scientists from master's and doctoral-granting institutions used the Internet, and in particular the WWW, for the retrieval of research information. The one from the master's-granting institution found it useful for gaining access to recent legislation from her desktop workstation. She said, "I can get all the House bills from the library if I want, but using THOMAS on the Web saves me a trip each time. Besides, I really do not want to use a microfiche collection, if I can help it!" She also commented, "Because I tend to use the same sources over and over, I don't need a librarian to help me."

She was the only academician interviewed who used the Internet as a student resource. In her classes, she frequently directed students to sites on the WWW to retrieve class information. "One of the most popular topics," she explained, "involves a search of the Internet for material about post-World War II Presidents, and most students discover and use the National Archives site for access to material from presidential libraries."

The other political scientist used THOMAS for gaining access to legislation and for searching the *Congressional Record*. He has set his default homepage on Netscape for quick access to THOMAS, and believes that "THOMAS is the greatest thing to come along since Troy Aikman joined the Dallas Cowboys!"

The historian from the doctoral-granting institution used the Internet to discover the types of primary source material which certain archives are acquiring and making available, whereas the historian from the other institution no longer "surfs the Net." He finds it difficult to locate high-quality material amidst the vast quantity of "junk." He preferred to use the library or his personal collection for access to books and journals.

None of the users of the Internet wanted librarians to provide lists of potentially useful Web sites. They wanted to know the direct value of the site to their teaching and research needs, but were also concerned about ease of access, uniqueness of the information provided, and the extent to which the information provided was reliable and valid.

COMPARISON WITH OTHER RESEARCH

Consistent with previous research, this study found that faculty members classified as either limited or nonusers of government publications perceived that the government publishes little or nothing of value to their immediate fields. They also believed that the amount of time spent in searching for government information is out of proportion to what they found.[7] As well, it seems that there are distinct patterns in the use of government information. Use tends to concentrate on certain types of publications and information, as well as agencies.[8]

Several historians from doctoral-granting institutions, in handwritten comments, reinforced a point made by Case in his study of historians' information use, namely that "the books, bibliographic databases, and reference tools that we [librarians] painstakingly provide are not the source materials that scholars most often seek. Reliance upon original evidence is especially important to historians...."[9] Those historians offering written comments regarded the primary source material provided electronically at best as a "teaser" and "indicator of what the WWW might provide in the distant future." They regarded the "distant future" as beyond their working careers. For now, they regard historical WWW sites as lacking sufficient primary source material for research by their students and themselves.

IMPLICATIONS OF FINDINGS FOR
LIBRARY MANAGEMENT AND REFERENCE

Because gateways such as THOMAS provide information useful to faculty members, students, and others, it is surprising that more political scientists do not regard such resources as a means of information access for themselves and their students, both undergraduate and graduate. Thus, alerting students to these gateways may have to come from bibliographic instruction and other services initiated by librarians. As libraries stress greater access to resources not locally held, they might mount THOMAS and other key gateways on their homepages and provide instruction in their use.

With the GPO encouraging depository libraries and other information providers and users to consult GPO Access, it is surprising that so few faculty members had used this gateway. Many documents librarians, this investigator has been told, appear to find it hard to search and prefer to consult other resources. Thus, it is difficult to draw any conclusions about the use and nonuse of GPO Access other than that the GPO itself might be surprised by such limited use. Clearly, the GPO may need to develop strategies, in cooperation with and independent of depository librarians, to encourage greater use of its online gateway. Such limited use may send a negative message to Congress, one which the GPO may not want sent. Undoubtedly, continued limited use may suggest to members of a cost-cutting and cost-shifting Congress that further funding of GPO is unnecessary or counterproductive.

The faculty members using the Internet and WWW tended to see librarians as fulfilling a unique and important role. They wanted the librarians fully informed of their information needs and engaged in a type of information delivery. Such a role may decrease direct use of library collections while shifting the role of librarians to expanding the nature and types of information available through the online public access catalog and homepage, assuming the library has one or both of these. At the same time, librarians will have to negotiate the information environment, selecting those resources that best complement the printed and CD-ROM collections and ensuring that information access focuses on criteria mutually agreeable to both librarians (their time and resources) and users (their computer sophistication and information needs).

TOPICS FOR FURTHER RESEARCH

The study reported here only provides self-reporting about faculty use and nonuse of paper-based and electronic government information. It does not place the findings in a context of use over time.[10] Further research, therefore, might collect trend data, monitoring if and/or how patterns of use change. Research might also update the studies on use of government publications and thereby place use of electronic government information in a more complete context than this paper does. As well, the research might examine faculty members in other geographical regions and departments, students, and the general public, depicting the types of publications and information, as well as gateways and other resources, most commonly used.

CONCLUSION

Both the Clinton administration and Congress emphasize a movement toward greater electronic government and the wider dissemination of government information. As well, many academic libraries are making an increasingly greater commitment to the provision of electronic resources. Studies such as this and The *ACLS Survey of Scholars*[11] suggest that the scholarly community has not embraced the Internet and electronic information resources to the extent to which students and others appear to use the Internet for recreational purposes. If scholarly communication among historians, political scientists, and perhaps others does not rate information available through the information superhighway as of more than "slight importance," that highway may comprise a side road at best. It is not integral to scholarly communication. This suggests that the perceived quality of the information must improve and more attention must be devoted to improving easy access and to training. Libraries will definitely have to expand their services and training programs to ensure that their electronic resources become more used and useful.

NOTES AND REFERENCES

[1] For an identification of these studies, see Peter Hernon, *Use of Government Publications by Social Scientists* (Norwood, NJ: Ablex, 1979); Beth Postema & Terry L. Weech, "The Use of Government Publications: A Twelve-Year Perspective," *Government Publications Review*, 18 (1991): 223-238.

[2] Postema & Weech, "The Use of Government Publications."

[3] "The Electronic Federal Depository Library Program: Transition Plan FY 1996-1998," *Administrative Notes: Newsletter of the Federal Depository Library Program*, 16 (18) (December 29, 1995): 1-25.

[4] See any issue of *Statistical Abstracts of the United States* (Washington, D.C.: Government Printing Office) for a map depicting the census regions.

[5] Hereafter, the American historians are referred to as historians.

6 Respondents mentioned use of the following Web sites:
- http://www.ohre.doe.gov/ (Office of Human Radiation Experiments, Department of Energy);
- http://sunsite.unc.edu/lia/president/pres-home.html (Presidential Libraries); and
- http://www.fas.org/pub/gen/fas/sgp/ (Federation of American Scientists).

[7] See Hernon, *Use of Government Publications by Social Scientists*.

[8] See Peter Hernon & Gary R. Purcell, *Developing Collections of U.S. Government Publications* (Greenwich, CT: JAI Press, 1982).

[9] Donald Owen Case, "The Collection and Use of Information by Some American Historians: A Study of Motives and Methods," *Library Quarterly*, 61 (1991): 61-82.

[10] As part of that context, future studies might probe use of the Internet and WWW within the context of use of technology. Donald Case, for example, in research conducted in 1988, found that historians "varied in the degree to which computers were integrated into their writing habits." He discovered that they were starting to word-process papers and correspondence, and to transcribe handwritten notes onto disks. A few social and economic historians, he noted, conducted database searching and performed statistical analyses. He found that the photocopier "—[a] means of creating physical copies of documents—... has most affected the work of the historian." See Case, "The Collection and Use of Information by Some American Historians," pp. 75, 76.

[11] Herbert C. Morton & Anne J. Price, *The ACLS Survey of Scholars: Final Report of Views on Publications, Computers, and Libraries* (Washington, D.C.: American Council of Learned Societies, Office of Scholarly Communication and Technology, 1989).

SURVEY OF FACULTY USE AND NON-USE OF U.S. GOVERNMENT PUBLICATIONS AND INFORMATION IN ELECTRONIC FORM

1. Estimate how many times you used the resources of the university library in 1995.

   a. ___more than 50   f. ___11-15
   b. ___31-50   g. ___6-10
   c. ___26-30   h. ___1-5
   d. ___21-25   i. ___0
   e. ___16-20

2. Estimate how many times in 1995 you used publications of the U.S government (informational matter published as an individual document at government expense, or as required by law) located in the library.

   a. ___more than 50   f. ___11-15
   b. ___31-50   g. ___6-10
   c. ___26-30   h. ___1-5
   d. ___21-25   i. ___0
   e. ___16-20

3. If you answered "h" or "i" to question 2, please indicate why your use is infrequent. Check as many as apply. (If you responded to the other options, move to the next question.)

   a. ___the government publishes little or nothing of value in my field
   b. ___unaware of the existence of such materials at the library
   c. ___unfamiliar with arrangement of the government publications collection
   d. ___rely on government publications located in a library other than on this campus
   e. ___obtain personal, paper copies of government publications
   f. ___obtain government publications and information through the Internet and World WideWeb
   g. ___do not need government publications on a regular basis
   h. ___the amount of time expended in trying to find relevant information in government publications is out of proportion to what I find
   i. ___the library staff members provide minimal assistance in use of government publications
   j. ___government publications provide more detailed information than I need
   k. ___rely on secretary, student or research assistants to gather any needed government publications
   l. ___the desired government publication is available in the library only on microform

m. ___government publications in microform are separated from the rest of the government publications collection

n. ___was not a member of this faculty last year

o. ___other (please specify)_____

4. Does the library have a homepage on the World Wide Web?
   a. ___yes   b. ___no   c.   ___don't know

5. If you answered "yes" to the preceding question, does that homepage provide access to electronic information of the U.S. government?
   a. ___yes   b. ___no

6. Either in your office or at home do you have a microcomputer which you can use to connect to the Internet and World Wide Web?
   a. ___yes   b. ___no

7. If you answered "yes" to the preceding question, do you use that linkage for: (Check all that apply)
   a. ___electronic mail
   b. ___discussion groups
   c. ___use of other library collections
   d. ___gaining access to research material
   e. ___searching for information
   f. ___downloading files
   g. ___document delivery (receipt of electronic publications)
   h. ___ other (please specify)_____

IF YOU DO NOT USE U.S. GOVERNMENT PUBLICATIONS OR ELECTRONIC GOVERNMENT INFORMATION AT ALL, SKIP TO NUMBER 17

8. Do you consult U.S. government publications/information in your field to obtain:
   a. ___current events and issues of interest
   b. ___general interest reading
   c. ___grant information
   d. ___information of historical value
   e. ___legal material
   f. ___research and technical reports
   g. ___resources that may be of value to students
   h. ___statistical data
   i. ___other (please specify)_____

9. In using U.S. government publications, how often do you ask library staff members for assistance?

   a. ___never   c.   ___frequently

   b. ___sometimes   d.   ___always

If you marked "a" to question 9, skip to number 11

10. For what kind of assistance do you ask the library staff? (Check as many as apply)

   a. ___help in locating a specific government publication

   b. ___reference assistance, i.e., aid in finding materials or information to answer a specific question or solve some problem on which you are working

   c. ___assistance in finding government publications not located on the shelf

   d. ___assistance in locating government publications not held by the library

   e. ___help in ordering for the library a government publication not contained in the collection

   f. ___help in locating electronic government information not held by the library

   g. ___other (please specify)_____

11. Do you use any of the following gateways on the Internet to gain access to a wide assortment of government publications and information? Yes___ No___. (If yes, please check the relevant one(s).)

   a. ___FedWorld (NTIS)   c.   ___LC Marvel

   b. ___GPO Access   d.   ___THOMAS

12. Specify the agencies from which you seek information.

13. What type of electronic government information do you seek? (Check all that apply)

   a. ___annual reports

   b. ___bills and resolutions

   c. ___reports of commissions, committees, and agencies—other than annual reports

   d. ___decisions and opinions (e.g., court)

   e. ___names and addresses, including phone numbers and e-mail addresses

   f. ___hearing transcripts

   g. ___information from Congressional Record

   h. ___laws and statutes

   i. ___press releases

   j. ___rules and regulations

k. ___speeches
l. ___statistical reports or data
m. ___other (please specify)_____
n. ___no pattern; use varies

14. Would you characterize the overall quality of government information on the Internet and World Wide Web as:

1   2   3   4   5
poor.......................excellent

15. How important is government information which you identify through the Internet or World Wide Web for keeping up in your field, teaching, or research?
    a. ___little importance or   c. ___moderate importance
           do not use
    b. ___slight importance   d. ___great importance

16. Do you believe that librarians can perform a unique and important role in providing access to electronic government information?
    a. ___yes   b. ___no. Briefly explain.

BACKGROUND INFORMATION

17. Are you currently engaged in, or have you completed within the past year, a scholarly activity intended for publication, which cites:
    a. a U.S. government publication(s) in the bibliography or footnote?
       ___yes ___no

    b. electronic information of the U.S. government in the bibliography or footnote? ___yes ___no

    If "yes" and if that paper has been published, please provide a citation:

18. Please specify your discipline:
    a. ___history   b. ___political science

19. What is your present rank?
    a. ___assistant professor
    b. ___associate professor
    c. ___professor

Thank you for your cooperation.

Appendix F

HOW TO FIND OUT ABOUT TAINTED RESEARCH

The following sources are helpful in finding out about research misconduct. They follow misconduct cases from the time that the charges are first made public until a finding is determined or the case is dropped.

Chemical & Engineering News. Washington, D.C.: American Chemical Society, 1923- . Published weekly. It contains news and articles of interest to those working with chemicals—more broadly interpreted than just chemistry.

Chronicle of Higher Education. Washington, D.C.: The Chronicle, 1953- . Published weekly (except the third week in August and the last two weeks in December). The Chronicle covers all aspects of higher education. It reports on cases of misconduct in all disciplines and from countries outside the United States. The Chronicle reports on charges of misconduct even for cases which are not later pressed.

Nature. London: Macmillan Magazines, Ltd., 1869- . Published weekly. It is the best source for news of British, Commonwealth, and European science. It also reports on significant news from the United States. Misconduct cases are covered from first news through reports of completed investigations.

New Scientist. London: Specialist Magazine Group, 1956- . Published weekly. It covers all science fields and is particularly good on news about Australia and New Zealand as well as Britain and other Commonwealth countries. News articles include reports and investigations of research misconduct.

Science. Washington, D.C.: American Association for the Advancement of Science, 1880- . Published weekly. It reports news in the first part of each issue: covers disputes, charges of misconduct, and reports on findings of investigations. It is an excellent source for keeping up with the U.S. science scene.

All of the journals above are widely indexed. For example, the following indexing and abstracting sources cover all of them.

Biological Abstracts	*Geological Abstracts*
Chemical Abstracts	*Index Medicus/Medline*
Engineering Index	*INSPEC*
Environmental Abstracts	*Science Citation Index*

Major newspapers, such as the following examples, frequently carry reports of research misconduct.

Boston Globe	*New York Times*
Chicago Tribune	

The following publications of the federal government describe cases investigated by the U.S. Public Health Service in which the individual charged with misconduct was deemed guilty.

The Blue Sheet: Health Policy and Biomedical Research News of the Week. Chevy Chase, MD: F-D-C Reports, Inc., 1957- . Published weekly except Christmas week. This newsletter covers all news about topics listed in the subtitle.

Federal Register. Washington, D.C.: Office of the Federal Register, 1935- . 5 times per week. Under "Findings of Scientific Misconduct," the names and decision are published as soon as possible after the case is closed.

National Institute of Health. *NIH Guide*, 1971- . 45 times per year.

Office of Research Integrity. *Annual Report.* Washington, D.C.: Department of Health and Human Services, Office of the Secretary, Office of Public Health Service, 1991- . The section entitled "Summaries of Closed Investigations" is a compilation of the cases from the quarterly *Newsletter* (http://phs.os.dhhs.gov/phs/).

Office of Research Integrity. *Newsletter*, 1992- . Quarterly. A section, "Case Summaries," names the persons judged guilty. It gives a general overview of the misconduct and sometimes lists the publications involved (ori/ori_home.html).

Listservs

These are a good source of information about cases closed and pending.

AAASEST@GWUVM.GWU.EDU (Perspectives on Ethical Issues in Science and Technology sponsored by the American Association for the Advancement of Science).

SCIFRAUD@CNISIBM.ALBANY.EDU

Appendix G

CODES OF ETHICS FROM PROFESSIONAL SOCIETIES AND GUIDELINES FOR INSTRUCTIONS TO AUTHORS

American Chemical Society. "Ethical Guidelines to Publication of Chemical Research," *Accounts of Chemical Research*, 27 (1994): 179-181. Also available at http://pubs.acs.org/instruct/ethic.html

American Library Association. "Code of Ethics," in *American Libraries*, 26 (July/August 1995): 673.

American Psychological Association. "Authorship," in *Publication Manual of the American Psychological Association*, 4th ed. Washington, D.C.: American Psychological Association, 1994, p. 21; "Ethics of Scientific Publication," pp. 292-298.

Association of American Medical Colleges, Ad Hoc Committee on the Maintenance of High Ethical Standards in the Conduct of Research. "The Maintenance of High Ethical Standards in the Conduct of Research," *Journal of Medical Education*, 57 (1982): 895-902.

Association of Independent Information Professionals. "Code of Ethical Business Practice," in *Intellectual Freedom Manual*, 4th ed. Chicago: American Library Association, 1992, pp. 67-69.

Committee on Editorial Policy, Council of Biology Editors. *Ethics and Policy in Scientific Publication*. Bethesda, MD: Council of Biology Editors, 1990.

Council of Biology Editors Style Manual Committee. "Ethical Conduct in Authorship and Publication," in *CBE Style Manual: A Guide for Authors*,

Editors and Publishers in the Biological Sciences, 5th ed. Bethesda, MD: Council of Biology Editors, 1990, pp. 1-6.

Endocrine Society, Publications Committee. "Ethical Guidelines for Publications of Research," *Journal of Clinical Endocrinology and Metabolism*, 66 (1988): 1-3.

International Committee of Medical Journal Editors. "Uniform Requirements for Manuscripts Submitted to Biomedical Journals," *New England Journal of Medicine*, 324 (1991): 424-428.

International Committee of Medical Journal Editors. "Retraction of Research Findings," *Annals of Internal Medicine*, 108 (1988): 304.

Professional Ethics Resources on WWW (http://www.ethics. ubc.ca/papers/professional.html). The Professional Ethics Resources includes the following:

- American Political Science Association's Guide to Professional Ethics in Political Science (http:// www2dgsys.com/~apsa/ethics/html).
- American Psychological Association ethics documents 1995 (http://www.apa.org/ethics/code.html).
- American Sociological Association 1996 draft revision (http.www.asanet.org/ecoderev.htm).
- Canadian Code of Ethics for Psychologists (http://www. sycor.ca/Psych/ethics.html#acchon).
- Canadian Information Processing Society Code of Ethics and Standards of Conduct (http://www.cips.ca/code.htm).
- National Association of Social Workers' Code of Ethics (American)(http://www.primenet.com/~dean.nasw.html).

REFERENCES

Alberts, Bruce, & Kenneth Shine. "Scientists and the Integrity of Research," *Science*, 266 (December 9, 1994): 1660-1661.

"American Association for the Advancement of Science. Member Opinion Poll. Summary Report of Key Findings. Scientific Ethics and Responsibility." March, 1992 (unpublished).

American Library Association Presidential Committee on Information Literacy. *Final Report*. Chicago: American Library Association, 1989.

Anderson, Christopher. "Bill Would Force Journals to Follow Misconduct Rules," *Nature*, 357 (May 7, 1992): 7.

Armstrong, C. J. "The Eye of the Beholder," in *Electronic Information Delivery: Ensuring Quality and Value*, edited by Reva Basch. Aldershot, England: Gower, 1995, pp. 221-244.

Bailar, John C., Marcia Angell, Sharon Boots, Karl Heumann, Melanie Miller, Evelyn Myer, Nancy Paler, Sidney Weinhouse, & Patricia Woolf (Committee on Editorial Policy, Council of Biology Editors [CBE]). *Ethics and Policy in Scientific Publication*. Bethesda, MD: Council of Biology Editors, Inc., 1990.

Basch, Reva. "An Overview of Quality and Value in Information Services," in *Electronic Information Delivery: Ensuring Quality and Value*, edited by Reva Basch. Aldershot, England: Gower, 1995, pp. 1-10.

Bates, Marcia J. "An Exercise in Research Evaluation: The Work of L. C. Puppybreath," *Journal of Education for Librarianship*, 19 (Spring 1979): 339-343.

Bechtel, H. Kenneth, Jr., & Willie Pearson, Jr. "Deviant Scientists and Scientific Deviance," *Deviant Behavior*, 6 (1985): 237-252.

Begley, Sharon, with Stanley Holmes. "How Many Scientists Does It Take to Screw in a Quark?," *Newsweek* (May 8, 1994), pp. 54-55.

Behrens, Shirley J. "A Conceptual Analysis and Historical Overview of Information Literacy," *College & Research Libraries*, 55 (July 1994): 309-322.

Bell, Robert. *Impure Science*. New York: Wiley, 1992.

Ben-Yehuda, Nachman. "Deviance in Science," *British Journal of Criminology*, 26 (January 1986): 1-27.

Berry, John N., III. "Open Inquiry vs. Closed Orthodoxy," *Library Journal*, 120 (November 15, 1994): 6.

Betts, Donald D. "Retraction of an Article Published in the *Canadian Journal of Physics*," *Canadian Journal of Physics*, 70 (May 1992): 239.

Beutler, Earl. "Assuring Data Integrity and Quality: A Database Producer's Perspective," in *Electronic Information Delivery: Ensuring Quality and Value*, edited by Reva Basch. Aldershot, England: Gower, 1995, pp. 59-68.

Beyer, Barry K. "Critical Thinking: What Is It?," *Social Education*, 49 (April 1985): 268-276.

Bittles, Alan H., & William M. Mason. "Letters to the Editor," *Human Biology*, 65 (October 1, 1993): 841.

Bodi, Sonia. "Critical Thinking and Bibliographic Instruction: The Relationship," *Journal of Academic Librarianship*, 14 (July 1988): 150-153.

Bodi, Sonia. "Scholarship or Propaganda: How Can Libraries Help Undergraduates Tell the Difference?," *Journal of Academic Librarianship*, 21 (January 1995): 21-25.

Bodi, Sonia. "Through a Glass Darkly: Critical Thinking and Bibliographic Instruction," *Catholic Library World*, 61 (May/June, 1990): 252-256.

Boucher, Rick. "A Science Policy for the 21st Century," *Chronicle of Higher Education*, 40 (September 1, 1993): B1-B2.

Bowers, Neal. "A Loss for Words: Plagiarism and Silence," *American Scholar*, 63 (Fall 1994): 545-555.

Braunwald, Eugene. "On Analysing Scientific Fraud," *Nature*, 325 (January 15, 1987): 215-216.

Broad, William, & Nicholas Wade. *Betrayers of the Truth: Fraud and Deceit in the Halls of Science.* New York: Simon and Schuster, 1982.

Brown, Phillida. "The Game's Up for Phoney Medical Research," *New Scientist*, 129 (February 9, 1991): 21.

Burd, Stephen. "Fraud Office in Trouble," *Chronicle of Higher Education*, 40 (November 24, 1993a): A21-A22.

Burd, Stephen. "New Policy of Naming Scientists Who Are Found Guilty of Fraud Renews Debate on Federal Role," *Chronicle of Higher Education*, 40 (June 30, 1993b): A24-A25.

Burd, Stephen. "Shalala's Criticism of U.S. Policies on Scientific Misconduct Troubles Some Lawmakers and Watchdog Groups," *Chronicle of Higher Education*, 40 (January 27, 1993c): A31, A34.

Buzzelli, Donald E. "The Definition of Misconduct in Science: A View from NSF," *Science*, 259 (January 29, 1993): 584-585, 647.

Buzzelli, Donald E. "Letters to the Editor: The Definition of Scientific Misconduct," *Chronicle of Higher Education* (August 16, 1996), pp. B3-B4.

Cantekin, Erdem I., Timothy W. McGuire, & Robert L. Potter. "Biomedical Information, Peer Review, and Conflict of Interest as They Influence Public Health," *Journal of the American Medical Association*, 263 (March 9, 1990): 1427-1431.

Caplan, Arthur. "False Claims Act," SCIFRAUD, electronic mailing list (February 3, 1996), pp. 1-2.

Chubin, Daryl E., & Edward J. Hackett. *Peerless Science: Peer Review and U.S. Science Policy.* Albany: State University of New York Press, 1990.

Colaianni, Lois Ann. "Peer Review in Journals Indexed in Index Medicus," *Journal of the American Medical Association*, 272 (July 1994): 156-158.

Colaianni, Lois Ann. "Retraction, Comment, and Errata Policies of the US National Library of Medicine," *The Lancet*, 340 (August 29, 1992): 536-537.

Cole, Leonard A. *Politics and the Restraint of Science.* Totawa, NJ: Rowman & Allenheld, 1983.

Commission on Research Integrity. *Integrity and Misconduct in Research: Report of the Commission on Research Integrity to the Secretary of Health and Human Services, the House Committee on Commerce and the Senate Committee on Labor and Human Resources,* 1996. URL: http://phs.os.dhhs.gov/phs/ori_home.html.

Congress. House. Committee on Government Operations. *Are Scientific Misconduct and Conflicts of Interest Hazardous to Our Health?* Report 101-688. Washington, D.C.: Government Printing Office, 1990.

Congress. House. Committee on Governmental Operations. Subcommittee on Human Resources and Intergovernmental Relations. *Scientific Fraud and Misconduct and the Federal Response. Hearing....*Washington, D.C.: Government Printing Office, 1989.

"Congressional Action on Research and Development in the FY1996 Budget." Web page of American Association of the Advancement of Science, updated June 5, 1996. URL: http://www.aaas.org/spp/dspp/rd/fy96.htm.

Cooper, Ellen R. "Identifying Errata and Retractions: Simplified Approaches for Serials Management," *Serials Review*, 18 (Winter 1992): 17-20.

"Court Computers Can Get Reporters in Trouble, If Not Careful," *Wisconsin News Association Bulletin* (January 18, 1995), pp. 3-4.

Crawford, Gregory A. "A Conjoint Analysis of Reference Services in Academic Libraries," *College & Research Libraries*, 55 (May 1994): 257-267.

Crawford, Susan, & Loretta Stucki. "Peer Review and the Changing Research Record," *Journal of the American Society for Information Science*, 41 (1990): 223-228.

Crawford, Walt, & Michael Gorman. *Future Libraries: Dreams, Madness, and Reality*. Chicago: American Library Association, 1995.

Crossen, Cynthia. *Tainted Truth: The Manipulation of Truth in America*. New York: Simon and Schuster, 1994.

Dalton, Rex. "'Fraud Police' Face Dilemma over Warning Medical Boards," *Nature*, 379 (February 8, 1996): 480.

Dan, Bruce. "The Paper Chase," *Journal of the American Medical Association*, 249 (June 3, 1983): 2872-2873.

Davis, Hazel M. Personal correspondence (reference librarian, Glendale College, Phoenix, AZ), April 1996.

Davis, Mark Stephen. "The Perceived Seriousness and Incidence of Ethical Misconduct in Academic Science." Doctoral dissertation, Ohio State University, 1989.

Davis, Ralph D. "New Censors in the Academy: Two Approaches to Curb Their Influence," *Science Technology & Human Values*, 13 (Winter/Spring 1988): 64-74.

"Dealing with Deception," *The Lancet*, 347 (March 30, 1996): 843.

Deming, Peter. "Plagiarism in the Web," *Communications of the ACM*, 38 (December 1995): 29.

Dingell, John D. "Shattuck Lecture—Misconduct in Medical Research," *New England Journal of Medicine*, 328 (June 3, 1993): 1610-1615.

Directory of Electronic Journals, Newsletters and Academic Discussion Lists. Washington, D.C.: Association of Research Libraries, Office of Scientific and Academic Publishing, 1991- .

Dworkin, Gerald. "Fraud and Science," in *Research Ethics: Progress in Clinical and Biological Research, Proceedings Organized by the Norwegian Academy of Science and Letters and Others*. New York: Alan R. Liss, Inc., 1983, pp. 65-74.

Engeldinger, Eugene. "Bibliographic Instruction and Critical Thinking: The Contribution of the Annotated Bibliography," *RQ*, 28 (Winter 1988): 195-202.

"Ethical Tremors in World of Science," *Los Angeles Times* (November 21, 1994), p. B8.

Fish, Stanley. "Professor Sokal's Bad Joke," *New York Times* (May 21, 1996), p. A23.

Fisher, Bernard, Carol Redmond, Roger Poisson, et al. "Eight-Year Results of a Randomized Clinical Trial Comparing Total Mastectomy and Lumpectomy with or without Irradiation in the Treatment of Breast Cancer," *New England Journal of Medicine*, 320 (March 30, 1989): 822-827.

Fisher, Shelagh. "Access to Information," *Library Management*, 16 (5) (1995): 27-34.

Flint, Anthony. "Conduct of Science Called Crisis," *Boston Globe* (June 22, 1994), pp. E1, E5.

"Foster Research Integrity," in *ORI Annual Report*, 1994, p. 8. URL: http://phs.os.dhhs.gov/phs. ori_home.html.

Friedman, Paul. "Correcting the Literature Following Fraudulent Publication," *Journal of the American Medical Association*, 236 (March 9, 1990): 1416-1419.

Garfield, Eugene. "Citation Indexes for Science," *Science*, 122 (July 15, 1955): 108-111.

Garfield, Eugene, & Alfred Welljams-Dorof. "The Impact of Fraudulent Research on the Scientific Literature," *Journal of the American Medical Association*, 263 (March 9, 1990): 1424-1426.

Geison, Gerald L. *The Private Science of Louis Pasteur*. Princeton, NJ: Princeton University Press, 1995.

Gilbert, Neil. "Miscounting Social Ills," *Society*, 31 (March/April 1994): 18-26.

Ginsparg, Paul. "First Steps towards Electronic Research Communication," in *Directory of Electronic Journals, Newsletters and Academic Discussion Lists*, 5th ed. Washington, D.C.: Association of Research Libraries, Office of Scientific and Academic Publishing, 1995, pp. 1-10.

Goode, Stephen. "Ph.D.s Flood Marketplace; Schools Refocus Programs," *Insight*, 11 (December 18, 1995): 16-17.

Goodstein, David. "Quotable: Every Scientist I Know Has Stories of Being Treated Unfairly by Anonymous Referees," *Chronicle of Higher Education* (August 2, 1996), p. B5.

Grinnell, Frederick. *The Scientific Attitude*. 2nd ed. New York: The Guilford Press, 1992.

Gross, Paul, & Norman Levitt. *Higher Superstition: The Academic Left and Its Quarrels with Science*. Baltimore, MD: Johns Hopkins University Press, 1994.

"Guess Who?," *Newsweek* (August 21, 1995), p. 10.

Hagstrom, Warren. *The Scientific Community*. New York: Basic Books, 1965.

Hall, Elmer C. "Report of Ad Hoc Committee to Evaluate Research of Dr. John R. Darsee at Emory University," *Minerva*, 23 (1985): 276-305.

Halvorson, T. R. "Selected Aspects of Legal Liabilities of Independent Information Professionals," in *Electronic Information Delivery: Ensuring Quality and Value*, edited by Reva Basch. Aldershot, England: Gower, 1995, pp. 171-188.

Hammerschmidt, Dale E., & Alan G. Gross. "The Problem of Biomedical Fraud: A Model for Retrospective and Prospective Action," *Journal of Scholarly Publishing*, 27 (October 1995): 3-11.

Handlin, Oscar. *Truth in History*. Cambridge, MA: Harvard University Press, 1979.

Haskell, Thomas L. *The Authority of Experts: Studies in History and Theory*. Bloomington, IN: Indiana University Press, 1984.

Hernon, Peter, & Ellen Altman. "Misconduct in Academic Research," *Journal of Academic Librarianship*, 21 (January 1995): 27-37.

Hernon, Peter, & Ellen Altman. *Service Quality in Academic Libraries*. Norwood, NJ: Ablex, 1996.

Herrenstein, Richard J., & Charles S. Murray. *The Bell Curve*. New York: Free Press, 1995.

Higgins, A. C. "A Review of Loewen, James W. : *Lies My Teacher Told Me*," SCIFRAUD, electronic mailing list (April 12, 1996).

Hilts, Philip J. "The Science Mob," *The New Republic*, 206 (May 18, 1992), pp. 24-31.

Hollander, Rachelle D. "On Issues of Scientific Misconduct," *Knowledge: Creation, Diffusion, Utilization*, 14 (December 1992): 193-196.

Horton, Richard. "Revising the Research Record," *The Lancet*, 346 (December 15, 1995): 1610-1611.

"Instructions for Authors: Manuscript Criteria and Information," *Journal of the American Medical Association*, 271 (January 12, 1994): 161-162.

Intellectual Freedom Manual, compiled by the Office for Intellectual Freedom of the American Library Association, 4th ed. Chicago: American Library Association, 1992.

International Committee of Medical Journal Editors. "Retraction of Research Findings," *Annals of Internal Medicine*, 108 (1988): 304.

International Committee of Medical Journal Editors. "Uniform Requirements for Manuscripts Submitted to Biomedical Journals," *New England Journal of Medicine*, 324 (February 7, 1991): 424-428.

Kaihla, Paul. "Academe on Trial," *Maclean's* (December 1994), pp. 42-46.

Kaiser, Joclyn. "Radiation Research Subjects Sue," *Science*, 270 (December 15, 1995): 1763.

Kantrowitz, Barbara. "Dissent on the Hard Drive," *Newsweek* (June 27, 1994), p. 59.

Kaser, Richard T. "Secondary Information Services: Mirrors of Scholarly Communication, Forces and Trends," *Publishing Research Quarterly*, 11 (Fall 1995): 10-24.

Keys, Marshall. "Beyond Gutenberg and Gigabites: Librarians and the Emerging Digital Revolution," *Resource Sharing and Information Networks*, 10 (1995): 21-32.

Kimball, Roger. "A Painful Sting within the Academic Hive," *Wall Street Journal* (May 29, 1996), p. A18.

Knoll, Elizabeth. "What Is Scientific Misconduct?," *Knowledge: Creation, Diffusion, Utilization*, 14 (December 1992): 174-180.

Kochan, Carol Ann, & John M. Budd. "The Persistence of Fraud in the Literature: The Darsee Case," *Journal of the American Society for Information Science*, 43 (1992): 488-493.

Koshland, Daniel. "Fraud in Science," *Science*, 235 (January 9, 1987): 141.

Kotzin, Sheldon, & Peri L. Schuyler. "NLM's Practices for Handling Errata and Retractions," *Bulletin of the Medical Library Association*, 77 (October 1989): 337-341.

Kozak, Ellen M. "Towards a Definition of Plagiarism: The Bray/Oates Controversy Revisited," *Journal of Information Ethics*, 3 (Spring 1994): 70-75.

Krug, Judy. Telephone interview (director of the Office for Intellectual Freedom, American Library Association), May 30, 1996.

Kuhn, Thomas S. *The Structure of Scientific Revolutions*. Chicago: University of Chicago Press, 1962.

LaFollette, Marcel C. "The Politics of Scientific Fraud," *Chronicles* (September 1993), pp. 21-24.

LaFollette, Marcel C. "Research Misconduct," *Society*, 31 (March/ April 1994): 6-10.

LaFollette, Marcel C. *Stealing into Print: Fraud, Plagiarism, and Misconduct in Scientific Publishing*. Berkeley, CA: University of California Press, 1992.

Lapidus, Jules B., & Barbara Mishkin. "Values and Ethics in Graduate Education of Scientists," in *Ethics and Higher Education*, edited by William W. May. New York: American Council on Education/Macmillan Publishing, 1990, pp. 283-298.

Last Chance Health Report. Charlottesville, VA: University of Natural Healing, 1990- .

Latour, Bruno, & Steve Woolgar. *Laboratory Life: The Construction of Scientific Facts*. Princeton, NJ: Princeton University Press, 1986.

Leibel, Wayne. "When Scientists Are Wrong: Admitting Inadvertent Error in Research," *Journal of Business Ethics*, 10 (1991): 601-604.

Levinson, Marc. "Not Everyone Is Downsizing," *Newsweek* (March 18, 1996), pp. 42-44.

Lewis, Bernard. *History: Remembered, Recovered, Invented*. Princeton, NJ: Princeton University Press, 1975.

Lindsey, Robert. *A Gathering of Saints: A True Story of Money, Murder and Deceit*. New York: Simon and Schuster, 1988.

Lock, Stephen. "Does Editorial Peer Review Work?" *Annals of Internal Medicine*, 121 (July 1994): 60-61.

Lock, Stephen. "Lessons from the Pearce Affair: Handling Scientific Fraud," *British Medical Journal*, 310 (June 17, 1995): 1547-1548.

Lock, Stephen. "Misconduct in Medical Research: Does It Exist in Britain?" *British Medical Journal*, 297 (December 10, 1988): 1531-1535.

Lock, Stephen, & Wells, Frank. *Fraud and Misconduct in Medical Research*. London: BMJ Publishing Group, 1996.

Loewen, James W. *Lies My Teacher Told Me: Everything Your American History Textbook Got Wrong*. New York: The New Press, 1995.

Luker, Ralph. "Plagiarism and Perspective: Questions about Martin Luther King, Jr," *International Social Science Review*, 68 (Fall 1993): 152-160.

Majerus, Peter. "Fraud in Medical Research," *Journal of Clinical Investigation*, 70 (1982): 213-217.

Mallon, Thomas. *Stolen Words: Forays into the Origins and Ravages of Plagiarism*. New York: Ticknor & Fields, 1989.

"Mankato, Minnesota Home Page," Academe Today [homepage of the *Chronicle of Higher Education*], section on "Resources on the Internet," April 15, 1996 (see http://www.lme.mankato.msus. edu/mankato/mankato.html).

Marshall,Eliot."ReanalysisConfirmsResultsof'Tainted' Study,"*Science*,270(December8,1995):1562.

Marshall, Eliot. "Suit Alleges Misuse of Peer Review," *Science*, 270 (December 22, 1995): 1912-1914.

Marwick, Charles. "US Government Inquiry Bodies Dismiss Scientific Misconduct Charges against AIDS Researchers," *Journal of the American Medical Association*, 270 (December 8, 1993): 2665-2666.

Marx, Jean. "Major Setback for Alzheimer's Models," *Science*, 255 (6 March 1992): 1200-1202.

McCormick, Mona. "Critical Thinking and Library Instruction," *RQ*, 22 (Summer 1983): 339-342.

McGee, Glenn. "Young Scientists Need to Feel a Personal Stake in Ethics," *Chronicle of Higher Education* (August 2, 1996), p. B3.

McGinty, Lawrence. "Researcher Retracts Claims on Plutonium Treatment," *New Scientist*, 84 (October 4, 1979): 3-4.

McMillen, Liz. "The Science Wars: Scholars Casting Critical Eye on the Laboratory Say Their Work Has Been Distorted," *Chronicle of Higher Education* (June 28, 1996), pp. A9, A13.

Miers, M. L. "Current NIH Perspectives of Misconduct in Science," *American Psychologist*, 40 (7) (1985): 831-835.

Miller, Keith. *Voice of Deliverance: The Language of Martin Luther King, Jr. and Its Sources*. New York: Free Press, 1992.

Mintz, Anne P. "Quality Control and the Zen of Database Production," *Online*, 14 (November 1990): 15-23.

Mood, Terry Ann. "Of Sundials and Digital Watches: A Further Step toward the New Paradigm of Reference," *Reference Services Review*, 22 (Fall 1994): 27-32, 95.

Morrison, Douglas, communication on SCIFRAUD, electronic mailing list (April 8, 1996).

Muller, Mike. "Why Scientists Don't Cheat," *New Scientist*, 74 (June 2, 1977): 522-523.

National Academy of Sciences, National Academy of Engineering, and Institute of Medicine. Panel on Scientific Responsibility and the Conduct of Research. *Responsible Science: Ensuring the Integrity of the Research Process*. Washington, D.C.: National Academy of Sciences, 1992.

Navarro, Mireya. "Dispute Turns a Researcher into an Inmate," *New York Times* (June 9, 1996), p. A22.

Neto, Ricardo Bonalume. "Brazilian Researcher Protests against 'Plagiarism' Fine," *Nature*, 380 (April 4, 1996): 371.

Nigg, Herbert, and Gabriela Radulescu. "Scientific Misconduct in Environmental Science and Toxicology," *Journal of the American Medical Association*, 272 (July 13, 1994): 168-170.

Norman, Sandy. "Database Quality and Liability: The UK Campaign," in *Electronic Information Delivery: Ensuring Quality and Value*, edited by Reva Basch. Aldershot, England: Gower, 1995, pp. 189-202.

Oates, Stephen B. "A Horse Chestnut Is Not a Chestnut Horse: A Refutation of Bray, Davis, MacGregor, and Wollan," *Journal of Information Ethics*, 3 (Spring 1994): 25-41.

"ORI Assessing Allegations Quicker, Increasing Case Closings," *ORI Newsletter*, 4 (December 1995): 1.

Owens, R. Glynn, & E. M. Hardley. "Plagiarism in Psychology—What Can and Should Be Done?," *Bulletin of the British Psychological Society*, 38 (1985): 331-333.

Paris, Marion. "Abandoning the Comfort Zone: Making Medical Reference Accountable," *American Libraries*, 25 (September 1994): 772-776.

Peters, Douglas P., & Stephen J. Ceci. "Peer Review Practices of Psychological Journals: The Fate of Published Articles, Submitted Again," *Behavioral and Brain Sciences*, 5 (1982): 187-195.

Petersdorf, R. G. "A Matter of Integrity," *Academic Medicine*, 64 (March 1989): 119-123.

Pfeifer, Mark P., & Gwendolyn L. Snodgrass. "The Continued Use of Retracted, Invalid Scientific Literature," *Journal of the American Medical Association*, 263 (March 9, 1990): 1420-1423.

Pfeifer, Mark P., & Gwendolyn L. Snodgrass. "Medical School Libraries' Handling of Articles That Report Invalid Science," *Academic Medicine*, 67 (February 1992): 109-113.

Poling, Alan. "The Consequences of Fraud," in *Research Fraud in Behavioral and Biomedical Sciences*, edited by David J. Miller and Michel Herson. New York: Wiley, 1992, pp. 140-157.

Price, Alan R. "The 1993 ORI/AAAS Conference on Plagiarism and Theft of Ideas," *Journal of Information Ethics*, 3 (Fall 1994): 54-63.

Price, Derek J. de Solla. *Little Science, Big Science*. New York: Columbia University Press, 1963.

Quittner, Joshua. "From God@heaven.org," *Time*, 145 (June 26, 1995): 65.

Rader, Hannelore, & William Coons. "Information Literacy: One Response to the New Decade," in *The Evolving Educational Mission of the Library*, edited by Betsy Baker & Mary Ellen Litzinger. Chicago: American Library Association, 1992, pp. 109-127.

Ratzan, Lee. "Retraction," *Wilson Library Bulletin*, 66 (March 1992): 31-32, 120.

Reference and Adult Services Division, Standards and Guidelines Committee. "Information Services for Information Consumers: Guidelines for Providers," *RQ*, 30 (Winter 1990): 262-265.

Relman, Arnold. "Economic Incentives in Clinical Investigation," *New England Journal of Medicine*, 320 (April 6, 1989): 933-934.

Relman, Arnold S. "Lessons from the Darsee Affair," *New England Journal of Medicine*, 308 (June 9, 1983): 1415-1417.

Rendell, Kenneth W. *Forging History: The Detection of Fake Letters and Documents*. Norman, OK: University of Oklahoma Press, 1994.

Rettig, James. "Can We Get There from Here," in *Evaluation of Public Services and Public Services Personnel*, edited by Boyce Allen. Urbana, IL: University of Illinois Press, 1991, pp. 9-20.

Robinson, Alex. "Science and Scandal: What Can Be Done about Scientific Misconduct?" *Canadian Medical Association Journal*, 151 (September 15, 1994): 831-834.

Roiphe, Katie. "Date Rape's Other Victim," *New York Times Magazine* (June 13, 1993), pp. 26-28+.

Ryan, Kenneth J. "Scientific Misconduct in Perspective: The Need to Improve Accountability," *Chronicle of Higher Education* (July 19, 1996), pp. B1-B2.

Sampson, Wallace. "Be More Selective in Books" (Letter to the Editor), *Library Journal*, 120 (November 15, 1994): 7.

Sarasohn, Jody. *Science on Trial: The Whistle-blower, the Accused, and the Nobel Laureate*. New York: St. Martin's Press, 1993.

Schmaus, Warren. "An Analysis of Fraud and Misconduct in Science," in *American Association for the Advancement of Science-American Bar Association National Conference of Lawyers and Scientists*. Project on Scientific Fraud and Misconduct. Report on Workshop Number One. Washington, D.C.: American Association for the Advancement of Science, 1988, pp. 87-115.

Schnabel, Jim. "Puck in the Laboratory: The Construction and Deconstruction of Hoaxlike Deception in Science," *Science Technology and Human Values*, 19 (1994): 459-492.

Schwitters, Roy F. "The Substance and Style of 'Big Science'," *Chronicle of Higher Education*, 43 (February 16, 1996): B1-B2.

"Scientific Fraud: In Bristol Now," *Nature*, 294 (1981): 509.

"Scientific Misconduct Identified in MEDLINE Citations," *ORI Newsletter*, 2 (4) (September 1994): 4.

Seitz, Frederick. "A Major Deception on 'Global Warming'," *Wall Street Journal* (June 12, 1996), p. A16.

"Setting the Record Straight," *Science*, 244 (May 26, 1989): 911.

Shapiro, Martin F., & Robert P. Charrow. "The Role of Data Audits in Detecting Scientific Misconduct," *Journal of the American Medical Association*, 261 (May 5, 1989): 2505-2511.

Shea, James, communication on SCIFRAUD, electronic mailing list (May 17, 1996).

"Should Journal Editors Play Science Cops?," *Scientist*, 3 (October 31, 1988): n.p.

Smith, Richard. "Time to Face Up to Research Misconduct," *British Medical Journal*, 312 (March 30, 1996): 789-790.

Snodgrass, Gwendolyn L., & Mark P. Pfeifer. "The Characteristics of Medical Retraction Notices," *Bulletin of the Medical Library Association*, 80 (October 1992): 328-333.

Sommers, Christina Hoff. *Who Stole Feminism? How Women Have Betrayed Women*. New York: Simon & Schuster, 1994.

Steinem, Gloria. *Revolution from Within: A Book of Self-Esteem*. Boston: Little, Brown, 1992.

Stevens, Norman. "Reviews," *Journal of Information Ethics*, 5 (Spring 1996): 82-91.

Stewart, Walter W., & Ned Feder. "The Integrity of the Scientific Literature," *Nature*, 325 (January 15, 1987): 207-214.

Stoan, Stephen K. "Research and Library Skills: An Analysis and Interpretation," *College & Research Libraries*, 45 (March 1984): 99-109.

Swan, John. "Sharing and Stealing: Persistent Ambiguities," *Journal of Information Ethics*, 3 (Spring 1994): 42-47.

Swan, John A., & Noel Peattie. *Freedom to Lie*. Jefferson, NC: McFarland, 1989.

Swazey, Judith P., K. S. Lewis, & Melissa S. Anderson. "University Policies and Ethical Issues in Research and Graduate Education: Highlights of CGS Survey," *CGS Communicator*, 22 (March 1989): 1-3,7-8.

Swazey, Judith P., Melissa S. Anderson, & Karen S. Lewis. "Ethical Problems in Academic Research," *American Scientist*, 81 (November-December 1993): 542-555.

Talent, John A. et al. "Himalayan Paleontological Database Polluted: Plagiarism and Other Anomalies," *Journal of the Geological Society of India*, 35 (June 1, 1990): 569-585.

Taubes, Gary. "Plagiarism Suit Wins: Experts Hope It Won't Set a Trend," *Science*, 268 (May 1995): 1125.

Tenopir, Carol. "Priorities of Quality," in *Electronic Information Delivery: Ensuring Quality and Value*, edited by Reva Basch. Aldershot, England: Gower, 1995, pp. 119-139.

Thaler, David. "Becoming Martin Luther King, Jr.: Plagiarism and Originality," *Journal of American History*, 78 (June 1991): 1-92.

Tillman, Hope N. "The Argus Clearinghouse," *Journal of Business & Finance Librarianship*, 2 (1) (1996): 71-75.

Totten, Nancy Thomas. "Teaching Students to Evaluate Information: A Justification," *RQ*, 29 (Spring, 1990): 348-354.

"UMass, Be Not Proud," *Boston Globe* (August 15, 1996), p. A22.

Wade, Nicholas. "A Diversion of the Quest for Truth," *Science*, 211 (1981a): 1022-1025.

Wade, Nicholas. "The Rise and Fall of a Scientific Superstar," *New Scientist*, 91 (September 24, 1981b): 781-782.

Wadman, Meredith. "Drug Company 'Suppressed' Publication of Research," *Nature*, 381 (May 2, 1996): 4.

Wainwright, Eric. "The Big Picture: Reflections on the Future of Libraries and Librarians," *Australian Academic & Research Libraries*, 27 (March 1996): 1-14.

"Weird Science: Kinsey's Pedophile," *Newsweek* (December 18, 1995), p. 62.

Weller, Ann C. "Editorial Peer Review: Research, Current Practices and Implications for Librarians," *Serials Review*, 21 (Spring 1995): 53-65.

Wesley, Theresa L., & Emily Werrell. "Making the Most of a Limited Opportunity," *Research Strategies*, 3 (Summer 1985): 108-115.

White, Herbert S. "Scholarly Publication, Academic Libraries, and the Assumption That These Processes Are Really under Management Control," *College & Research Libraries*, 54 (July 1993): 293-301.

Whitley, William P., Drummond Rennie, & Arthur W. Hafner. "The Scientific Community's Response to Evidence of Fraudulent Publications: The Robert Slutsky Case," *Journal of the American Medical Association*, 272 (1994): 170-173.

"Widespread Misrepresentation Found in Fellowship Applications," *ORI Newsletter*, 4 (December 1995): 2.

Williams, Martha. "Database Publishing Statistics," *Publishing Research Quarterly*, 11 (Fall 1995): 3-9.

Woodsworth, Anne, & James F. Williams, II. *Managing the Economics of Owning, Leasing and Contracting Out Information Services*. Brookfield, VT: Ashgate, 1993.

Woolf, Patricia K. "Accountability and Responsibility in Research," *Journal of Business Ethics*, 10 (1991): 595-600.

Wright, N. D. "A Citation Context Analysis of Retracted Scientific Articles," Doctoral dissertation, University of Maryland, College Park, 1991.

Zangrando, Robert L. "A Crying Need for Discourse," *Journal of Information Ethics*, 24 (Spring 1994): 65-69.

Zangrando, Robert L. "Historians' Procedures for Handling Plagiarism," *Publishing Research Quarterly*, 7 (Winter 1991/1992): 57-63.

Zurer, Pamela S. "Misconduct in Research: It May Be More Widespread than Chemists Like to Think," *Chemical & Engineering News* (April 13, 1987), pp. 10-17.

NAME INDEX

SUBJECT INDEX

ABOUT THE CONTRIBUTORS

Ellen Altman was Visiting Professor, Department of Library and Information Studies, Victoria University of Wellington (PO Box 600, Wellington, New Zealand) until July 1997. Dr. Altman has been a faculty member at the Universities of Kentucky, Toronto, and Indiana. She was Professor and Director of the Graduate Library School at the University of Arizona. She has been Feature Editor of *Public Libraries*, the official publication of the Public Library Association of the United States, since 1992. She is also Co-editor of "JAL Guide to Professional Literature" in the *Journal of Academic Librarianship* and a member of *Library Quarterly's* Editorial Board. Professor Altman has served on many professional and governmental committees. She received the Distinguished Alumni Award from Rutgers School of Communication, Information and Library Studies in 1983, and has been included in *Who's Who in America* since 1981.

Philip J. Calvert is Senior Lecturer in the Department of Library and Information Studies, Victoria University of Wellington (PO Box 600, Wellington, New Zealand <philip.calvert@vuw.ac.nz>). He has worked in public and academic libraries in England, Fiji, and Papua New Guinea, subsequent to which he worked for a library supply company in Europe. His main teaching areas are in information technology and library automation. His recent research projects have included studies of library effectiveness and of service quality. He was Editor of the journal *New Zealand Libraries*.

Peter Hernon is Professor, Simmons College (Graduate School of Library and Information Science, 300 The Fenway, Boston, MA 02115 <phernon@vms-vax.simmons.edu>). While doing some of the research and writing for this book, he was Visiting Professor, Department of Library and Information Studies, Victoria University of Wellington, Wellington, New Zealand. This book is his 32nd; he is also the author of more than 100 articles. Dr. Hernon is the Editor-in-Chief of the *Journal of Academic Librarianship*, the Editor of *Government Information Quarterly*, and the Co-editor of *Library & Information Science Research*. He has received various awards and recognition for his research and other writings, and for his contributions to the profession.

Laura R. Walters is the Head of Collections at the Arts and Sciences Library of Tufts University (Medford, MA 02155). She has a Masters in Library and Information Science from Simmons College and a Ph. D. degree in anthropology from Brandeis University. She is a National Science Foundation grant recipient. Dr. Walters is active in the New England chapter of the Association of College and Research Libraries (ACRL), currently serving as its Secretary. She also serves on ACRL's Anthropology and Sociology Liaison Section.